D0988644

E

THE ACTOR WITH A THOUSAND FACES

MARK OLSEN

PHOTOGRAPHS BY
TOM PALUMBO AND MARK OLSEN

APPLAUSE
NEW YORK • LONDON

THE APPLAUSE ACTING SERIES

TO BEN

An Applause Original

THE ACTOR WITH A THOUSAND FACES
  by Mark Olsen

Copyright © 2000 by Mark Olsen
  ISBN 1-55783-306-0

All rights reserved.

No part of this publication may be reproduced or transmitted in any form or by any means, electronic or mechanical, including photocopy, recording, or any information storage system now known or to be invented, without permission in writing from the publishers, except by a reviewer who wishes to quote brief passages in connection with a review written for inclusion in a magazine, newspaper, or broadcast.

Printed in Canada.

Library of Congress Cataloging-In-Publication Data

Library of Congress Catalog Card Number 99-65410

British Library Catalogue in Publication Data
A catalogue record for this book is available from the British Library

APPLAUSE BOOKS
1841 Broadway
Suite 1100
New York, NY 10023
Phone (212) 765-7880
Fax: (212) 765-7875

CONTENTS

FOREWORD

This book is of great importance as a contribution to our Theatre heritage. It is a must for every actor, mime, clown, dancer, composer and director who truly cares and loves the Theatre Arts. It is addressed to those future talents that aspire to integrate their emotional life with self-discipline, emerging as someone worthy of being called a fully integrated human being and a genuine artist.

Mark is one of the rare individuals who landed some twenty-two years ago to study Mime and Movement Theatre with me at Le Centre du Silence Mime School in Boulder, Colorado. Fresh from academia, he devoured knowledge with a great appetite, like a hungry lion. Then he dared to embody it, emerging with his own original approach and giving it freely from his generous heart.

His words written here were chosen carefully in order to share his practical wisdom and precious knowledge. He is well equipped to write from his guts and from his rich experience in this demanding Theatrical career. He teaches fearlessly his profound conviction, and speaks and demonstrates from his own experience. Mark's eloquence is contagious and it endears him to anyone who encounters his presence.

Read and learn from his experience and if you apply what he proposes, you will surely discover the magical way of being a genuine artist. In return, share with others, the passion, the joy, and the love.

What else can I say about Mark Olsen? He is a Man (hero) of a thousand faces and one.

– SAMUEL AVITAL
Founder and Director of Le Centre du Silence Mime School, and the discoverer of Bodyspeak the Avital Method

I NTRODUCTION

M y first exposure to ensemble work was as a child. It was not in the theatre, but at a Native American rain dance. Due to an unusual set of circumstances, my family and I were permitted to witness this extraordinary event on a distant part of the reservation under a blazing sky from which, my skeptical mother pointed out, the Indians were as likely to obtain water as from a stone.

The men gathered around a small tent–like structure inside which one of the elders had placed a box. Loud drumming began as the men, surrounded by their chanting women, began to pound the earth with their feet. Suddenly, and without looking, one of the dancers reached into the box and, to my terrified disbelief, withdrew a writhing rattlesnake. Each of the performers followed suit, and as the chanting and drumming built to a frenzy each performer seized the snake at a point just below the head and gripped it between his teeth. With snakes clenched in their mouths, the performers danced.

The dance grew in delicious abandon, but my exhilaration at this spectacle was rapidly replaced by a sense of awe as the sky began to cloud over. Within fifteen minutes a light sprinkle of moisture had turned into a full–fledged rainstorm. Needless to say, we had not brought an umbrella.

I have tried to bring that potential for collective magic to the theatre ever since. Each time I succeed, the experience refreshes my contact with that first mystery in the Arizona desert. It is my hope, with this book, to share some of that mystery in simple practical terms.

Imagine you are involved in an extraordinary theatre production that allows for extensive research and rehearsal. Imagine further that the action and production elements are fully integrated in such a way that the creative process and the ensuing results are enormously satisfying for everyone, especially the public. Now, imagine that one night, during a performance, an unusual shift occurs: you and your fellow actors merge with the action of the play; you begin communicating with a resonance and a clarity surpassing anything you have ever experienced. You sense that the audience recognizes the shift and has unified into a heightened awareness. Even the stage hands are drawn to the wings.

Everyone performs with heightened commitment and with the perfect measure of truth. The play no longer seems a play, but a vibrant ritual, drawing forth laughter, tears, gasps, shudders, and astonished sighs. It's as though everyone in the building, has been lifted from ordinary reality into a sublime journey; breathing and soaring together through a progression of palpable moods, reflections, and insights.

Time vanishes until finally, at the end, the assembled gently return like a flock of great birds to a meadow. The audience, grateful for the journey, sits in stunned silence until they leap to their feet roaring with applause when you and the other actors appear for your bows. Everyone involved recognizes this applause as a celebration honoring the mystery of collective transcendence. My professional life has been dedicated to developing just such an awareness, what I call the ensemble flow. I have seen many world-class *individual* performances, but the dynamic of an ensemble effort is what I find most compelling. In both my training and my experience I have come to realize that, regardless of language or style, collective endeavors have a profound impact on people.

In this state, during an ensemble flow, actors are liberated from conventional restrictions. By adopting the global theme of Joseph Campbell's The Hero With a Thousand Faces, actors penetrate the mysteries of ensemble work and learn to relinquish selfish performance habits. Their reward is access to a deeper source of inspiration, enabling them to become actors with a thousand faces.

However, before you can walk you must crawl; and before you can consciously perform in an ensemble, you must train. The first part of this text will supply numerous exercises and variations of exercises that are essential steps toward creating the strength, flexibility and common language necessary to cultivate a coherent and effective ensemble. It enumerates the fundamentals of warming and tuning the body, voice, emotions, and the imagination. The second part of *The Actor With a Thousand Faces* assumes that most of the groundwork from part one has been accomplished and can now be applied to the exploration and creation of ensemble works.

The principles of the text are founded on my own knowledge accumulated from well over 20 years as a professional in the theatre, as well as the widespread methodology of directors and theatre groups which embody the collective ideal. Their visions may be diverse, but their goal is the same: to affect audiences in such a way that they advance not only their art, but everyone's.

I became interested in theatrical expression at an early age and for reasons I could not explain at the time, I was completely fascinated by European approaches. Luckily for me, I received guidance from very creative and caring teachers, one of whom changed my life by insisting I stay with the work in her drama class, and another who had studied with the Berlin Ensemble and instilled in me the essential ensemble values.

I played some very demanding roles in high school and was developing a growing awareness of the craft along more or less traditional lines. Then, one evening my friends and I went to a neighboring high school to view their annual mime show. I had never seen anything quite like it. I was entranced and stunned and knew with every fiber of my being that I had to know more about this form of expression. Soon afterwards, I joined a fledgling mime troupe and spent my last year of high school as an apprentice and performer in the troupe.

My college years were spent in pursuit of my goal to become the best actor in the world. However, late at night, after everyone had retreated to their dormitories, I would sneak into the theatre and spend hour upon hour in silent expression. I was making progress as an actor, but upon graduation it was clear to me that my heart was seeking an alternate route.

Thus began my journey into the realm of mime, mask, clown, and even stand-up comedy. My dear friend and mentor Samuel Avital, awoke in me my artistic fire and my appetite for more training and experience. This led me to encounters with many teachers and performers, all of whom contributed to my growing level of skill.

I was working as an artist in residence for the city of Dallas, touring locally with a mime troupe, performing in comedy clubs with my comedy partner, and studying with any and all influences that were available. Finally, just as I was opening my solo show in Los Angeles, I received a call to audition for the Swiss mime and mask show MUMMENSCHANZ.

I went to New York, auditioned, and was cast. The honor of being cast as a member of the international touring cast was deeply moving. I entered into the specialized training with complete and utter commitment. The show was very demanding in all aspects, the rewards, however, were immense. I traveled to distant parts of the world, receiving exposure to the theatre and the training methods of many cultures. I met remarkable men and women, all of whom have had a great influence on my life.

Upon returning to New York, having been travelling and performing for two years, I chose to plunge into a series of specialized trainings. I studied meditation, massage, Tai–Chi, Alexander Technique, sacred dance, mask–making, mime, Roy Hart vocal work, acting, film–making, and more. I found teachers of great nobility, tricksters, taskmasters, and chums. I feasted on theatre, dance, music, and art. I made New York my academy.

I was being asked to be a guest artist at a variety of respected instututions and found that teaching was something that flowed from me effortlessly. I began to realize that all of my years of travel and training and working with various teachers were leading me to this new role as a teacher. I also came to realize that the work I enjoyed doing and seeing and indeed the work that was nurtured in me through master teachers was, without exception, reinforcing the values of ensemble flow. My directing and acting and teaching ever since has been a journey of exploring and applying those values.

Unfortunately, our natural urge towards group ritual can sometimes become distorted, leading to involvement with negative surrogate structures like gangs and cults. Technology has not been of much help in this regard. Many of the advances in communication have, ironically, made us less interconnected. The opportunities for positive group interactions continue to become increasingly scarce. We are starved for meaningful group dynamics.

Theatre, on the other hand, has always had the ability to provide the nourishment of meaningful interaction. What makes it so effective is not only the experience itself, but the very powerful subliminal message that accompanies it. A message so powerful, in fact, it has motivated governments to take action against it; so powerful, it has survived centuries of repression and revision; so powerful, it must be handled with great care and foresight. The message is: by working in groups with a singular artistic aim, people can learn to overcome fear, to create mutual trust, and to gain knowledge through compassionate understanding. Ensemble theatre, then, when approached with serious but joyful intent can nourish an important part of our soul and provide the keys to our essential humanity. Those who commit to the work and stay with it beyond the first layers of discomfort, will find great joy in mastering the essential over the anecdotal, the universal over the topical, and the resonant over the hidden heart.

HOW TO USE THIS BOOK

Although *The Actor With a Thousand Faces* is for both the student/professional and teacher/director, it is addressed to the student in all of us. I have yet to meet an accomplished teacher who was not also an avid student. It is designed to be a resource for any theatre group wishing to explore ensemble work. This includes, but is not limited to: educational theatre, children's theatre, classical theatre, musical theatre, and avant guarde theatre of all classifications.

Some of the exercises, especially those in the "warm–up" section, can be done alone. The text assumes an interest in ensemble work, but is not limited only to those actors currently involved in a theatre group. Many of the exercises are beneficial to the individual actor and will enhance skills and deepen artistic awareness regardless the circumstances. It is fine to learn and practice those exercises on your own, but remember that they are designed as part of a process within the dynamic of a group and provide optimum benefit when done in that context.

The Actor With a Thousand Faces is not intended as a "how to" primer for the creation of theatre groups; although, much of the material will indeed be useful in that regard. The primary thrust of the text remains geared toward the dynamic of an active group. If you are not now involved in an ensemble, perhaps this book will provide the information and inspiration for you to create one.

What constitutes a group? A group could be as small as two or three people or as large as a hundred. It could be as informal as a gathering of friends or as formal as a designated class for a university theatre program. The formation of a group with the intention to work implies at least a rough formulation of an aim. *The Actor With a Thousand Faces* is a book designed for groups or individuals whose aim is to improve or initiate ensemble flow in performance. Its sole intent is to promote ensemble awareness for the purpose of quality stage-craft.

In my experience there can be much healing and growth derived from this work, but this book is not designed as a therapeutic program. Groups wishing to explore those elements need to work within the structures formulated by a bona-fide group therapist. I cannot emphasize this enough, because abuses can and do occur when the aim of the group shifts toward other agendas.

Kept within the proper context, all the exercises herin contained are safe and, with only a few exceptions, easily done by anyone with normal movement function. The work should be approached with focus and clarity and with a large dose of common sense. I do not advocate extreme states of exhaustion, militant attitudes, or fetishism in any form. Please know that this work is intended to promote equilibrium, mutual respect, open dialogue, freedom, inventiveness, and the extraordinary joy of living. If even for a few moments, within a flow of human energy those elements are blended with artistic intent to create an ensemble flow, then my intent will have been accomplished.

With any group, the question of leadership quickly arises. For some groups the leader is obvious by authority of age, experience, or success. Others will need to elect a leader, or perhaps several leaders whose duties and services reflect their areas of expertise. Sometimes leadership is something that evolves through time and usually as a result of a personality that emerges as an effective diplomat or visionary.

For the purposes of this book, it must be assumed that one or several "leader types" have been chosen or evolved in order to facilitate some of the exercises. If a leader has not emerged and the group wishes to forge ahead, it will be important that the role of leader be divided among the willing participants. Some of the exercises can be done without the guidance of a leader, but most can not.

It is useful to have had theatre experience before launching into these exercises, but it is not absolutely essential. What is essential is a commitment to the process of the collaborative journey.

SAFETY AND SECURITY

A secure and safe environment is essential to allow people to engage each other in deep and meaningful ways. To establish that environment requires a mix of structural security in terms of the actual workspace and psychological security in terms of the emotional atmosphere. The same remains true if you are presently working alone or have yet to be involved in an active group. The workspace must always be safe and secure. Here are a few tips that will help fulfill both needs:

1. Never attempt to participate if ill, exhausted, or under the influence of drugs or liquor.

2. Always warm-up and cool down.

3. Difficult maneuvers like safe and effective falling, fighting, rolling, balancing, and shared weight or shared energy techniques need to be learned from a trained professional and preferably early on in the training process.

4. Take a short break every hour or at least every two hours.

5. Establish a quick group freeze command that will stop the group in an instant. This helps to prevent accidents you may see coming.

6. Wear proper movement attire that facilitates free movement and remains close to the contours of the body. Avoid street clothes or jewelry in the workspace.

7. Don't wear socks, stockings, street shoes or sandals.

8. Inform the group leader if you have current or chronic injuries. In consultation with the group leader you must assess if your involvement needs to be limited in any way. Some common injuries that will certainly necessitate diminished involvement are: Broken bones of any kind, sprains, torn ligaments or cartilage, whiplash, and any cuts or abrasions that are deep enough to require medical attention.

9. Work with focused controlled energy. Over–enthusiasm, however well–intentioned, can and often does create unsafe and unproductive work.

10. Wear knee and elbow pads if movement work will entail a fair amount of falling and/or rolling.

11. Enter and exit the building in groups of two or more whenever possible.

12. Create a contact sheet for the group that not only has the names and phone numbers of each participant, but the appropriate numbers to call in case of an emergency.

13. Keep a First Aid kit and ice-packs handy at all times.

14. Lock the workspace during each session and never bring valuables into the space.

15. Leave emotional baggage outside the workspace.

SPACE AND TIME CONSIDERATIONS

Space is very important to the process of creating an ensemble. A group's work will inevitably reflect the relationship it develops to the workspace. Therefore, much of the beginning work in creating an ensemble is directed toward creating an effective workspace.

The ideal space for ensemble work is a large, well ventilated, soundproof room with a sprung dance floor, a mirror on one wall with a pull curtain, high ceilings, several functioning windows for fresh air and natural light, proper heating and air-conditioning, a secure storage closet for mats, props, video and audio equipment, a table, folding chairs, and sufficient overhead non-fluorescent lights controlled by a dimmer.

There should be bathrooms, showers, and a water fountain within easy access and the space should be placed in a quiet, secluded, or at least protected part of the building, away from the hubbub of the ordinary world.

Unfortunately, very few spaces can meet the criteria. Some spaces in newer universities professional studios come close to this description, but realistically, most available spaces will be far from ideal.   Some spaces are small with inadequate lighting, some have no mirrors, some have low ceilings or pillars and many have no windows.   Some have carpeted floors, parquet floors, or even concrete floors.

While it's important to come as close to the ideal space requirements as possible, it's equally important to remember that the chemistry of the group will eventually adjust to any space. Nevertheless, the process is much quicker and smoother if the space is fully conducive from the start.

All exercises must be tailored to suit the demands of each particular space. It's not advised, for example, to do a lot of jumping and rolling movement if a group is working on a concrete floor.

Time is another element that must be carefully considered. The most obvious challenge in working with groups is to find times when the entire group can meet. Here again, there's no magical time slot which guarantees success. Nevertheless, it is generally accepted that nighttime energy is more conducive to creative flow.

Ideally, the group should be able to meet for three to four hours, five nights a week for anywhere from sixteen to eighteen weeks.   Under these ideal conditions, it's fair to assume that the group could achieve a high degree of ensemble awareness.

In my experience, however, true ensemble dynamics cannot be achieved with less than three meetings weekly. The actual time spent at each meeting is secondary to actually connecting, bare minimum, three times a week. The reality of each situation, however, will ultimately dictate the time considerations. The rule of thumb to remember is to find as many times as possible where the whole group can work together. Continuity is important.

GROUP DYNAMICS

The chemistry and effectiveness of any one group depends on the integrity and focus of each individual in the group. I have observed an interesting paradox regarding group dynamics, whereby, individuals by virtue of their surrender to the workings of a group setting, do not lose their individual identity as one might expect. Instead, they become more confident and secure as individuals, able to define themselves more clearly through group interaction.

In the early stages, however, the threat to the ego and the various challenges brought on by the pressures of a group dynamic often trigger unusual, awkward, and sometimes hilarious manifestations from the individual. We all have a tendency to play out various roles within the ever-changing contexts we encounter in life. Most of the roles are old habits designed to enhance our status and to manipulate the surroundings to favor our needs.

Awareness is a very powerful tool that can help to gently dissolve old behavioral habits and to arrive at newer and more useful strategies aligned with the goals of the ensemble. Therefore, as various habits spring forth to test their effectiveness upon the group, it's important to recognize at least a few of the standard manifestations.

Some of the roles played out in the group are innocuous and will fall away rather quickly. Others can be a serious obstacle to the aims of the ensemble and must be dealt with in clear and open terms. The following offers a list of some of the more common roles. You may recognize yourself in this list, so be compassionate with yourself and others and, above all, keep a sense of humor.

THE COMPLAINER

This character simply loves to complain. In fact, if things are going smoothly, they'll complain that there's nothing to complain about. They hurt all over, never get enough strokes, and never fully find joy in the moments of their life. They're forever noticing how their current reality differs, however slightly, from their expectations.

If they're attacked for always complaining, they'll complain they're being attacked. However, if these characters are made aware of their role (with kindness and humor) they'll actually find ways to turn their little hobby into hilarious self-effacing humor and the kind of constructive criticism that benefits the ensemble. They transform curmudgeonly traits into real work.

THE USURPER

This person puts inordinate amounts of energy into finding weaknesses in whomever has been selected as the leader. They may not even be aware of it at first, but their hidden agenda is to dethrone the leader and place themselves in the leadership position. They may start out as complainers, but as time wears on and as they build resistance to their own commitment to the work at hand, they often become increasingly hostile and disruptive. Very often usurpers are tyrants in the making.

The usurper must be dealt with quickly and effectively. In my experience, there are several ways to deal with such a situation. The leader can call everyone's attention to the role being played out and then, with compassion, help the usurper to understand their desires as sophisticated work resistance. The leader can pull the usurper aside and make them aware that they're playing this role.

The leader can delegate to them some tasks that appear to have great importance, but in reality will keep them occupied until they overcome their need to play out this role.

If none of the various tactics make enough impact on the character, they must be dismissed from the group. Their ego needs will never allow for a true ensemble to be formed.

THE HIDER

This person hopes to hide within the group. They use the ensemble like a security blanket to avoid confronting their goals and personal weaknesses. They're usually very nice people who provide the minimum in participation and tend to happily go along with what everyone else wants to do.

It's my experience that hiders hide because they have so much repressed energy that they fear the slightest exposure will trigger an avalanche of feelings and dreams and ideas so overwhelming that they'll never recover to a state of equilibrium. So, to avoid the discomfort of such a scenario, they will prefer to live in an obscured state, feeding vicariously off the dynamics of the group.

Each person is unique and must be approached as such. Nevertheless, it's helpful to make the hider aware that hiding is selfish and vain. (Hiders want to see themselves as selfless and humble.) They're selfish by not sharing the fullness of themselves with the others in the group. They're vain to think that their emotions, dreams, ideas, etc. are any more valid and precious than others. Once the hider confronts their game and chooses to reframe or rethink their habitual behaviors, they often come out into the light and blossom wonderfully.

THE PROFESSOR

This character prefers to analyze verbally each moment of every endeavor. This analysis, albeit stimulating and certainly appropriate under certain circumstances, tends to draw focus from the group aim and slows any momentum that may be developing. These characters relish the opportunity to bring to the attention of the group all manner of useless data. Sometimes this character will take on the role of teacher and try to get others to understand unusual parallels or philosophical perspectives they've proudly come upon in their research.

The professor can be helpful at times and shouldn't be summarily dismissed. I suggest focusing the inclination by finding projects and various tasks for this person to do. Occasionally, allow them free reign during an ensemble work session, it usually serves to point up the hazards of too much professorial pontification.

This character will usually arise from a person who has habitually relied upon intellect to distance them from new experiences or to prevent them from experiencing the awkward vulnerability of intimacy. They mean well and, if made aware of their penchant for over-intellectualizing and lecturing, they'll usually find ways to prevent this character from habitually emerging.

THE PREDATOR

This character is always on the make. Their involvement with the group is motivated by their sexual interests. They'll use group exercises as an excuse to seduce their intended prey. This character is difficult to dismiss, because they're usually very talented, magnetic individuals who have a lot to offer the group. Unfortunately, if their habitual character cannot shift from the predatory stance, they'll eventually disrupt and damage the ensemble energy.

There are other kinds of predators. Some are on the make for a quick financial score or to impress a boss or to launch personal careers. This kind of ambition can be harnessed and dealt with for a time until the person either admits their character, and by doing so, diffuses its destructive capability, or leaves the group.

Predatory traits exist in all of us. We are territorial by nature and want to establish the boundaries within our control. Held in check, these natural tendencies are harmless. If tolerated in a predatory character, however, they can become invasive, disruptive, and hurtful. Dealing with predatory characters can divert precious time and energy from the established aim of the ensemble.

THE CLOWN

This person loves to amuse and annoy. The standard clown character is sometimes endearing and usually produces very little perturbation. If the clowning around becomes disruptive or a means to avoid doing the work at hand, then they must be made aware of their unfair behavior. If the clowning is chronic they'll have to be removed or their involvement greatly curtailed.

THE SHARK

The Shark does precisely what the character name suggests. They circle someone who they sense is less capable than they are in some area, and they attack them. They often attack as part of a larger more general critique session, always cautious to avoid being detected as a shark. They're usually very bright people who, for one reason or another, have developed their intellect as an arsenal, poised and ready to shoot down anybody who might be learning, misinformed, or just having a bad day. (A standard quality in the Commedia dell'arte character, Docttore.)

Sharks should be exposed for what they are and encouraged to use their intelligence to teach and defend others. Gradually, their shark–like manifestations will become linked with compassion, a step that will make their contributions to the ensemble, extremely valuable.

THE HIPSTER

This character wants to be a rock star. Too much effort is placed in the pursuit of looking and acting cool. They tend to view the world according to the latest fashions. While their involvement with popular culture can be very useful and stimulating, it must be limited so as to insure the integrity of the ensemble and to avoid fluctuating the aim according to the whims of fashion.

THE CHALLENGER

This character is very similar to the Usurper, except this person has no clear agenda, they simply have developed a strategy to get attention by challenging. Their essential character trait is actually very useful and would be entirely positive if not for the fact that the challenger characters to which I refer, rarely, if ever, challenge themselves.

It soon becomes apparent that their demands for proof, for extra attention, for instant results, is a smoke screen, cleverly devised to hide the fact they're afraid of discovery and are in fact, resisting looking at their own progress.

In my experience, this character needs the freedom to play out their challenges now and again. They also must be completely denied this freedom, from time to time, and given very physically demanding tasks to accomplish. With their involvement so completely focused on measurable, attainable goals, they'll gradually build the confidence necessary to jump into creative realms where the paths to the goals aren't measurable and the work sometimes doesn't feel like work.

THE MARTYR

This character is a standard in the theatre. They put the needs of the show, the cast, the artistic staff, and anyone else remotely connected to whatever project is ongoing completely above their own needs. This includes eating, sleeping, and having any kind of life.

They seem to feed on crisis and revel in the myriad opportunities theatre affords them to work while they remain perched on the brink of starvation, and exhaustion. They can often be seen holding the hand of a classmate who is going through a rough period emotionally, or staying up all night to help the understudy learn lines for a role. They seldom work for money and, if they do, they spend it on throwing a cast party at their place the weekend before eviction.

These characters have always been attracted to the crisis mentality of theatre and their presence in a group is relatively harmless. Their chances for making a valuable contribution, and their ultimate growth potential, however, depends upon them breaking their martyr cycle and learning how to conserve their energy and allowing others to take responsibility for their own lives.

When the martyr awakens, special care must be taken that they don't suddenly flip the other direction and become aloof and self–centered. That too can be a subtle trap and another version of the same character trait.

There are, of course, many other characters that surface within the group dynamic. They are amusing and sometimes endearing and usually harmless. Recognizing the primary ones will help to reveal the secondary ones and before long, everyone will have moved to a more honest portrayal of themselves. Keep in mind, this level of honestly needs to be focused toward an aim or sequence of aims for the group to arrive at the kind of coherence that characterizes a true ensemble.

Again let me reiterate that the participants should not fall into the trap of becoming a psychological encounter group. The roles I mentioned above are useful to resolve conflicts and to keep the artis–

tic aims of the group intact. They must not be used as a means to demean or diminish self-esteem. The best approach is to find which description best describes your tendencies and then with humor and ease, let yourself expand out of the role.

HAVING A LIFE

Creating an ensemble can sometimes resemble the workings of a religious order. For example, there's often a temporary withdrawal from the world as the various individuals struggle to find a common aim. As the hearts and minds of these different participants begin to merge, under the careful guidance of a leader, the experience can be unsettling and can indeed begin to have an impact on one's ability to appreciate and function in the established order as defined by society.

Personally, I'm not in favor of lengthy withdrawal from the world. I think it is unnecessary, especially for theatrical endeavors. It's always wiser to stay closely linked with the marketplace of the world at large, regardless of the trends. This insures a healthy perspective on one's work, protecting against unrealistic or delusionary opinions of oneself.

LEADERSHIP AND AUTHORITY

A group of people gathered to define or pursue a common goal, be it athletic, artistic, scientific, or businesslike in nature, need leadership. In the theatre, that's commonly the job of the producer or the director. In training situations, however, it may fall more directly on a teacher or similar authority hired to facilitate the training. In some instances the leadership role may be shared by several people who either have the talent or the experience to fulfill the role.

Usually the leader is a respected peer whose natural leadership abilities flow easily from his or her personal authority. In addition, a good leader must have some of the character traits Shakespeare gives to his Henry V: the ability to ignite passions, to stir the hearts of those around, to lead by example, and to inspire loyalty to the artistic vision. In addition, one should remember that leaders are human and therefore fallible. Unrealistic expectations on the part of the group or the leader is always disastrous.

Some leaders assume the role of the tyrant and get short-term results by using threat and fear tactics that squelch opposition. Tyrannical leaders are usually hiding deep insecurities and often hold self-interest over the interests of the group. In these situations, there'll be an initial semblance of an ensemble, but it will always be short lived. Tyrannical leadership can never be rooted in the hearts of the participants, and so withers away quickly.

The better choice is for the leader to be open and honest about any weaknesses and clear and confident about strengths. They should act as the discussion facilitator, the project focusing lens, the visionary, and the one who, by consensus, has the last word when disagreements arise. If the leader is to be successful in this style of leadership, their efforts must be perceived as fair, consistent, and in the best interest of the whole. They must have the respect of the members of the group by virtue of their past accomplishments, personal authority, and daily actions. And they must get results.

Regardless of the leadership style, participants must also be willing to take responsibility for the efforts of the whole. This means to be sensitive enough to respect individual needs, secure enough to voice personal opinions, and flexible enough to sacrifice personal problems and desires. Responsibility for the group is a natural by-product of the group dynamic after a time. The members of a true ensemble are highly individual and yet can at any time speak for the whole group.

Finally, members of an ensemble must be allowed to have outside lives. Some people, motivated by their enthusiasm and perhaps, in part, from an altruistic desire to reach ever higher levels of communication, may welcome their lives being consumed by the ensemble experience. And indeed, many group experiences are so powerful that the outside world begins to pale by comparison. Nevertheless, my experience has proven to me that people enjoying life outside the framework of the ensemble, regardless of how mundane, add dimension and depth to the work of a group

The time demands for creating an ensemble can range from a single session in a workshop where the participants get a taste of the experience to groups of people working together over the course of years, even decades. One does not negate the other. In both ends of the spectrum, the ensemble experience itself remains as elusive and delightful as always.

One's relationship to true ensemble expression and experience remains a very individual choice. That's why I feel it necessary to emphasize there's no need to view ensemble work, regardless of the cult-like attributes, as a reverent and holy work requiring many years of dedication and detachment from the world at large. Some groups may find it necessary to do that to facilitate their aims. It's not, however, a prerequisite.

HONESTY, CLARITY, AND ETHICS

We all have differing value systems. Sometimes the values change as we grow older, and sometimes the values change suddenly. Sometimes they mutate over decades. What remains constant in my work, and in the kind of ensemble work I hope to inspire, is a strict code of ethics regarding matters of the heart.

It's unfair and unnecessary for someone in a leadership role, for example, to take advantage of the established trust in an ensemble by embarking upon romantic or sexual interludes. By the same token, it is unfair and unnecessary for someone to distort the role of the leader by projecting onto them romantic or sexual fantasies.

I think it's healthy to have feelings toward people, regardless their perceived status, but it's inappropriate and ultimately unethical to act upon those feelings within the framework of the ensemble. It's equally unethical to be inordinately sanctimonious and prudish. That kind of repressive behavior, in my opinion, encourages dishonesty and deceit. Instead, there's a fine ethical line to be walked, allowing freedom of expression, but respecting the rights and feelings of all involved.

I suggest that members of a group wishing to sense true ensemble awareness should lead their quest for the truth by first surrendering to the more powerful and practical pursuit of honesty. Truth as a concept, especially early on, divides people. It tends to be linked to subjective notions that are themselves linked to cultural biases, parental conditioning, and philosophies of personal comfort. Honesty, on the other hand, unites people and allows for mutual respect, humor, warmth, and true growth. There may be moments of consensus that feel true at the time, but moment-to-moment honesty allows for much deeper learning.

Honesty isn't an easy state to achieve. To be honest with someone implies first that one must be honest with oneself. To be honest to oneself isn't easy, because there are usually many subtle delusionary systems in place that need to be assessed and honestly revealed. An honest leader, for example, is someone who is capable of admitting they don't know, but has the resources to soon find out.

Clarity of thought, speech, and action is a worthy goal. Honesty is useless unless it can be communicated in clear, unmuddied terms. However, clarity need not translate as overly "simplistic" or "mundane." A complex metaphor, for example, spoken clearly at the correct moment can have an extremely powerful influence on people. Whether simple or sophisticated, everyone must work to maintain clear open lines of communication among all members of the group. That clarity should then be applied to the forms of theatrical expression. Good intentions and fabulous experiences within the ensemble amount to nothing unless they clearly communicate something of value to the world at large.

Keep in mind that mistakes will be made; feelings will get hurt from time to time; sessions will bomb; some terrific groups will self-destruct and others, less terrific, will be tight-knit for years. There are no guarantees. Still, the pursuit of an ensemble experience is worthy and one that gives hope for the future of culture and community. That hopeful idea is best and most beautifully described in the following story.

THE ELEPHANT STORY

A famous Sufi story tells of four blind men who have heard of the existence of an unusual creature near their village. They elect to go find it. They separate and spread out in all directions. After each has successfully encountered the creature they return to the village and relate their experiences.

Sufi One tells the others the creature is very wide and very very round. Sufi Two disagrees and tells the others the creature is very thin and has a snake–like appearance with soft skin near the mouth. Sufi Three disagrees, saying his creature was like the trunk of a tree only it had thick stubby roots and moved around from time to time. The last Sufi scoffed at the others and told them *his* creature was flat, like a huge leaf, and flapped to and fro.

They were confused by their varied reports and began to argue vehemently in support of their own experiences. Luckily, another Sufi nearby, who had overheard the entire discussion, remarked that it might be possible that each had experienced a part of something much bigger and that if they combine their descriptions they may find their creature. Hearing the wisdom of their fellow seeker, they combined their descriptions and it soon became apparent to all that they'd found an elephant.

The purpose of this story is to illustrate why it's important to work in groups from time to time. A combined vision helps to elim-inate the natural inclination to assume that one's own small piece of experience is representative of the whole picture. Once the pieces are shared, the whole image can come into focus and reveal insights that might otherwise have remained hidden.

What follows is a practical text designed to provide a usable resource of ritual theatre exercises and a sequence of teaching that suggests how to equip a group of individuals to formulate an aim and to create an authentic ensemble. I wish you success and joy in your journey. May your efforts benefit us all.

PART I

THE JOURNEY BEGINS BY WARMING UP

The need for a warm–up must not be underestimated. Warm–ups are needed to prepare the voice and body for activities beyond everyday demands. They change the body from a cool relatively stagnant state to a warmer more active state.

Warm–ups in the theatre, as in athletics, are also used for injury prevention. The events on the stage, particularly battle scenes and action sequences involve a degree of risk. A body and voice in a warm and ready state has a much better chance of coping with those demands. In addition, warm–ups are a very effective device for creating bonds and bridges between separate personalities. People who gather as an ensemble are like any other group: each person carries with them an entire universe of perceptions, dreams, memories, fears, and social conditions which contribute to the creation of artificial barriers, layers of subjective distance. If the members know one another, the buffers of expectation can often add to that distance; creating a gap that is difficult to close.

In the beginning, it is unwise to attempt to bridge gaps directly. It is better to start with something simple and innocuous, like a warm–up. A group warm–up is an activity which is preparatory and non–threatening. The equity of sweat and breath in a context that does not imply judgement allows various personality types to blend and gradually close the distance between them. This bridgework between the group members can allow significant progress toward ensemble flow.

The style of warm–up and the exercises used are usually determined by the leader. Generally speaking, however, they should include the following three things: systematic contact with the primary joints and major muscle groups in the body: the face, the neck, the trapezius muscles at the top of the shoulder, the shoulder joint, elbow, wrist and finger joints, the sides, the waist, the hips, the knees, ankles and toes, the upper and lower abdominals, the lower back, mid to upper back, the quatracepts or thigh muscles, the hamstrings and calf muscles and the muscles of the hands and feet. Weaved into the warm-up of the various joints and muscles should be exercises that focus the mind and activate the breath. Finally, if the work is going to be particularly demanding or intimate, it is important to include exercises that activate the emotional center.

Many of the exercises in this book will be useful for such a comprehensive warm-up. Ideally, they should be arranged and sequenced according to the expertise of the leader and the particular needs of each specific group. However, to facilitate the early stages of the work, I will at the end of part one, provide several suggested sequences from which to choose.

The warm-up will become increasingly important to the creative life of the participants as their work assumes a particular character. If masks are worn, for example, the neck and shoulders will need extra limbering and preparation, if the work utilizes quite alot of running around, it will be important to use the warm-ups as an aerobic preparation to secure ample wind power for the performance. These selective aspects of the warm-up will present themselves quite naturally as the work advances. In the beginning, however, enjoy the warm-up as a means to get everyone focused and ready to start the ensemble journey.

PHYSICAL POSTURES

The first step to developing an ensemble is to create a common language. A common language helps formulate the way of working for the group. Later it evolves into the style associated with that particular ensemble. One of the most reliable foundations on which to build this common language is through physical postures. Postures resonate universal moods and emotions which then work quickly to link the participants to a kinetic grammar that can be easily transformed into creative expression.

The standard postures have been adopted from a wide variety

PHOTO: MARK OLSEN

The "A" Frame Posture in Performance.

of cultures and disciplines. They have, for the most part, been in use for hundreds of years, refining the body and enhancing theatrical expression.

As you begin this work, move slowly and smoothly, keeping the breath stream open, the eyes alert, and the mind focused. Unlike certain muscle–building activities, do not assume that pain is an indicator of good work. If pain accompanies any posture, particularly those involving the spine, ease off and check your alignment. If the alignment appears to be correct, and you still experience pain, then you are not ready to do the posture. Discomfort or a rigorous challenge to the body is good, not sharp or agonizing pain. Be content to gradually build up to it.

Some postures are obviously designed for expression while others are less expressive, designed instead to reinforce proper structural alignment. Nearly all of them, however, contain elements of both. Please take special care to master this first stage of work before going on. The postural language of the body and its connection to the rest of the instrument are the roots that secure the growth of the tree.

Begin working on the postures by incorporating two or three of them into a basic group warm–up. Gradually, over the course of several weeks, add the others. Because postures are often static, they can go dead very fast. They can lose their effectiveness and become dull, lifeless, and uninteresting. Everyone must remain extra vigilant to keep the postures vibrant and alive. I do not prescribe an exact learning sequence for these postures because everyone's physical structure is different. Some people will find a posture easy to accomplish while others will be struggling just to approximate it. Nevertheless, I have organized the descriptions into an order that represents a fairly reliable and gradual progression.

STANDING POSTURES

1. ZERO POSITION

This is a neutral "ready" position, energized, balanced, and full of potential energy. It's a handy position to arrive at a uniform ready posture during warm-ups or in other more theatrical situations.

The feet are at an easy forty-five degree angle with the heels touching gently. The weight is evenly distributed between both legs and placed slightly forward of center on the feet. The knees are aligned, but not locked. The hips should be centered directly over the legs. The torso should be aligned with the hips and allowed to float upwards slightly.

Floating the torso does NOT mean to puff the chest out or to stiffen the ribs. It is instead, a delicate stretching upwards out of the hips with a sense of lightness as the chest relaxes and the back extends upwards.

The arms should be relaxed at the sides with the fingertips touching the outside of the thigh. The elbows should be lifted slightly and the shoulders relaxed and centered slightly forward. The neck and head should also line up over the hips. Allow the head to float up until the eyes are looking at an imaginary horizon line.

Keep in mind this isn't the "attention" posture of the military, but simply a neutral ready position which breathes and retains a degree of flexibility.

The spine is lengthened with the natural convex curves at the neck and lower back allowed to exist without undue pressure to straighten the neck or tuck the pelvis.

2. PARALLEL ZERO

Exactly like the zero position except the feet are placed parallel, hip-width apart, with the weight evenly distributed to include the use of the little toe for balance. This will insure that the foot doesn't collapse inward, forcing a misalignment of the knees. Let the arms drop relaxed and slightly rolled forward.

3. THE A-FRAME

Place the feet wider than shoulder width, turned out from the hips at an easy forty-five degrees. Keep the knees straight, but not locked. The arms can now assume a variety of positions which will evoke different moods. Try folding them in front of the chest, hands on hips, held loosely in front or back.

4. THE HORSE STANCE

A standard position in nearly all martial arts, the horse stance is balanced, strong, and develops a great deal of lower body strength.

There are two basic variations. First, stand with the legs wider than hips width, bow the knees outward, sit straight down into it until the knees line up with the toes. Keep the back straight and the weight poured into the outside or blades of the feet. Do not let the tailbone arch back; keep it centered and dropped to the floor. Stay in this position for a full minute.

Second, stand with the legs wider than the hips and instead of bowing them outward, tuck the pelvis and wrap the muscles inward as though you were indeed riding a horse and using the legs to grip. Place the weight on the blades of the feet. Sitting deep within this position and with the back aligned, wait for a full minute.

As you get stronger, you will be able to stay in these positions for longer and longer periods of time.

5. THE CAT STANCE

This is another common martial arts posture develops strength, balance, and agility.

From zero position, step back with the right leg and drop the tailbone as if about to sit on a barstool. Now draw the left leg closer in with the heel lifted allowing only the ball of the foot to touch the floor. The image often used for this posture is that one foot, in this case the right foot, is the deep root of the tree and the other foot is the tap root.

Be sure that the knee of the support leg isn't over the toe. If a line were drawn from the knee to the floor, it would touch the center of the first and second toe. If it touches the floor, the person must adjust the posture to protect the knee.

The arms can find a variety of positions to accentuate various

PHOTO: JIM CALDWELL

The "Lunge" in Performance — The Duel from *Hamlet*.

(Houston Shakespeare Festival. Directed by Sidney Berger.)

qualities of this posture. The front foot can also improvise a bit with various positions as long as the primary root support remains solid. Maintain this cat stance for several minutes, until the muscles begin to heat up and shake. Repeat the position on the other side.

6. THE LUNGE

This very useful position is frequently used in theatre and as well as certain sports. The correct lunge is a combination of good leg flexibility and proper structural alignment.

Stand with the left leg turned out from the hip, foot pointing to the left and the right leg pulled in, foot pointing straight ahead. Both heels should be touching. Now take a long step forward, leading with the right foot. Keep the torso lifted and centered on the hips. The hips should be facing forward and the back leg should be straight, but not locked, with the heel fully on the floor.

As the hips rotate forward, the back foot will naturally roll to a forty-five degree angle. This is fine as long as the foot doesn't collapse, rolling onto the ankle, or the heel doesn't come off the floor.

The front knee should be aligned with the toes. If the knee goes further than the toes, the structural alignment is off. If not corrected early, misalignment of this kind could result in severe damage to the ligaments of the knee.

When done correctly, a person in a deep lunge should be able to balance a plate on the extended front thigh. The stretch for a deep lunge happens more in the groin than in the legs. If you wish to deepen or lengthen the lunge, instead of leaning over or pressing the front knee forward, think instead of sitting down into the lunge while allowing the back leg to slide to the rear.

Arm placement should be dictated by the conditions of the lunge. Unless instructed otherwise by a director for dramatic reasons, avoid bending over at the waist. An open lifted torso presents a much better picture for this position.

Make sure to master the lunge on both legs. Working only one side can result in poor alignment and imbalance.

7. ANGULAR STANDING POSTURES

By breaking up the line of the body into angles, the body becomes more interesting, more complex. Sculptors and painters have known this since the days of ancient Greece. Many of the ancient Greek statues present the body in a stunning variety of angles.

Stand with the left leg slightly in front, drop the weight into the right hip, rotate the chest slightly to the right and incline it downward to the right, turn the head to the left. This approximates the sensuous S-curve which has reappeared throughout cultural history (whenever a society aspired to the classical ideals of physical beauty and harmony).

Angular postures are also associated with the postures of famous movie stars and high fashion models. As an exercise, find photographs that capture a specific mood or drape the body in interesting ways. Place your own body into the exact postures and stay there until you can recreate each posture with ease.

Some angular postures are not linked to classical beauty, but instead depict specific characters in a particular period of history. The Italian Commedia dell'arte, for example, has a panoply of stock characters that all adhere to angular postures signifing the character.

One very good way to capture the essence of a character is to place yourself into that character's posture, staying and playing there until related movements suggest themselves. For example, to find Arrlechino, the famous trickster character from Commedia, you must first step back on the right leg, getting into a deep cat stance. Now move the front leg to the left side. Rotate the right hip until the lower back arches and the right buttock sticks out a little toward the front. Then lift the toes of the left foot off the ground, place the right hand loosely on the right hip and the left arm held aloft in a theatrical flourish. Cock the head in quick darting motions like a monkey.

Reproduce the posture on the other side. Now hop back and forth between postures. Play with the leg and arm movements as you switch back and forth, sometimes pointing, sometimes flexing the feet. Gradually you'll feel the sly, devilishness of this character and begin to move according to rules absorbed from the posture and changes.

Note: Angular body presentations are the most interesting to watch onstage. They carry an innate tension, necessary for creating dynamic stage pictures.

SITTING POSTURES, CHAIR

Strange as it may sound, most people do not really know how to sit in a chair, much less on the floor. They assume the way they've always sat is correct because the familiarity of their habitual posture tells them that it feels right. It's possible, however, to have the wrong sense of what's right.

By reevaluating physical alignment in various sitting postures, one begins to open up to new possibilities and new relationships.

The basics of aligned sitting are nothing more than a balanced relationship to gravity. However, if the chest is pinched, the head locked, the pelvis frozen, or the rib cage slumped deep into a cushion or chair back, there can be no balanced relationship to gravity.

Start by sitting on the edge of the chair. Place the feet directly under the knees and the knees about hip-width apart. Keep the spine long and the pelvis flexible. The head should be aligned with the hip bones as though a straight line were drawn up from the hips to the center of the ear. The eyes should look out at an imaginary horizon line, the arms dropped onto the lap in a relaxed manner.

Allow the chest to melt downward while the spine lengthens. As you inhale, allow the pelvis to rock backward slightly and as you exhale, allow the pelvis to rock forward. The word "allow" is important since you do not want to get in the way by forcing. Instead, release in the hips and let the breath itself do the movement.

Now lean forward from the hips, keeping a lengthened spine all the way over until the lower rib cage touches the thighs. Keeping that length, come back up to the sitting position. You should feel slightly taller. Again, keeping the breath flowing naturally, find the easy rocking motion of the pelvis which in turn helps to free up and balance the head at the upper end of the spine.

This balance game with an elongated spine is also to be played in the sitting positions on the floor, though it becomes harder

PHOTO: TOM PALUMBO

Sitting Positions (FROM LEFT TO RIGHT): **The Bundle, The Squat, The Princess, The Prince, the Bench, the "4," The "Z."**

because there are more variables. Nevertheless, this unforced relationship to gravity should prevail whenever possible.

Now find a meeting place between the ideal balance and the more expressive sitting postures. Using a chair and remaining loose and lengthened, explore the many variations of sitting postures such as perching, lounging, straddling, slumping, draping, leaning, gripping and so forth.

By viewing sitting as well as standing as a relationship to gravity, one avoids the temptation to "lock in" a posture which will rob it of its grace and potential energy.

SITTING POSTURES, FLOOR

Sitting on the floor, for most Westerners, is an arduous task. The back feels strained, the feels cramped, and there never seems to be a position that's truly comfortable. To find the natural sitting postures on the floor, however, one needs only to watch a young toddler. A two-year-old who is still experimenting with walking and sitting develops a wide variety of options. Nearly all are with a lengthened spine, a balanced head, and a free and unlocked rib cage.

For those of us well beyond the experimentation stage, our habits have imposed limitations that greatly restrict our choices.

The following positions offer a few options. For dancers and people with limber bodies, they'll be fairly easy. For others, they'll be more demanding and therefore must be approached in gradual stages.

1. THE BUNDLE Start by sitting on the floor with the feet parallel. Pull the knees up toward the chest, wrap the arms around the knees, and pull gently on the knees while lengthening the lower back. Stay in the posture until you feel balanced and relaxed.

2. THE PRINCE From the bundle position, tuck the right leg under the left allowing the knee to fall naturally to the floor on the right side. Place the right hand to the side of the body about ten inches away from the right hip and drape the left arm on top of the left knee which has remained bent in the elevated position. Keep the head elegant and free. Repeat this posture to the other side.

3. THE BEACH From the prince position, place both hands behind the back for support. Keeping the feet on the floor, bend the knees toward the chest. Lengthen the spine while pressing down on the shoulders to avoid slumping. A variation on this posture is to bend the arms, with the torso supported by the elbows. Be careful not to let the chest sink down and the shoulders pull high. Keep the spine lengthened.

4. THE PRINCESS From the raised arm support of the beach position, let the knees fall to the right side and release the left arm forward, which brings the torso forward. The bottom of the right foot should be near the left knee and the left foot folded back in proximity to the left hip. Return to the beach position and repeat the posture to the left.

5. THE "Z" SIT This is a variation on the princess pose that allows the hips to open up while providing a stretch for the thigh. Start by sitting in the princess pose. Pull the left leg as far back around to the left as it will go. Next, bring the bent right leg directly in front of the hips. Sit up out of the hips and lean forward slightly. Place the hands on the floor and keep the shoulders relaxed. Repeat to the other side.

6. THE "4" POSITION From the "Z" posture, bring the back leg forward and straighten it. The other leg should be bent with the foot touching the inner thigh of the extended leg. In an odd way, this shape resembles the number four. This is a particularly important position in the recovery from a roll. If the momentum brings the torso upward, the bent leg will rotate naturally to allow the body to rise up over the shin bone, thus protecting the knee from hyperextension. Experience the posture on both sides.

7. THE SQUAT Once mastered, the squat elongates and relaxes the muscles of the lower back, maintains long and flexible achilles tendons, and is considered by most people in the postural integration field to be a prerequisite for good standing posture.

To squat correctly, place feet parallel with the inside arch of the feet aligned with the outside of the hipbones. Think of sitting down on a stool, and then, without arching the back, *allow* the buttocks to descend smoothly, keeping the shoulders and neck relaxed.

The descent is tricky. Avoid letting the weight pour into the balls of the feet. Instead, think of it placed in the heels. Above all, DON'T LET THE KNEES BUCKLE INWARD! (This rotates the ankles and twists the tendons of the knees.)

Once you have fully folded down into the squat, check to make sure the weight is poured slightly to the outside or *blades* of the feet. Now lengthen the spine, rest the knees in the armpits and relax into it. You'll discover various positions of the squat, but two of them are the most apparent. One is with the spine long and the head erect. The other is with the spine rounded, the head tucked, shoulders curled up inside the legs.

While in the squat, there are a number of exercises which can take advantage of this position. You can, for example, place the hands together in a prayer position, wedge the elbows on the inside of the thigh just below the knee, and press down. The elbows will force the legs open and provide a good stretch for the groin. Do this slowly by inhaling and then pressing open the legs during the exhale. Repeat several times.

You can also use this position to strengthen the feet. Simply raise up onto the balls of the feet and descend again slowly and controlled. Do this thirty times and you'll begin to feel just how beneficial this exercise can be. Be careful to limit the movements *only* to the feet. Avoid the temptation to lift the hips or chest.

If you cannot get into the squat fully or if it is painful, rely for a short time on your hands. Place the hands to the front or back of the body to stabilize the balance. This way you can gradually work into the position over the course of a month or two. Another effective way of working into the squat is to hold onto a door handle or some other stable object, like a heavy table, and then descend into the squat. By holding on, you can fold down to the level that remains comfortable and slowly control the stretching with your arms as you ease into the position. Don't force anything! Modern furniture and certainly shoes with heels have contributed to the unnatural shortening of the Achilles tendon. This can, and will lengthen over time, so don't rush it.

8. SECOND POSITION Borrowed from dance, proper alignment is essential to accomplish this posture as is considerable flexibility in the hips, lumbar, and hamstrings. Sit with the back against a wall and the lower spine lengthened. Spread the legs apart as far as they'll go until you feel the first layer of stretch. Turn the legs out by rotating the leg in the hip socket so that the inner thigh turns toward the ceiling.

Stretch the upper torso in all directions, working to free up the lower spine. Work to maintain a straight back and an elegant lengthened neck. If you can manage this posture with a degree of ease, move away from the wall and recreate it. This posture is excellent for depicting children, puppets, dancers, and so forth.

9. THE FETAL POSITION Nearly everyone knows this position, a re-creation of the position the fetus most often chooses while in the mother's womb. I have included it in case someone may have missed it or forgotten it somewhere along the way.

Laying on your side, draw the knees up to the chest, curl the spine gently, and let the arms pull inward to whatever position feels most natural. Allow all tension to drop away.

In some people, due either to posture or physical size, the head is strained while resting on the floor. If this occurs, loosen the position by spreading out slightly onto the stomach. This should clear the lower shoulder and allow the head to rest easy.

10. THE FOLDED LEAF A standard position of rest, the folden leaf allows maximum breath expansion into the chest cavity while the skeletal structure is in repose. It can be expressive in postures of supplication or worship, and is one of the best remedies for sudden nausea or dizziness.

There are many ways to get into it.

1. From lying down on the back, simply roll to one side, pull the knees up to the chest (fetal position), roll over onto

the knees, resting the forehead on the floor. The arms and hands extend onto the floor either by the head or next to the hips.

2. From a stand, take a step back and descend straight down, landing the weight on the rear knee. Pull the other knee back, fold both knees so the buttocks are resting on the heels, bend forward from the hips until the forehead rests on the floor and the arms rest in their favorite position.

3. From a squat, tip forward onto the hands, bring the knees to the floor, tuck the toes under, and lay the head down. This position can be used to stretch the muscles around the shoulder and scapula by extending the arms out overhead and using the fingers to "walk" along the floor, thereby extending the stretch.

Above all, this is a position of passive rest. Small adjustments can be made to distribute the weight, but be sure to find a still point where you can simply relax into it.

11. THE COBRA Borrowed from the Hindu Hatha Yoga tradition and a standard stretch in almost all Yoga workouts.

Start by lying down on the stomach with the hands on the floor, palms down, directly under the shoulders. Using the eyes as guides, look up and let the head follow smoothly and slowly, lifting it as far as it can go. The shoulders will then follow, lifting while using only minimum pressure from the arms. Next, arch the upper back as the head curls up to face the ceiling. You should do a long slow inhale during the entire lift sequence.

Do not think of this as a coiling motion, but rather an unfolding. Allow the spine to *lengthen* into this posture. If you feel any sharp pain in the back, reduce the lift by a few inches and use more arm strength to support you. This is designed primarily to stretch the upper spine and to open the cavity of the upper chest.

Descend to the floor as you slowly exhale, laying the chest onto the floor as if it were a carpet unrolling. Do this several times making sure to breathe fully with each phase of the posture.

PHOTOS: JIM CALDWELL

Some Theatrical Postures In Performance

(*A MIDSUMMER NIGHT'S DREAM*, HOUSTON SHAKESPEARE FESTIVAL.
DIRECTED BY CAROLYN BOONE.)

12. THE PLOW   A series of positions, also borrowed from the Hindu Hatha Yoga tradition, the Plow is especially effective at stretching the spine, lengthening the hamstrings, and opening up the area around the kidneys.

To begin, lie down on a mat or a semi-cushioned surface. (The raw floor surface can be too hard on the spine in the early stages.) Next, bring the knees up with the feet on the floor near the buttocks. Place the hands at the sides of the hips and press the fingertips lightly onto the mat.

Using a rocking motion of the hips and some help with the fingertips, swing the knees up and over, resting them next to the ears. Everything at this point should be very relaxed and easy. The hips must be high enough and forward enough to allow the knees to drop easily by the ears. (Some people advocate the use of the hands to support the hips. I don't because I think it facilitates a crutch whereby the stomach muscles never quite develop the proper support.

At any rate, once you're there, concentrate on even but deep breaths. You will feel the last row of floating ribs expanding with the breath. It's slightly uncomfortable at first, especially if you let the entire torso crunch downward. Keep a slight sense of lift in the hips and there'll be more room for breath.

Now let the toes touch the floor behind the head. Inhale, straighten the legs; exhale; relax back and let the knees rest by the ears. Again, straighten the legs on the inhale, and relax back on the exhale. Do this about five times.

Next, roll down the spine one vertebra at a time using the breath as a guide. Inhale deeply and as you do, visualize the uppermost vertebra on which your weight is resting. Now exhale and come down to the space *between the vertebrae*: stay there, relaxed, and inhale. As you exhale, roll down *one* vertebra and inhale again, deeply, then exhale, and as you do, roll down *one* vertebra, and so on down the entire spine.

There are two places where it gets difficult and you'll be tempted to skip over a few vertebrae: mid-back and lower-back.

Do not skip over them. If your stomach muscles are weak, you will, perhaps, need the assistance of your hands on the floor to control the descent of the torso. Try, however, to maintain strict adherence to the "single vertebra" breathing technique. When you have reached the last vertebra connecting to the coccyx, let the knees relax down, placing the feet onto the floor. Once there, let the entire back relax as you breathe slowly and fully.

One additional note, as you work down the spine, the head will want to roll upwards with the chin towards the ceiling. Allow this to happen. In fact, even in the full curl with the knees by the ears, the head can be tilted a little upwards. This avoids overstretching the spine and follows the natural needs of the body.

Because of the degree of stretch this position allows, it's advisable to follow this up with a *contra-stretch* such as the Cobra, or, as described below, the Bridge or the Back Arch.

13. THE BRIDGE Use the same starting position as the Plow. Take the hips and knees up and over as in the Plow, only this time place the *thumbs* under the hips with the fingers wrapped around to the front. Bring the elbows in underneath the hips for support. Keeping the hips high, let the feet arc over and land back onto the floor where they were in the beginning. You will see that you've created a little bridge with the pelvis arching upwards. Stay here and breath in and out deeply. To maximize the stretch, walk the feet closer to the buttocks and lift onto the toes as the pelvis lifts higher.

14. THE BACK ARCH In the starting position again with the knees up, feet on the floor by the buttocks this time place the hands by the ears with the fingers pointing toward the top of the head and the thumb near the ears.

Make sure the feet are well in towards the buttocks and then raise up onto the toes slightly. Lift the pelvis up into a bridge and then pour the weight into the legs as you begin to lift the upper back with the arms. *Do not lift straight up!* This is too much strain on the wrists and elbows. Instead, maintain the weight pouring into the legs by pushing *laterally* toward the knees. Don't allow the knees to buckle!

Once the arms have nearly straightened, bring the pelvis to center, pouring the weight into the arms and centering the weight evenly between the arms and the legs.

The back should be arched high with the hips at the apex of the bend. The head should hang loose and be free to look around. Stay here for several full breaths.

To descend, simply reverse the process: pour the weight out of the arms by shifting laterally into the legs. Then as the upper back descends, lift the head and return the weight to the arms as the back gently lands onto the floor.

This is a major stretch for the spine and, as such, should be followed or preceded by an equally effective spine stretch in the opposite direction.

15. KNEELING POSITIONS There are a wide variety of choices for these basic positions. All are very useful in the theatre. We're perhaps most familiar with the "L" shape kneel whereby a person is simply standing on the knees with the lower legs tucked behind. This is often used as a religious posture for prayer or supplication.

A variation on this is simply to bend the knees and let the hips rest on the heels. This has a more passive feel to it and especially in the Orient, is a common sitting position. The toes in this position can be either pointed or flexed, giving the position more subtle variations.

A single leg can be removed from the position and placed in front. This gives the shape more kinetic potential and strengthens the line of the body. The foot can be placed open to the side or directly in front of the hips, depending on the desired effect. The upper body can now lean on the thigh in various positions, giving more variety of expression. Again, the toes add a dimension of passive rest or potential movement depending on whether they're pointed or flexed.

One note of warning: the knees are delicate and as such need some degree of special care. Avoid any movements requiring you to land on the knees. Crashing down onto the knees may have a certain dramatic effect, but is structurally dangerous. If you need to get to a kneeling position quickly, find ways of getting there where the weight and forces of momentum will be absorbed by another part of the body.

16. SPIRALING UPWARDS This is actually a series of positions which reflects one of the simplest and most economical ways of getting from a prone position to a stand. It's designed to flow from one position to another with a minimum of effort.

To begin, lie down on the floor or a mat surface, back down and chest facing the ceiling. Relax. Turn the head to the right or left. If you have looked right, lift your left knee upwards until fully bent. Then let it fall to the right, shifting the weight of the hips and turning the lower body slightly. Next, lift the left arm and place it palm down on the right side of the body.

Doing the first three moves gets you into a position which enables you to pull the legs up to the chest into a fetal position. After you've done this, use only the effort needed to turn the body onto the knees. *Keep the head and neck relaxed throughout this exercise*!

You're now in the Folded Leaf Position. Pour the weight into the upper arms as you widen the legs to hips width and place the toes down onto the floor. Now pour the weight back into the legs and onto the feet. You should now be in the Full Squat position. Keeping the head and neck relaxed, lift the buttocks up until the legs are almost straight. Now begin to build the spine one vertebra at a time. Come up slowly and smoothly.

The head should be the last thing to come up and it should be placed center, with the eyes to the imaginary horizon line.

If you were to start this spiral ascent by turning the head to the left, all the directions relative to that would simply be reversed, of course.

BREATH WORK

T he foundation for all work in the theatre is breath. The breath is the link to the emotions, to relaxation, to power, and to vitality (as well as to staying alive!) It's also a key ingredient in creating an ensemble.

We don't normally use our full lung capacity. When the body is suddenly exposed to a higher dose of oxygen than it's used to, a number of new sensations result. Most sensations are pleasant; those few unpleasant sensations are usually short–lived. If, however, you feel extremely lightheaded or nauseous, descend to a folded leaf position and breathe slowly. Resume the exercise only after your system has stabilized.

I recently had a student come to me and ask advice on how she might improve her cario–vascular endurance. She is an older, return-ing student who also has a mild case of asthma. I could tell from her approach to the subject, she was wanting a program to "attack" the problem, to get in there with a hefty aerobic regimen that would serve to get her quickly into shape. My advice came as a surprise to her. I recommended that she embark upon easy sessions of yoga, perhaps a little swimming and relinquish the willful need to "fix" her breath. I recommended letting her growth in other areas be a source of pride. Her shortness of breath wasn't a major obstacle and I could see it was more important for her to be kind and loving to her breathing apparatus. (It so happened that I was the third teacher to recommend yoga to her, so I think she got the message)

The point of this story is to remind you that you musn't assume a boot camp mentality regarding any of this work, but especially regarding breath work. Also, remember every person is different and will respond differently to each exercise. Had the request for advice come from another student, my response would have been very dif-ferent. Therefore know that some of these exercises will be a perfect fit for you and you will derive great benefit while others might fall away without an imprint. And that's fine. Just because an exercise isn't connecting deeply with you, does not mean that it isn't provid-ing something of real value to another in the group.

The breath work is designed as a means to focus the mind, to connect with the emotional system, to expand the range of expres-sion, and to link with fellow participants. So smile, take a deep breath and begin.

1. CIRCULAR WARM THROUGH

This is an easy warm–up that isolates the major divisions of the body and helps develop control of those specific muscle groups. It also works as a good awakener for the body before going into more demanding warm–up or task–oriented activities.

Start from stillness in the Zero position. Begin by tilting the head forward with the chin near the chest. Inhale as you roll the head upward in a small clockwise circle, and exhale as the head completes the circle going down. Continue, letting the head spiral in increasingly large circles until the largest one is reached at ten. Reverse direction and repeat. Keep all other parts of the body still, allowing only the head and neck to move.

Next, roll the shoulders in forward circles ten times, inhaling going up and exhaling on the downward path of the circle (maintaining the progression of small circles to large). Repeat the opposite direction. Be sure to keep the arms straight and to breathe with each rotation.

Now lift the arms out to the sides in a "T" formation, release the arms from the elbow down, letting them dangle, and with the elbows held as if pinned in space, circle the lower arms like propellers. Do this ten times each direction (*without* an exact breath pattern or attempting to go from small to large rotations).

Straighten the arms directly in front of you and make fists. Circle the fists toward the inside ten times, inhaling deeply; then repeat to the opposite direction exhaling deeply.

Take a small lunge onto the right leg and begin to vigorously swing the left arm from the shoulder, making large circles while opening and shutting the hand. Do this ten times and then repeat, circling the other direction. Next, take a small lunge onto the left leg and repeat the exercise.

Grab a large imaginary beach ball. Keep the arms extended and open as you begin to form small clockwise circles that gradually get bigger until they reach the fullest extent at number ten. Reverse the circle pattern and then repeat the exercise to the other side.

Drop over from the waist and swing from side to side in a

relaxed manner. The arms should brush the floor slightly; the knees should be gently bent and the neck relaxed. Build the pendulum of the sweep, inhaling as the torso swings upward and exhaling on the downward stroke, until it takes you into full circles. Circle ten times one direction breathing on the upper swing and exhaling on the downward swing, and then do ten the other direction.

Imagine you're standing in the center of a huge barrel. Wrapped around your waist is a big fluffy towel. Your job is to dry off the inside of the barrel without moving from the center spot. This exercise should fully engage the pelvis, hips, and waist. Enhance the exercise with occasional directives to "hurry up," or to "reeeeeally scrub" the inside of the barrel.

Lift one knee until the thigh becomes level and then circle the leg from the knee down ten times one direction and ten times the other. Do this with both legs.

Stand with all the weight on the left leg and place the right leg slightly in front in a forced arch. Pour about 30 percent of the weight into the ball of the right foot and then circle the knee. As you look down, the foot should be in the center of a circle drawn by the knee. This exercise limbers up both the knee and the ankle joint. Do this ten times in both directions and on both legs.

Finish by briskly breathing in and out while stamping the feet and circling various parts of the body at random. You should feel refreshed, loose, and ready to work.

2. CIRCLE RUN

In a large room, preferably where participants can go barefoot, create one large circle with the leader at the center. Upon completion of the circle, have every other participant step out and form an inner circle. Have the outer circle turn to their right and the inner to their left. Staying on the balls of the feet, everyone should begin a steady slow jog in place.

Stabilize the rhythm until everyone is synchronized. Without speaking, begin to demonstrate how they're to breathe with this rhythm: In In – Out Out. The inhales are done through the nose the exhales through the mouth. Keep this breath rhythm going in per–

fect time with the feet. When everyone has synchronized in place, the leader should make a gesture to instruct each circle to begin running in the respective directions.

Keep the run an easy jog and make sure everyone maintains the same even rhythm. Now allow the exhale to have a slightly louder sound, somewhat like a stage whisper. Keep the run going in this manner for several minutes.

Staying in the center of the circles, the leader should give a sharp double clap indicating they're to return to running in place. Next, introduce a change in the breath by adding a third exhale to the original rhythm, creating a triplet: In In/Out Out Out. After the new rhythm is established, the leader should have everyone turn the opposite direction and begin to run again. Maintain the run for several minutes.

After one or two more rhythm changes, invented by the leader, slow the circles down to an easy walking pace. This time everyone will be producing a relaxed, open "Ha" sound on the exhale. The opening rhythm will become: In In, "Ha Ha." Try the voiced exhale version of the exercise for several minutes each direction.

3. PANTING

A great aerobic workout for the diaphragm muscle. Over time it can increase lung power and improve the ease with which many of the participants speak.

On hands and knees, start with a simple pant, keeping the tongue and jaw relaxed. Pretend to be a dog on a hot summer day. The panting at this stage is fast and light, designed primarily to locate and activate the diaphragm in preparation for more demanding work. Take frequent rest stops during this part.

After ten minutes, everyone should be warmed up enough to try the next phase. Go into a fullscale hyper panting mode, as if running a race. Keep the head and neck relaxed and have the freedom to move the back if you feel like it. You may indeed experience some cramping; the diaphragm will sort of freeze up after the first minute or so. This is normal and nothing to be alarmed about.

The challenge in this exercise is to maintain the panting effort long enough for the diaphragm to reactivate. After about two minutes of nothing but interrupted attempts at sustained panting, something unusual occurs: the diaphragm seems to be ready to commit to even longer efforts. This pattern goes on for some time, the panting builds until the diaphragm becomes quite warm and flexible.

The length of this panting race really depends upon the individuals participating. Five minutes, however, should be enough for any beginner. After a brief rest, the panting race can begin again. This time the participants should vocalize during the moments of frustration and discomfort. The sounds should be free and uninhibited, reflecting the exact sensations experienced in the body. Again, beginners might want to stop after five minutes.

Afterwards, you will want to lie back and gently massage your abdomen. Take long deep breaths and stretch the body in all directions until ready to go on to the next task.

4. HOME BASE

This is one of my favorite exercises for breath. I first encountered it while studying voice techniques with the Roy Hart Theatre in France. It incorporates both release and control functions while engaging the players in a delightful game. The game aspect of the exercise provides for a much higher degree of commitment and accomplishment.

Find a spot in the room you can call Home Base. It could be a speck on the floor, a tape mark, or anything nearby that can easily help identify the spot as a place to return through easy visual identification.

Make sure there are no obstacles in the space that could impede a chaotic traffic pattern. Make sure the home bases approximate an even distribution. An uneven congregation of people at any one place in the room can make the exercise difficult.

Once you've found home base, it is there and *only* there where you get "inspiration." That is, you may *inhale* at home base. You may not *exhale* there and must lean off the central axis or step to one side for the exhale. Have everyone experience this breathing mode for a few minutes.

You are to take a full breath and to paint the space with your exhale. Visualize a specific color and, like a human airbrush, travel all over the room painting your masterpiece.

The only restriction is that you may *not* inhale anywhere except at home base. You can see this presents quite a challenge, especially if you're brave enough to venture across the room. You must dash to home base in time to inhale before you implode, catch your breath by exhaling off the central axis and then take another big breath before jumping back into your masterpiece.

Before starting, it is important to be aware of everyone else in the space and to take pains to accomplish the painting without running into anyone. It is advisable to select a leader to direct the events and to act as a safety. The exercise can begin with this simple command from the leader: "At home base, inhale, now paint!"

A strong double clap from the leader can serve to signal everyone to return to home base. Allow a few moments for recovery and then the leader can ask to see individual colors painting the space. Start with the primary colors. Let all the red painters take off, moving through the space until they have to dash for home. Upon their return, send the greens and so forth.

After the primary colors, the leader can send out various pastels, gold or silver, black and white, and any other colors; finally finishing by telling all the remaining colors not yet mentioned to paint the space. Finish this section with one last full–group painting journey.

The next section engages the voice. This time instead of painting with color, you're to paint with sound. You'll take off at full speed while sustaining a clear, well focused open "Aah" sound; once the run begins, the pitch should not vary. As before, you can only inhale at the home base.

It's usually too dangerous for everyone to go at once, so the leader should roam the room and tag people. When they are tagged they're to take off running and painting with their sound all around the others who are standing at their home base. The leader should allow several people to go at the same time, overlapping just a bit to keep a constant flow of sound in the room. It's important that the sound choices are limited to comfortable pitches and are bright, focused sounds.

With a large group, the leader may have to eventually say, "Alright, all those people whom I did not tag – Go!" It's perfectly legal, by the way to tag the same people more than once.

This is a great situation to really challenge the more reserved or vocally locked members of the group.

In addition to the joy of running while sustaining sound, most participants are surprised to learn they can travel much farther and remain away from home base much longer while they're engaged in sustaining sound. Others report a wide variety of sensations, ranging from distress to ecstasy. It's important that the group be allowed a few minutes to discuss their experiences. The assimilation which occurs during such discussions is an important step in the learning process.

Variations on this game include having only a limited number of home bases, placing home base on a body part of someone else who in turn has a base on someone else, travelling in teams, or even reversing the game whereby the home base is the spot for exhale and sound production and the space is the place for inspiration and inhalation. After playing the game several times, other variations may present themselves.

5. YOGIC FULL BREATH

One of the first discoveries people usually make when they begin breath work is that they rarely, if ever, take a full breath. A truly full breath acts as a cleanser for the lungs, clearing out old pockets of stale air that has accumulated. It also provides a much appreciated boost to the oxygen level of the bloodstream, which in turn refreshes and revitalizes the entire system.

In addition, the practice of taking full breaths can expand the lung capacity and provide more power and support for the performer. The additional oxygen maintains good mental clarity and physical vitality and even provides a healthy skin tone. For anyone looking to work at their peak, the yogic full breath is a simple but important tool.

There are a wide variety of postures used in the Hatha Yoga tradition which are wonderful for alignment and flexibility. They also lead to deep levels of meditation. The full breath I refer to here requires only that a person be able to sit normally in a regular chair.

Sitting near the edge of the chair, place both feet squarely on the floor. Lean over from the hips until the lower back begins to lengthen and then return to the upright position, maintaining the length in the back. Place the hands palms up on the top of the thigh with the fingers resting toward the inside. This should square the shoulders and allow the elbows to fan out slightly. Make sure the head is centered and free to move easily in any direction.

This position is a *fluid* one and should not feel restrictive or locked in any way. Its purpose is to allow ample room for the lungs to fully expand. Therefore, feel free to make any adjustments which would better accommodate your structure.

Once in a comfortable but aligned position, begin to exhale all of the air from the lungs. When the air is completely gone, give one last squeeze to force out any hidden residue. The urge to inhale will be very strong. Instead of taking a breath, however, release all holding mechanisms (especially in the throat) and *allow* the breath to rush in on its own. The natural vacuum will create the conditions for a sudden and deeply felt breath. Repeat this vacuuming procedure several times.

Next, without doing an exhale, take in as much air as you can possibly hold in the lungs. Try to fill every last inch of space; paying close attention to filling all around the collar bones. Again, rather than *doing* an exhale, allow the exhale to occur on its own. In both extremes, natural law will work to equalize the air pressure. Try this full inhale several times.

For the full breath we combine the two while encouraging some movement in the torso. The exhale should be a long luxurious process with the torso lifting upwards to counter the temptation to collapse the chest. Once the full exhale is reached, the release allows a rush of air to equalize the breath. The moment the breath is equalized, begin a long slow luxurious inhale. As the air begins to fill the lungs, undulate the spine and move the torso in small circular patterns, inviting the air to enter parts of the back, to fill cavities on the sides, and to completely inflate both lungs to their fullest.

This time, instead of the sudden release, open the mouth, relax the jaw, and allow the air to escape in a steady stream through an open, unvoiced "Ahhhh." Pay close attention to the shoulders and neck, working against the temptation to grip with the muscles. Keep this open exhale going until reaching the full exhale; release, allowing the equalized breath and begin the full inhale once again. Do this full breath at least ten times, stretching the limits of both the inhale and exhale, while taking a luxurious sensual delight in the entire process.

It's normal, especially in the early stages of learning this exercise, for occasional coughing to occur. This is part of the process and actually a sign that residue is being released. Over time the coughs will abate and the overall health and capacity of the lungs will improve immensely.

6. BREATH STEPS

This exercise involves the whole body in the experience of the two basic time signatures: 3/4 and 4/4 time. It's an ensemble experience which demands not only a high degree of individual skill but also a high degree of sensitivity to the larger ensemble facets of the exercise. It's necessary for the leader to have a full grasp of the exercise because it demands a great deal of leadership in the early stages.

With everyone facing the same direction, begin by introducing the breath step that utilizes 4/4 time. This step is very simple at first: from the zero position, take a demi-lunge out onto the right leg as you count "one", step back into the left leg which is the "two"; place the right foot behind you while lifting the left foot slightly, making it the "three" count, and then bring the left foot down in front to complete the "four." Keep the torso centered and repeat this several times until it becomes smooth.

The step gets slightly more complicated as the other elements of breath and gesture are added. In the 4/4 step, the accent is on the first lunge. It's at this accent point that the person should exhale and extend the arms in a friendly welcoming gesture, though inviting a hug. During the other three steps they should inhale through the nose, saving the exhale for the accent beat.

When this basic pattern is mastered, the advanced level can be attempted. During the three return beats with the nasal inhales, the arms should be folding in toward the chest, backs of the hands touching slightly. This gesture should be thought of as a gathering of energy in preparation for the exhale beat where the stored energy is released. The exhale is to be audible with the face fully open. Second, the chest should be expansive and the head centered over the shoulders. Third, the arms should be rounded slightly and filled with a dynamic of sending energy out into the world.

When at least 80 percent of the group has mastered the 4/4 pattern, it is time to introduce the 3/4 pattern. This is actually a simple waltz beat which is done in the same pattern as previously described. In this one, however, the accent beat is done with alternating feet. Here's how it goes: from zero take a semi–lunge on the right, the left step is in place and on the ball of the foot, followed by the right step in place on the ball of the foot, followed by another semi–lunge on the left foot, followed by the two steps in place, and so forth.

The breath, gesture, and attitude is identical to the other rhythm. This pattern moves much more quickly. Therefore, the arms and breath need to be coordinated to make this work. The count is obviously a simple, one–two–three, one–two–three, one–two–three.

Once again, when most of the class has managed to learn the 3/4 step it's time to move on. At this point, have everyone gather into a big circle. With a leader in the center of the circle, practice the two rhythm patterns one more time. (Change the lead leg in the 4/4 pattern a few times.)

After about ten minutes of solid practice, everyone should be ready to try the combination pattern. To prepare, the leader should have every other person in the circle take a giant step forward. They'll constitute the inner circle while the remaining people become the outer circle. Have the inner circle turn and adjust so that there's about five or six feet between them and the outer circle. The two concentric circles should now be facing one another.

The inner circle will do the 3/4 waltz pattern while the outer circle, at the same time, will do the 4/4 pattern. You must be in complete synchrony with your own circle while at the same time listening to the overall rhythm created by the combined patterns.

You'll need a count to get started together. Keeping the rhythm slow and steady, the leader should count off: "One–two–ready – *and*," The first attempts are usually chaotic as everyone struggles with the demands of the exercise. After a few corrections and reminders, however, the group will begin to gel. When it works, the group will perceive an interesting new rhythm which is created by the combination of the two time signatures.

As a final nuance to the exercise, the leader should instruct everyone to produce a vocalized tone during, and *only* during, the moment the two rhythms match up. This establishes a cadence which helps everyone stay together.

Once the circles have managed to reach a level of competence and security in this pattern, break it up by having the inner circle do the 4/4 time and the outer circle doing the 3/4 time.

The group reinforcement and the many opportunities to try the two rhythms all but guarantees success. Naturally, the combined use of breath, voice, intention, and gesture can be unsettling at first, but after repeated attempts and with growing unity of the group rhythm, even the most awkward student will make measurable progress. In a very short time, a new–found rhythmic confidence will emerge for everyone. This confidence informs all other aspects of the actor's development.

7. BREATH MACHINE

Creating a machine by interconnecting body parts in a variety of ways has long been a standard of ensemble training. It's simplest form, one person enters the center of the space and begins an easy movement which can be repeated over a long span of time. One by one, everyone steps in, attaching their own movements to another so that it very soon gives the impression of a machine with interconnecting parts. It's helpful to allow sounds to be produced during the early experiments with this exercise.

After the group has a sense of how to create a machine, and especially after they've established the appetite for creating interesting, precise movements, it's time to introduce the breath work.

Before beginning, the leader should explain that the participants are about to experience something very demanding. It's not unusual for one or more students to end up feeling nauseous and light headed. These symptoms are temporary conditions that will disappear very quickly at the end of the exercise.

Begin again to create a machine, only this time make breath the essential ingredient of the exercise. Everyone should be making movements similar to the first attempts while incorporating breath as the primary motor driving the movement.

Allow for several machines to be created, taking a rest between each and discussing any problems, ideas, and improvements that might be warranted. Then, as a final creation, when most of the movement choices are in the managable range, sustain the machine action well beyond the usual stopping point. Everyone is free to add vocal sounds to the work. In most cases, the sounds reflect the sheer effort involved in maintaining the breath and movement.

Let this continue until it's clear the machine must stop. Afterwards, lie on the floor, rolling and stretching. Allow for a full ten minutes of decompression time and at least another ten minutes for open discussion.

8. THE BREATH OF THE BODY

This next exercise is a great tool for learning a number of things. First, it demonstrates clearly that the body has its own intelligence. Second, it shows the precise and natural action of the diaphragm muscle. And third, it introduces a very quick and useful technique for stabilizing the breath.

Because of the latter feature, this exercise is usually best introduced after some physical activity. Do *not*, however, attempt it immediately following a heated game or any activity where everyone is winded and flushed. Allow for a cool down before attempting this exercise.

Begin on the floor on your back. Bring your knees up with the feet flat on the floor in alignment with the hips. Place the hands on the lower abdomen and relax the neck and shoulders. While in this passive position, observe the natural movement of your breath. Don't interfere, simply observe.

After only about 30 seconds, the leader should say the following: "I'm going to ask you to *not breathe*. I don't mean for you to hold or in any way stop your breathing. I mean just to get entirely out of the way of the body and let the body take its own breath. Wait for it. The body will not let you pass out. When it needs air, the body will take a breath entirely on its own."

Additional coaching or explanation may be necessary, but the essential requirement is that all participants simply observe, awaiting the organic impulse to take a breath. This passive activity creates a deep relaxed state and a curious sense of wonder as the body activates its own demands for air.

After a few minutes, the leader should direct the attention to the observation of the diaphragm muscle. Invite all to sense the action of the diaphragm when the body takes a breath. For some, it will be the first time they've been able to isolate the diaphragm from other muscles of the abdomen. This revelation can greatly quicken growth in vocal support, saving what might have been months or even years of confusion, trial, and error.

End the session with some stretching, yawning, and brisk cleansing breaths.

CONDITIONING WORK

Performing is very often an athletic event. The demands on the body, the mind, and the emotions require performers to be in top condition. For groups who want to progress beyond superficial explorations, physical conditioning is imperative. A good performer must prepare for the work as though preparing for an Olympic event. The following is a series of rigorous exercises that will help develop the necessary stamina and strength to allow a group to function at a much more exciting level.

As in any conditioning, it is wise to be brutally honest with youself with regards to your current state of health. If you are a video game slug or a couch potato and want to jump into these exercises full force from the start, you are courting disaster. Please take an honest inventory of your exercise activity and partake of the following work accordingly.

In other words, if you are a dancer or an athlete or an actor in top shape, the following exercises will feel good and will help you to build upon the momentum of conditioning you have already in place. If you are a bookish scholar or a mildly active personality, be smart and ease into the conditioning program.

Please don't treat these as mindless calisthenics. Give each exercise a focused emotional and mental component. Too often, demanding physical work can descend to a kind of gym–class mentality and the imagination and the inner life of the performer goes on holiday. Granted, these aren't the most imaginative or stimulating exercises you will encounter, but that is all the more reason to infuse them with life and verve.

Thus begins the "sweat equity" of the training process. Everyone, regardless of age, background, or talent must sweat and struggle with these exercises. Naturally, some will be easier than others and some people will have more of an aptitude for this work. Nevertheless, with everyone working to improve and to grow stronger physically, the foundation for bonds will begin. Ah, sweat, the great equalizer!

1. SQUAT HOPS

An exercise borrowed from Japanese theatre training techniques. Do not do it if you have weak or injured knees. It's important to be fully warmed up before participating in this exercise.

To begin, line up at one side of the room and then descend into a squat position. Make sure the alignment of the back, knees, and feet all meet the requirements described for a good squat position. Next, extend the arms in front of the face, link the thumbs, and extend the fingers upwards, the palms facing away. Next, tilt the hands toward the middle bringing the two index fingers together to create a triangular space between thumbs and fingers. Remaining in this shape and with the shoulders relaxed, the breath stream open and the eyes focused on the center of the triangle, begin hopping across space to the opposite side of the room.

Prior to the actual execution of this exercise, it should be explained that a sound will be incorporated. During the landing of each hop, the person should release a loud focused "eya" sound (accent on the "ee"). The eyes should not wander from the triangle and everyone should maintain a consistent rhythm and a serious focused intent as they move across the floor.

Once mastered, this exercise is one of the best ways to achieve a strong focused mind and a quick effective workout for the legs and feet. Avoid overdoing it. Twice across the average room is sufficient during the early stages of training. Over the course of two months, work up to three times the beginning distance.

2. SINGING PUSH UPS

Lie face down on the floor and place the hands directly under the shoulders. Staying relaxed, inhale, then push up on the exhale. The body should create a raked platform with the hips aligned, the spine straight, and the arms fully extended, but not locked. It's important not to bend the head upwards, which pinches the spine at the neck and reduces blood flow. Instead, keep the neck extended as part of the entire shape, the eyes facing the floor. Everyone should do at least ten slow push-ups just to get the form and to coordinate the breath with the movement.

The next sets, however, are done with song. This way, the breath and the rhythm of the push-up become integrated; and since every-one *must* sing along loudly, the breath stream participates in a more active way. Just as importantly, it takes push-ups out of the punish-ment mode and creates a more friendly atmosphere for this old stan-dard.

Start with the "ABC" song, since nearly everyone knows it. Other songs to consider are: "Frere Jacques," "I'm a Little Tea-pot," "Mary Had a Little Lamb," or any other lighthearted and well- known song with a steady rhythm.

3. BEAR CRAWL

After a warmup, place your hands on the floor and distribute the weight evenly. Keep a springy cushion-like feeling to the elbows and knees. Stabilize the breath in this position and then go for a "walk."

Allow the walk to be unhampered by any technical considera-tions at first. This freedom will give you a chance to simply explore the feeling of walking on all fours. Let the walking continue until the first signs of fatigue.

During a rest, the leader should explain that the next version of the walk demands a diagonal design. That is, the left leg will step fol-lowed by a step with the right arm, followed by a step with the right leg and then a step with the left arm and so on. (Some of the more coordinated students will have little difficulty with this: others may find it extremely challenging.) Continue slightly past the first signs of fatigue.

Following the next respite, you will be asked to walk in parallel fashion: the right foot stepping followed by the right arm and then the left foot stepping followed by the left arm and so on.

This is somewhat easier to coordinate, although just as demanding on the body. When you have walked long enough to get a stride going, the leader should invite people to speed it up; to see just how fast they can go. (For safety concerns, be sure to watch where you're going.)

Finish by alternating on your own between the diagonal and parallel walk. Imagine yourself as a big bear as you move about the room. Finish this exercise with some easy rolling and stretching to relieve the strain on the upper body joints.

4. SOLO ARM WRESTLE

Clasp both hands together in front of the chest. Keeping the breath stream open, begin to push the arms against each other. Let them wrestle at full power in all directions. This is good for strengthening both arms and chest. Take several breaks and be careful not to over-constrict the upper chest and neck.

5. ROCKEFELLER CENTER

There is a famous statue of Prometheus overlooking the skating rink at New York's Rockefeller Center. The figure appears to be balanced on one buttock with limbs aesthetically extended.

Borrowing from this basic shape, sit on one buttock and extend the arms and legs in a graceful manner. This is very demanding and those people who have weak abdominal muscles will have great difficulty achieving any semblance of grace. If you cannot achieve the full extension, bring the arms in near the legs. Upon reaching the fully lifted position, everyone should smile, breathe smoothly, and hold for at least thirty seconds.

When the grunts and complaints start to percolate, the leader should switch everyone quickly to the other buttock to re-enact the shape. Again, hold the position while having fun with the image of being this giant statue overlooking the skaters.

I sometimes have us all completely shift the image and create the illusion of running in slow motion. Still elevated onto one buttock slowly move the arms and legs as if running under water. Look behind you and see an imaginary enemy and double your effort to get away. This sudden change of image helps to sustain the exercise for a longer period of time.

6. TORTOISE ON ITS BACK

Lie down on the back and pretend you're a giant tortoise struggling to right itself.All four limbs and the head should participate. Maintain very slow movements. Fully extend the limbs at least once during the exploration.

This is a great workout for the abdominals and is a lot of fun. After about five minutes, bring the knees to the chest and rock side to side and then repeat.

7. WALKING ARCHWAY

By now everyone should know how to do a back arch. Some people will have more flexibility than others and consequently will enjoy greater ease in both getting into the posture and in holding it. This exercise is for those advanced people only. Do not attempt this exercise until the back arch posture is fully mastered with ease.

Begin by carefully pushing up into a full back arch. Once you have arrived at the full height and have secured the stance, breathe evenly and begin to walk in the direction of the arms. It takes a moment to adjust to the coordination demands and to the unusual use of the back muscles. Walk around for thirty seconds to a minute, then descend slowly.

Follow this up with some contra–stretches. While the back is warm, push up once again into a back arch. This time, walk in the direction of the feet. This is slightly harder due to the strength needed in the arms to push the body forward. Afterwards, soothe the back with contra stretches and some gentle rolling along the floor.

8. CLEARING THE SIX DIRECTIONS

In a strong horse stance, inhale and gather all the force you can muster and place it in the solar- plexus. Pull the arms in with the inhale, placing the hands just to the sides of the chest. With a burst of energy and a loud open sound, open the palms out and push the energy outward, directly in front of the body. While doing this, visualize the space expanding away from you.

Next, and still in the horse stance, inhale and gather up. Using the arms, explode the energy behind you. Do the same to the right side of the body, the left side, downwards below the feet, and finally upwards above the head.

When the final burst of energy has cleared toward the sky, slowly stand up out of the horse stance. Shake the body out and enjoy a moment in the center of your clearing.

9. THE DRAGON

Drop down into a deep horse stance, place the hands on the knees. Keeping the spine long and the stance solid, begin to circle the upper body. Draw a large circle with the torso, keeping the head center and in alignment with the rest of the spine. Inhale during the upper hemisphere of the circle and then exhale during the lower one. Inhale through the nose and exhale loudly, as if spewing fire. Do this direction and this breathing cycle for ten complete circles.

Without changing the stance, stop after the tenth circle and redirect it toward the other direction. This time, inhale during the bottom hemisphere and exhale during the upper half. Again, perform this dragon–like movement ten times, keeping the stance strong, the hands firmly on the knees, and the breathing fully dynamic.

When finished, stand slowly out of the stance and massage the legs and knees and the lower back by the kidneys.

10. FROG JUMPS

Descend to a wide base squat. On a signal from the leader, push up into the biggest jump you can do. Just before reaching full height, bend the knees upwards in a quick pumping action. This will allow for a slight hang time in the air and lend a frog–like form to the jump. The secondary impulse at the top of the jump essentially recreates the squat shape that was the initial base. Be sure to let the legs drop naturally to control and absorb the landing impact as you descend into another squat.

Repeat at least ten times.

1

2

3

4

5

6

Up Side . . .

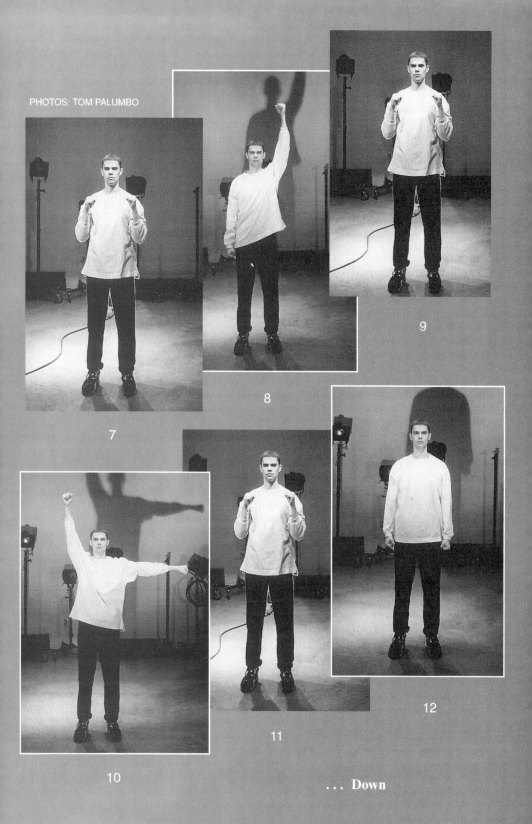

PHOTOS: TOM PALUMBO

9

8

7

10

11

12

... **Down**

11. MOVING WALLS

Go to a wall that is securely constructed and well braced. Place both hands against the wall, bend the knees, and try with all your might to move the wall. Change pushing positions to try and find the most leverage and strength. Push at full capacity for a minute, rest thirty seconds and then push again. Do this for at least ten minutes.

COORDINATION AND RHYTHM

Contrary to popular notions, coordination can be learned. Certain motor functions are easier for some people than others, but with a little effort and a lot of patience, even the class klutz can begin to develop grace and coordination. The following exercises are selected because of the range of demand and the high degree of effectiveness.

1. ZIG–ZAG–ZOG

This game is fun for everyone; consequently it's a good starting game when dealing with coordination. Everyone should stand in a circle and face one other. Keep the circle wide enough to provide ample elbow room. Have everyone say the words "zig–zag–zog" several times so they can sense how the words feel when said in sequence.

The leader should explain to everyone that they're expected to do three things at once: they must hop, clap and point to someone else in the circle (with eye contact), and say "zig" or "zag" or "zog" according to where they're in the sequence. For example, one person starts by doing the hop–clap–and–point and saying "zig" towards the person they have targeted. That person in turn does the hop–

clap-and-point and must say "zag" towards their target person and so on back and forth or around the circle.

It's perfectly acceptable to return an impulse to the person who targeted you or to zig someone next to you. It's not acceptable to look at one person while you zig someone else. Clear, direct communication is one of the demands of the game.

Have someone start "zig" and let the game try itself out for a few minutes while everyone adjusts. Then stop the game and explain its a game of elimination. If anyone says one of the words out of order, fails to clap, hop, or point, delivers an unclear signal or hesitates, that person must step out of the circle.

Before long the circle will shrink to only two people. They must face off and play until one makes a mistake. Encourage cheers and positive reactions for the winner.

If a group is large and two circles were created to accommodate everyone, there'll be two champions, one from each circle, and they can face off for a final bout, cheered on by their respective teams.

Once the game is learned by everyone, after practice, it will move with astonishing speed. Eliminations, however, will decrease as everyone's reflexes and concentration improves. The overall time of the game, therefore, will increase and this should be considered when selecting the game.

2. UP SIDE DOWN

A simple arm coordination exercise, quite easy once learned. The learning stage, however, stirs up considerable frustration and very quickly reveals people with less than healthy learning habits. It's advisable to have a leader who has comfortably mastered the sequence.

Again, this will be easy for some and extremely difficult for others. The people who learn it first can act as assistants in helping others. It's important, during all stages of this exercise, to keep talking to an absolute minimum. Some people talk and joke as a resistance to doing the work.

The leader needs to explain quite openly this is a coordination exercise that will generate frustration for some. Tell everyone to simply live with the irritation and seek relief only in the mastery of the exercise.

Start by standing with the arms at the sides. Make a light fist with each hand and bending at the elbow, bring the fists up to a comfortable position in front of the shoulders. This is the basic "return position" that each arm will experience during the exercise.

From this position straighten the right arm so it becomes extended toward the ceiling. Return to the original position and then straighten the arm downward, extended toward the floor. Again, return to the basic position. Do this simple movement several times.

Next, raise the left arm overhead and return just as the right arm did. Now, however, instead of heading downward, extend the arm out directly to the side. Return to the basic position and then extend downward followed by a return. Do this simple movement several times, making sure to maintain the simple Up Side Down sequence *without adding an additional side extension before returning to the "Up."* In other words, after each down stroke and return, only extend upwards as the next move.

After a few moments of practice, the leader explains they're now to put the two together. The right arm will be maintaining only the up and down stroke while the left is doing the up side down stokes. They're to be moving simultaneously and returning to the bent elbow position after each extension.

After some initial fumbling and frustration, several participants will begin to notice a pattern, created by the combination of the two rhythms. When this pattern is felt, the person will begin to absorb the exercise in a new and more secure way.

The next step is to reverse the arm rhythms. Do this, however, only after everyone has mastered the first pattern. There may be groans and exasperated sighs from many who fear the other side will be harder to accomplish, now that they're used to doing it one way. The truth is, however, it's easier. They inevitably transfer their coordination to the opposite side in half the time it originally took.

Once both sides have been mastered, do the exercise while walking, talking, or reading. Invent your own additional complications to the pattern, be playful and see how the patterns can be merged to create two-person patterns and interesting group shapes.

3. POLY-KNEES-IA

Pun intended, this exercise was inspired by the rhythm dances of Polynesia and other Oceanic cultures. In those cultures, many of the basic myths and folktales are told through rhythm and symbolic gestures.

Unlike those dances, however, this exercise does not attempt to tell a story. Quite simply, it provides a basis for two people to link up in a rhythmic dimension and then simultaneously engage the speaking function. This combination is, in fact, one of the essential aspects of acting. There are countless variations on this theme, of course, but the ability to carry on a conversation while doing rhythmic stage business or handling props is a fundamental acting skill.

Pick a partner and sit on the floor with the legs crossed, facing one another. Make sure you're sitting close enough for the knees to almost touch. Participants who have weak backs or happen to be inordinately stiff in the lower body can sit with the back supported by a wall surface.

Each person uses four "drum pads" during the exercise. They are: the inner right thigh, the inner left thigh, the right knee, and the left knee. Start by gently slapping the right thigh with the right hand, and then the left thigh with the left hand, and then the right hand on the right knee and the left hand on the left knee. Do this several times, easy and smooth, returning in rhythm each time to the starting slap at the inner right thigh. Within a few minutes everyone should be able to approximate a simple drumroll in this manner.

Each team should then work to synchronize so that both partners are doing the rhythm at the same time.

The next step complicates things a bit and begins the real work of linking the partners. The rhythm will now change to include a crossing slap to the partner's opposite knee. To do this creates a new pattern altogether.

The new pattern, which starts exactly like the old one is this: r-thigh, l–thigh, r–knee, l–knee, cross to partner's r–knee, (your own) l–knee, (return to your own) r–knee, l–thigh, begin again with r–thigh, etc.

When this rhythm is produced at a smooth tempo with both partners in synch, crossing together and beginning the sequence together, lift your head up from the legs, look at each other, and have a conversation.

Only after the previous exercise is mastered should you add the next, more advanced combination. Here the single cross becomes a double and again changes the sound of the overall pattern: repeat the sequence for the single cross except the sequence will now read: cross to partner's r–knee, l–knee, r–knee, cross to partner's l–knee, r–knee, l–knee, begin again with r–thigh, etc. With the double, once you've switched to the knees you stay there to complete the phrase, returning to the thigh only when time to start the sequence over again. When you and your partner synchronize and master the double–crossing rhythm pattern, do as before and converse.

If this becomes relatively easy, create your own additions which might include hand slaps, whistles, and all sorts of unusual movements. I've seen some patterns develop that were fascinating in their complexity and thrilling in their execution. One pattern took nearly a full thirty seconds before the first repetition was completed.

4. RHYTHM RUN

Combines the cardiovascular workout of running with the exploration of rhythm. The drum pads for the hands are the sides of the thighs, the upper chest, and the hands coming together in the traditional clapping mode. The feet striking the floor provides the additional drum pad sound.

I have discovered that the most widely used and useful rhythm in the theatre is what drummers call the "flam." It's a tight two- beat rhythm which is forced into the time allotted a single beat. This is the rhythm of placing the hand on a wall switch and then clicking the light on; it's the beat where the cup clinks the saucer followed by the first word of dialogue; it's the stop of the body followed by the take with the head; the backswing preparation followed by the duck before enacting a stage combat move, and countless other circumstances where a two-beat occurrence is compressed slightly to accommodate the single time.

If it were written it might read as: ba-da. It's a simple rhythm that can make all the difference in the world in terms of comic timing and clear stage communication. Unfortunately, for some it's often confused with the a down beat and an up beat. The rhythm run helps to clarify the rhythmic subtleties of the "flam."

The leader must establish an easy one-two rhythm; everyone should run in place, to match it. Using the hands on the thighs, begin to incorporate a flam beat by striking the thigh a half second before the foot on that leg strikes the floor. It should make a clear "ba-dum" sound.

The single beats of the feet will now become flam-beats with the familiar ba-dum, ba-dum, ba-dum, rhythm. When this can be done in place by everyone, have them run around the room, maintaining the same easy pace and practicing the flam rhythm. Stop after a few minutes.

Next, do the exact same thing, only this time have the hand slap the knee on the upbeat. The rhythm will now sound less like a gallop and more like: ba-and-ba-and-ba-and, etc. Master this rhythm and then let them take it out for a run.

After a few minutes, the leader should introduce what I call the "triple flam-beat"" Which is actually easier than it sounds. Make a flam beat with the hands on the sides of the thigh. Now try to add a beat made with the foot. This will sound something like: ba-da-bum. The flam will complete just before the foot strikes the floor. Try it out on both legs.

During an easy jog, let the hands do the flam before each foot beat. This rhythm will sound very much like a galloping horse. As the pattern becomes easier, allow the hands to produce the flam rhythm on the upper chest as well as the thigh. Incorporate occasional up beats by clapping. Before long you'll have created your own rhythm run, expanding your sensitivity to rhythm while getting a good aerobic workout.

IMAGINATION WORK

The spirit of a performer is most often moved by moments when the imagination is fully engaged. Actors delight in the joy of playing, especially if it's a highly demanding form of play, because, at the essential level, that is why they want to act. They feel connected to the core of the craft in these instances and, once engaged, tend to learn at a more rapid rate. The imagination, quite simply, makes learning fun.

A useful side-effect of this fun is the development of specific skills and improved confidence in improvisation, tactical behavior games, and in ensemble awareness. The following is a collection of games that fully engage the actor while providing good training:

1. SPLIT ROOM

The group is split into two halves and sent to opposite sides of a large room. A center line needs to be established either with tape or any other readily available means.

The leader (or teacher) stands at the edge of the centerline and "side-coaches" during the exercise.

One side of the room is given a quality, atmosphere, or state of being and the other side is given the exact opposite. Both sides are encouraged to sincerely establish the reality on its side and then, eventually, cross over to the opposite side. Once on the opposite side, they're to enact that quality until the leader claps twice and commands both sides to return to neutral.

Aside from being fun, this game challenges the imagination to participate in the genuine enactment of opposite qualities. The transition at the centerline from one side to the other is particularly interesting, presenting a unique sensory challenge for the actor.

It's best to start with two very obvious extremes such as heat and cold. The leader simply announces to one side that they're in an extremely hot atmosphere and tells the other side that they're in one that is unbearably cold. They are instructed to struggle with their

SPLIT ROOM

PHOTOS: TOM PALUMBO

condition until, unable to bear it any longer, they have to cross over to the other side.

With this particular one, it's tempting to indicate the extremes, that is, showing the states of extreme as if there were a need to tele-graph it to the outside world. Avoid indicating and instead, experi-ence it fully and allow the body to express honestly, without regard to the performance.

By the same token, fear of indicating can make your experience too passive and lacking in any active choices. To be effective, you must make active choices. It might help to consider that you cannot truly play a generic quality like "cold," it is too passive. However, you *can* play, "what do I do to get warm?" Do you see how restructuring the thought process a bit, helps to activate the choices and keeps the attention off the "how am I doing" factor.

(Actually, this entire game is a great diagnostic tool for quickly assessing under which conditions you and your fellow actors tend toward indicating as a means of expression)

Following a brief break, where indicating can be discussed and discouraged, go at it again, this time enjoying the new levels of sub-tlety that'll certainly surface as as you strive to erase your indicating.

Below is a list of successful opposites culled from previous attempts. Keep in mind, however, that this game is by no means lim-ited to the qualities listed. Feel free to use the ones in this list and to expand upon it with your own inventions.

OPPOSITE QUALITIES FOR SPLIT ROOM EXERCISE

HOT/COLD

HEAVY/LIGHT

GROTESQUE CHARACTERS/SOPHISTICATED SOCIALITES

TINY PEOPLE/GIANTS

ANGRY AND PETULANT PEOPLE/HAPPY AND LOVING PEOPLE

EXTREMELY DENSE ATMOSPHERE/NEAR WEIGHTLESSNESS

MONKEYS/HUMANS

OUTCASTS/HIP TRENDY PEOPLE

WILD PARTY/SOMBER FUNERAL

PUPPIES/CATS

SLOW MOTION/FAST MOTION

ARROGANT PEOPLE/HUMBLE PEOPLE

SINGERS WARMING UP/DANCERS WARMING UP

A note on sidecoaching: Repeat the instructions in different ways while reacting to the game with occasional phrases of support. This will give more confidence and assure them they can deepen their experience and commit even further to the elements of the game.

2. FLOOR CHANGES

Especially effective with large groups, Floor Changes can be incorporated into the Split Room game. To begin, the group should go for an easy walk, changing directions at random. Keep the pace slow.

Next, the leader should announce that the surface of the floor has just changed to (fill in the blank). A good opener is *freshly mowed lawn*. Let everyone experience this for about thirty seconds before changing to other surfaces.

A word of warning: portraying slippery surfaces invites a lot of uncontrolled movement and quick falls to the floor. Be careful not to hurt yourself or anyone around you.

Below is a list of surfaces that have been effective.

LIST OF FLOOR SURFACES

Freshly mowed lawn

Hot sand at the beach

Barefoot through patches of broken glass

Knee deep thick oozing mud

Giant trampoline

Ice

City street

Autumn leaves

Crunchy snow

Knee deep in Jello

Clouds

Hopscotch arena

Thick carpeting

Mine field

Snake-infested swamp

Sticky syrup

Raw eggs

Jello

3. PAINTING THE WORLD

This exercise can expand and contract to meet the current needs of the class. It helps to free the body and voice by engaging the imagination in the act of painting. With the mind fully visualizing the array of colors and shapes created, all students will feel liberated from the confines of self-consciousness and more free to express themselves in movement and sound.

First establish a diameter of space where you can work. Next, the leader should instruct the participants to notice that on the floor they'll find two imaginary buckets of paint, one on each side. The colors of paint are up to the individual. Make the effort to see each bucket and to visualize the specific colors. Be sure to make exact choices of color and to stick to them throughout the first exercise.

Next, dip your hair in a bucket of paint and begin to paint the space in front of you. Employing both buckets as well as the desire to create a masterpiece, begin to free up the entire body with particular emphasis on the upper torso.

This can expand to include other areas of space, more buckets of paint, painting to music, or shared painting projects. And, of course, incorporating other parts of the body takes it to greater levels of physical challenge. Painting with the hip, for example, can go far toward freeing the locked pelvis.

4. SPINS

Spinning is great for developing the kind of leg strength necessary for any kind of action or combat–oriented work. The legs are the roots and trunk of the tree and must be quite strong to support the kinds of avoidances, attacks, and impact illusions of most stage combat.

Also, spins are good theatrical moves because they give the illusion of large movement without having to cover a lot of space. Of course, dance technique introduces the body to a variety of useful turns, called pirouettes. The spins I'm introducing, however, are closer in form to sports or martial arts.

To begin, everyone should start with the legs slightly farther apart than the shoulders and the weight fully on the balls of the feet. The spine is aligned and the head centered. The hands are held in front, palms facing out at the level of the shoulders. For the sake of clarity and easy reference, we can call this the "tiger" pose. This is an energized position and should feel neither locked nor saggy.

Next, activate the position by quickly shifting weight back and forth between both feet, keeping the feet near the floor. Then, the leader of the exercise says: "Quarter turn...hep!" At the "hep!" command, the body should turn exactly one quarter turn to the right. The key is to make the *entire body* turn without jumping up, traveling on a single horizontal plane while maintaining the original tiger pose.

The commands should continue in quarter turns in random order to the right and the left for at least a full minute. Next, introduce and demonstrate a half turn. That is, the body spins from the bouncy tiger pose exactly 180 degrees with the minimum of effort while trying to keep the head level. Repeat the random commands for a minute or so.

Once this is mastered, you can begin to incorporate three-quarter turns and finally full turns. Remember that the body should move as a unit and should spin quickly and land sharply on a dime, ready and waiting for the next command. When this is learned, the leader can then mix the commands. A typical command sequence would sound something like this:

"Quarter-turn, hep!....Quarter-turn, hep!...Half-turn, hep!...Quarter-turn, hep!...three-quarter turn, hep!...three- quarter turn, hep!...Full-turn, help!...Quarter-turn, hep!...Half turn, hep!"..."Other direction quarter-turn, hep!..." And so forth.

The next spin is on the heel of the foot, a very fast spin and relatively easy. What's difficult, however, is breaking the addiction to spinning on the ball of the foot. To do this spin, simply stand with the heels close together and the feet at a forty- five degree angle. Let the weight center on the right heel, bend the knees slightly, push off to the right using the left foot, and spin around as the right foot lifts into a flex position.

Repeat the instructions to the left side. Once you've mastered the sensation of spinning on the heel to the right and left, begin to add some controls. For example, try spinning with the legs remaining straight, or the legs bent, or stopping in quarter, half, three-quarter, and full turns. Try leading with the head, keeping the head centered, or trailing the head. Create your own variations.

5. FOXHOLES

Not an army chore, but a game that greatly challenges the legs and will help to develop considerable leg strength. To begin, the leader explains that everyone is to imagine that the floor is pocked with numerous crater-like foxholes. They're in danger if they stay too long in one foxhole and must move along quickly to others, avoiding possible gunfire.

What makes this a challenge is that the jump into and out of the foxhole is done in a specific manner: to jump into a foxhole, the person must leap with the arms and legs fully extended and land softly onto one leg. Then that same leg supports the body entirely as it descends into a squat position, contracting the arms and free leg in order to give the illusion of crouching low within the foxhole.

The exit from the foxhole is just as demanding. The jumper must use the same leg to support an expansive leap out of the hole, then stay low during the run to find another foxhole, preferably one with people already crouched.

The leader simply reminds them that they cannot stay too long in one foxhole and must keep moving. Early sessions of this exercise cannot last long for the simple reason that very few people have fully developed leg strength. With practice, however, the exercise can extend well beyond the five-minute mark.

6. SWOON LAGOON

The Swoon's a great exercise for experiencing shared weight as well as for strengthening attention to nonverbal signals. Caring for someone in distress, or being in the position of needing care, often cuts through social barriers and allows for clear communication and uncluttered kinetic learning. The Swoon Lagoon offers a game that cleverly approximates that sensation of distress and activates some very basic human responses.

At the top of the exercise, there should be a brief demonstration of the proper way to fall into someone else's arms: one should be in control of the fall and only fall to the point of shared weight. If someone falls too quickly or too hard, the receiver won't be able to control it and the fall will be dangerous and certainly awkward. Also, the person falling should tilt or collapse either to the side or to the diagonal, allowing the receiver to support the faller's *shoulders, back, and sides of the chest.* The legs should be used as a base of support, which helps create the illusion of falling while providing very real support. Of utmost importance is the clear pass of silent signals which must communicate, "I am falling toward you." and, of course, "I am ready to catch you."

Proper distance is an important factor in a successful swoon. Even if you're a particularly big person, try *not* to fall toward someone from six feet away!

After a brief practice session of falling and catching one another, begin to walk silently around the space in random directions. Your task is to non-verbally communicate to someone walking nearby that you are going to faint or swoon. The receiver of this signal must maneuver near you and manage to catch you before the swoon loses control and forces you to the floor. The receiver simply catches the swooner, helps them back to center, and then continues walking in a different direction.

This exercise may be awkward at first. As everyone grows accustomed, however, it becomes much easier. When everyone seems to have a fair grasp of the exercise, allow it to take on more dramatic tones incorporating breath, sounds, and imagined reasons for the swooning. Before long, a true "swoon lagoon" will emerge which is at once delightful and hauntingly sad.

7. CREATURE FEATURE

Developed to help young actors break out of their habitual patterns of movement, this exercise has the additional advantage of teaching them how to "listen with the body."

I employed this exercise with a group of young actors at an acting school in Toronto. At first, the exercise was a means to stretch the imagination and break free from habits. As the exercise progressed, however, I began to see that for some inexplicable reason, this particular group was ready to jump all the way into the exercise.

Knowing we were going to complete the training with the production of a movement piece, we began to delve into the exercise with more alert sensitivity. It wasn't long before we realized that we had created a unique and somewhat primordial world. From this one exercise came fully half of the show which resulted in inventive body masks and characters emerging from rock shapes in a bizarre, but exceptionally exciting piece we called, "The Primordial Picnic."

As in many of these exercises, if the timing and energy is right, they can evolve and grow into remarkable and sometimes stunning works for the stage.

The leader should begin by instructing the participants to move in a completely free-form fashion with the understanding that they're to come to a stop when they hear the command "freeze." It's helpful to establish a few practice runs.

When everyone has adjusted to hearing the freeze command, start off into a free-from movement exploration. At some point the leader should call the first freeze. While in the freeze, make the sound you feel best matches the posture you're in. Now, develop a walk and then evolve into a sound-and-movement creature that moves about the space in a particular rhythm. Your creation can and should be abstract at this point.

Do this process several times, with the leader changing the time frames of the movement section and urging everyone to try out many different ways of moving. If you find you're always moving fast, choose to move slowly; if always rigid, relax; if always on your feet, go to the floor; if always in one place, take in the whole room and so on.

Take a short break after about four of these freeze creatures. During the break the leader should explain that you're going to create another creature, but this time you're going to "find your fellow species." That is, as everyone moves about the room in whatever ridiculous creature they've developed, they'll be searching for another creature similar in essence to themselves.

When they link up with another creature, they're to make subtle compromises in shape, reforming into exact members of the same species. The rhythm, sound, and silhouettes of the creature should, in the end, be identical.

Next, after the initial blending has occurred, develop a method of walking through the space. This can lead you to decide if you're a hunting creature or the hunted. When this stage of the game has been reached, a totally new dynamic develops that's even more theatrically engaging.

Finish each full creature feature with a brief show and tell: the groups should stay in their general area and the leader instructs them one at a time to demonstrate their creature. Afterwards, allow two or more groups to interact. It's great fun to see the hunters stalk their prey and the hunted work out their mechanisms of defense.

There will be times when someone's creature is so distinct, there are no fellow species in the room. In that case, it's perfectly acceptable for that creature to remain a loner.

In the advanced stages, the creatures can be inflected in one direction or another, they could be monsters, or insects, or animals, or aliens, or dinosaurs, to name a few.

8. THE PUPPETEER

Everyone starts by lying down on the floor in any position. The leader explains to the group that they're now puppets with strings attached to the head, shoulders, elbows, hands, center chest, butt, knees, and feet. The old master puppeteer is entering his shop to animate his favorite puppet.

The leader should start by narrating the action:

The old puppeteer walks into his studio one evening and there, he opens a box that reveals his favorite puppet. You are that puppet, in the same position he left you only days before. He gently picks up the frame that controls the strings and decides he wants to visit his puppet again. He lifts only the head at first letting it move in an animated, slightly curious manner. (*The leader should allow the group to experience this for a minute*). He's now exploring the arms and hands. (*another hold while everyone enjoys the experience*)

Continue in this fashion until all the parts of the body have been singularly explored. Afterwards, the leader narrates once again:

The puppeteer is beginning to play with the puppet, bringing it to life. He lets it walk, run, jump, bow, dance, and gesture. (*This often evolves into a very impressive and sophisticated array of movements*) The puppeteer is tired now, carefully he places you back in the box. He then leaves the room and you are alone. Soon afterwards, however, his three-year-old grandson has wanders into the shop, finds the box, and decides he wants to play with Grandpa's favorite toy. You are now being controlled by this little child. (*There is little need for prompting at this point. They'll have a lot of fun enacting all of the erratic and comical movements they imagine*) Finally the little boy gets bored and carefully he returns the puppet to the box, puts on the lid and leaves the room.

The puppet exercise can now be expanded according to your own inventions of what types of people control the puppet. It might be interesting to have the puppet controlled by a young girl, by a character from a popular cartoon program, by a computer, and so on.

Playing puppets unlocks the imagination and can get very physical. Because of the nature of the exercise, it should be closely monitored to avoid any unwanted collisions or injuries.

9. ROBOTICS

Much like the previous exercise, this one is designed to isolate specific muscle groups. The movement dynamic will be much more controlled in order to achieve the illusion of robotic exactness. Robotics is particularly useful for people whose acting choices tend to be muddy and unfocused.

I stopped teaching the robot technique for years because I had so many negative memories attached to it. As a developing mime artist, I became fascinated with this technique, as did many mime artists at the time including Shields and Yarnell whose duo act landed them a short-lived television series. I became very accomplished at it and for a time, while I was working as an Artist in Residence for the city of Dallas, I was performing regularly all over the city.

Well, you can be a robot for only so long before you start to go bonkers. The problem was that everywhere I went, people wanted me do to the robot. I made the mistake of developing this remote controller idea whereby someone in the audience would pretend to be controlling me by this device. (I would simply manage to keep them in my peripheral vision and read their facial and body language to determine what their commands were) People thought I was some kind of psychic genius! Of course, this was extremely popular and as I ventured forth into other territories, I would inevitably hear a volley of requests to see me "do the robot man!"

I eventually took it out of my repertoire all together so my other work would have a chance to develop. The past few years I have gradually re-introduced it into my teaching, primarily to teach isolation work, but also it does offer a doorway into a unique part of the imagination. So take heed. Work well to master it, but don't let it become popular.

Start in zero position, and begin to move the head in simple rotations right or left. The movement should be accomplished with the quality of a precision machine. A small degree of tension is needed to sustain robotic motions and to capture the sharpness of the starts and stops. Be careful, however, to use only the minimum amount of tension necessary. Otherwise, the illusion will call attention to itself and reduce the overall effectiveness.

Explore fully the movement of the head, limiting the exploration to right angles and perpendicular lines. When this has been done (usually after fifteen minutes), begin to explore all of the potential robotic movements of the chest. The chest can be isolated and commanded to expand and contract, to shift side to side, to tilt in all directions, and to rotate right and left. Once the basic possibilities are mastered, usually after months of disciplined application, they can be orchestrated in a variety of interesting combinations.

Follow this pattern of exploration as you isolate the pelvis, the arms, and the legs. Keep the mind occupied with wanting to enact perfect movements in all isolations and in all combinations. After several sessions of exploring isolations in place, it's time to incorporate a walk.

Keep the body humming with just enough tension to give the impression of a machine plugged in and ready to go. With the legs remaining straight, begin to slide the feet in a "pressurized" shuffle. Because the whole body is engaged in maintaining the motor effect, the power for the walk originates high up in the hips. The feet should be slightly flexed and any turns should be precise pivots on the ball of the foot or on the heel.

It helps to incorporate a few robotic rotations of the hands and of the head as you walk. The robotic illusion works best if you keep the rhythm of all other moving parts at the same tempo as the walk and moving at unpredictable times.

Always come to a precise stop. During the stop, it's fun to incorporate a few elements of the isolation exploration experienced earlier. As people get more and more proficient at creating the illusion of robotic movement, they're also becoming adept at isolating and controlling every muscle in the body.

One word of warning: For some odd reason, this style of movement becomes highly addictive. Students report that after mastering certain aspects of it, they feel obsessed with the need to remain in robotic exploration for inordinate lengths of time. This can lead to excessive detachment and a preoccupation with pure movement at the expense of more lively impulses. Therefore, limit work sessions to a half hour at the most and always follow it with some free-form release-oriented work.

RELAXATION

Relaxation is the cornerstone of your work as an actor. It's vital to all aspects of the craft, including the process of getting the work. Therefore relaxation should be incorporated into actor training as much as possible. Unfortunately, most people have never really experienced deep relaxation. They have, however, experienced a fair notion of high anxiety and stress. Unfortunately, because of this familiar background of stress, their measure of relaxation is calibrated according to a warped system. What they sense as relaxation is usually only a level of relief from habitual stress.

True relaxation, and certainly deep relaxation, is a state of being altogether free of habitual stress. It's an experience entirely unique unto itself. Experts consider it healthy because of the contrast and perspective it can bring to the entire organism which is usually subjected to many hours of sustained stress.

Like anything else, moderation is the key. If deep relaxation is experienced in prolonged doses it can be as disruptive as stress. The body demands a certain equilibrium and the overall vitality of the organism depends greatly upon the *dynamic* relationship between relaxation and stress.

The demands of acting are, for the most part, stressful. Therefore, it is necessary to master certain tools so you can incorporate more relaxation into your work. Stanislavski recognized the stressful conditions of acting and truly believed that relaxation was the foundation for quality acting.

The following exercises are designed to introduce various levels of relaxation. They're useful as primers, as reminders, and as gradual refiners of the nervous system. They're no substitute, however, for the relaxation that comes with confidence; or with being prepared, clear, healthy, self-possessed, and unashamed. Some people become enamored of the exercises themselves and will need help to transfer the relaxation into their work. This is a particularly unfortunate occurance, but it does happen that some people become so comfortable with the classroom setting and with the comfort of being guided, they literally create a strange co-dependent relationship with their training. Make sure to give equal attention to discovering relaxation during the performance event. If you can't reproduce at least some of the relaxed state under pressure you are wasting your time.

1. THE SIGH

This is not only an excellent relaxation tool, but it can be very useful to prime the engine prior to any kind of work that requires a lot of emotional volatility or vulnerability. I often lead a cast in this backstage prior to the start of a dramatic work. It gets the voice warm, the breath going, the nerves calmed, and the emotional system lubricated.

While walking around the space, changing directions, and maintaining an easy gait, incorporate a few simple sighs. Allow the body to move in any way during the sigh. Gradually extend the length of the sigh until the body, in response, feels the need to go all the way to the floor.

Once on the floor, lift various body parts with the inhale and then sigh as that part is released onto the floor again. Continue in this manner using a variety of postures for several minutes.

Now lie on your back with the knees up and the feet parallel on the floor. Inhale long and luxurious and then activate a long continuous sigh. After a few full sighs, begin to include some voice. Let the voice engage more and more until the sigh becomes unforced, yet fully voiced. Do this for several minutes.

After a few moments of silence, the leader will guide you through a number of specifically qualified sighs. The leader will start by saying, "*Give me the sigh of*_____" and then fill in the blank with one of the following:

Compassion for someone else's pain

Relief

Self-congratulations

Preparing for a difficult task

Preparing for sleep

Exasperation

Seeing something beautiful

Relief from pain

The leader should encourage the participants to repeat the sigh at least five times.

The voice will engage fully on some of these and only partially or not at all on others. You should try out several sighs linked to a quality, searching for emotional accuracy and freedom. Feel free to add to the list qualities of your own.

2. SHAKING

Animals include shaking as part of their natural impetus toward comfort and physical relaxation. Watch a cat stretch and notice the movement is punctuated with vigorous shaking. Borrowing from the natural wisdom of the animal kingdom, there are advantages to shaking out various parts of the human body as well. Shaking delivers a massage-like vibration to the muscles and joints. It vitalizes the breath and promotes circulation. While some shaking exercises incorporate a partner, the vast majority are enacted by the individual, making it an ideal, non-invasive relaxation tool.

3. SPARKLING HANDS

This is called Sparkling Hands because, at a particular point in the exercise, the hands will feel tingling, as if sparkling. It's a pleasant sensation and one that establishes the appetite for more of the same throughout the body.

To begin, stand in an easy second position. The knees should be in an unlocked demi-plie. Make sure you've removed all loose fitting rings, watches or bracelets. Keeping the hands relaxed, begin to shake them easily in all directions. This warms up the wrist in preparation for a much more vigorous shaking.

While everyone is shaking the hands, the leader will explain that in a moment there'll be a signal, a loud command or sound which will initiate phase two of the exercise. When the signal is given, everyone is expected to jump in the air, land in a deep plie and shake the relaxed hands as vigorously as humanly possible. The hand position for this shaking is with the palms facing the chest the thumbs facing up. Shake the hands, alternating, as fast as possible.

While shaking, breathe in and out at a vigorous pace. The signal given by the leader launches a flurry of shaking hands and fast breathing. It helps to have the leader cheer everyone onward by saying some of the following phrases: *"Breathe! Keep going!"* and *"Back straight! Shake 'em as fast as you can. Faster!"* *"Relax the shoulders!"*

After thirty seconds, the leader will give another sharp command or sound, halting the shaking. Immediately let your hands float through space, caressing the air. The hands will feel "sparkly." This sensation lasts for approximately one minute and is a delicious mix of relaxation and invigoration. Over time, it can eliminate excess tension in the hands and establish the appetite for similar relaxation in other parts of the body.

4. THE SHAKE OUT

Expanding on the previous exercise, this one incorporates more body parts until the entire body's involved. Start at the feet, grabbing one foot at the ankle with both hands the knee bent toward the outside. Relax the foot and vigorously shake it from the ankle. Do this while saying to yourself in a quasi-desperate tone, *"Get it off! Shake the foot off! If they find me with this foot it's all over! I was just borrowing it. Get the foot OFF!"* Finish after thirty seconds and then repeat with the other foot.

The legs are next. Balance on one leg and using only the muscles of the hip and leg, vigorously shake the other out. Repeat the internal commands to get rid of the leg before being caught with it. Repeat on the other leg.

Stand with feet parallel, back straight, knees slightly bent, and arms held in front as though grabbing a low steering wheel. Take an inhale and on the exhale execute a series of quick, short punches with the hands in a fist shape. While continuing to punch, descend into a low deep knee bend, keeping the buttocks relaxed. The exhale should be a "voiced" exhale with a relaxed open "Ah" sound.

The shaking in this position relaxes the lower back and buttocks and gently urges the voice down into the body. Do this at least ten times.

Take an easy step forward with the right leg, bend the knees slightly, and take in an ample inhale. On the exhale, shimmy the shoulders and undulate the back downward with the chest rolling onto the right thigh. Roll back up until the spine is straight and repeat several times, incorporating the voice. Halfway through the sequence, switch feet and continue the shimmy, rolling the chest onto the left thigh.

Now shake out the whole body. Keep everything relaxed and use only the energy needed to produce a vigorous shaking of every part of the body. Jumping up and down during this helps to engage the entire instrument. When done correctly, this whole body shake-out can approximate the sparkly sensation which represents an elevated, yet relaxed state of readiness.

5. THE SLAP OUT

This exercise is a favorite of many of my students. During the middle of a demanding semester or when I sense that stress levels are
high or bodies are extremely sore, I will announce this exercise and
instantly the room fills with rounds of approval and delighted expectation. Never, ever, mention this exercise and then change your
mind. The jury will say you had it coming to you.

Pick a partner of similar size and weight. Partner A will go
behind partner B and begin the exercise. Start with fast alternating
"drum-roll" strokes on the top of B's head. This should be gentle, yet
firm enough to be effective. Continue with the patting rhythm
behind the head and ears, the back of the neck, and the top of the
shoulders.

Shortly after reaching the shoulders, lift the finger tips and
deliver the patting strikes with the palm of the hands. This should
provide a deeper and more effective vibration to the back. As the
shoulders are being worked on, B should slowly drop the head and
continue rolling over as far as possible. Keep the legs parallel, knees
bent, and the neck relaxed.

Continue with the vibrating slaps all over the back and hips,
eventually working down one shoulder and arm all the way to the
hand. Work back up the same arm across the shoulders and slowly
down the other side to the other hand. Come back up the arm, slowly down the back and to one hip.

Just before the slap out descends down one leg, B should pour
the weight into the opposite leg, maintaining only light contact with
the floor. The vibrating slaps have more effect when working down
an "empty" leg. After the foot, work all the way back up the leg,
being careful not to hurt the knee. As the slaps move across the hips,
B should transfer the weight to the opposite side, allowing A to continue smoothly down the opposite leg and foot. Return up the leg to
the hips and finish with a once over of the back.

Go to the shoulders at the base of the neck and place the fingertips on either side of the spine. Gently rake away from the spine
and to the sides of the body in quick vigorous strokes. Be sure to use
the tips of the fingers and not the nails. Do this stroke all the way
down the spine until reaching the top of the pelvic girdle. Then place

the left hand on the top of the left shoulder and two fingers on either side of the lower spine. Pressing firmly into the muscles along the spine, "walk" up the spine with the fingers, guiding with the other hand. B should roll up the spine as it is articulated by the walking fingers, one vertebra at a time.

The walking fingers should continue all the way up the neck and finish with a final pressure at the base of the skull. B should be at a full stand. Then, repeat the long opening strokes away from the spine, starting again at the top of the shoulder. B should keep the knees bent to avoid being pushed over by the pressure of the raking strokes.

As a finish to the slap out, turn the hands to soft brushes and brush quickly and vigorously down the sides and back of the body. Go all the way from the top of the head to the feet. Both partners should exhale on each downward brush.

Switch positions and repeat the exercise.

6. TOSSING THE DICE

With hands in an easy fist, shake them as if about to throw dice. Let the tricep muscle relax and shake at will. The vibration of the shaking tends to create a warm relaxing sensation to other parts of the upper torso. Employ more imagination by making a "chicka–chicka" sound, like the sound of shaking dice.

LEADER: Explain to the group they're going to throw the dice in a moment. First, however, demonstrate the proper throw position: step into a lunge, chest lifted and arms extended wide with energy pouring out the fingertips. Further inform them that at the moment of release, they are to produce an open, yet unvoiced, exhale sound.

Start with a vigorous "chicka–chicka" and then launch into a hearty throw. Repeat this several times, changing the lunge leg.

Incorporate the voice by asking everyone to pick a number say it when they throw the dice. Invariably, you'll hear a ton of "seven" and "three" on the first throw. Keep them alert by asking for a new number before each throw. Finish by announcing that this is the last throw and this one they'll actually win!

If everyone bursts into joyous expression, the exercise is capped and you're ready to go on. If not, spur them on with a mild admonishment like: *"Come on people! You just won a thousand dollars. Invest something in this winning! Really call out your number and then let yourself experience and express this wonderful moment of winning. Let's try it one more time!"*

This usually results in a full release which, if done correctly, gives everyone the opportunity to engage the entire instrument in a fully realized emotional physical experience. The consequence of which results in relaxation and an increased appetite for fully invested acting moments.

7. ROLLING

Animals are a great resource for relaxation techniques. Their movements of stretching and shaking can be readily observed as spontaneously occurring responses designed for relaxation. Less obvious is the use of rolling as a relaxation response, employed by nearly all members of the animal kingdom. We tend to discount this movement because although it's servicable to the animal's immediate ends, it is, by our standards, quite limited.

Rolling has been explored to great advantage in both martial arts and in numerous acrobatic sports. In these instances, rolls are designed for specific and highly dynamic results.

The rolling for relaxation, however, is a non–dynamic, luxurious roll. It's used to free the breath, massage the muscles and tendons, and momentarily reclaim that effortless "yummy" feeling often experienced in childhood. In this form, it very closely resembles the simple rolling movements of certain animals.

Pair up and move to one end of the room. If the room is big enough three or four teams can begin at an even distance, the other teams lining up behind them. If you are going first, lie down on the floor on your back, lift the arms up overhead, and relax. When everyone is in position on the floor or the mat surface, begin to inhale and then roll over slowly, curling up into a fetal position during the exhale.

At this point your partner is asked to simply crouch down and hug you as you exhale. He or she should release the hug on the inhale and gently guide you onto your stomach during your next exhale. The partner then brushes your back with open hands in long swift strokes from the center of the back outward toward the limbs. This is done during the long slow exhale.

Afterwards, allow for a long, luxurious inhale, curling up into a fetal position (again a brief hug or cradling from your partner), and then roll over onto your back for the slow exhale. The partner should provide similar brushstrokes down the sides of the body and the limbs.

One full roll has been completed and we are again at the starting position, ready for the next one.

Each team should roll all the way across the floor with the active partner making sure the rolling is going straight enough to avoid collision with the other teams. Once the rolls have completed one pass along the floor, the other partner should lie on the floor and repeat the exercise across the floor in the opposite direction.

After the team effort technique is practiced for a while, the rolling can occur at a slightly faster pace. Integrating the breath with the rolling and the brushstrokes takes practice and coordination. Once mastered, however, it produces a remarkably liberating state of relaxation that's well worth the effort.

This same rolling technique can be done solo, without a partner. The directive is to roll in the same breath pattern but to pay a great deal of attention to the attempt to melt into gravity; to spread out completely onto the floor. After several rolling passes across the floor, incorporate the voice into the exhale portions. The voice itself will unlock and translate that relaxation as feedback, which will further reinforce the body, which, in turn, will again inform the voice and create a welcome loop of relaxation.

MEDITATION

There's a wide variety of meditation techniques available today: chanting, transcendental, contemplative, ritual prayer, visualization, yoga, and much more. I have sampled them all and have incorpo-

PHOTO: TOM PALUMBO

Experiencing "Coherent Hands."

rated some into my daily life. All of them, at the fundamental level, are designed to enhance mental clarity and reduce stress. Many, however, are attached to religious traditions which in some circumstances may complicate the work of the actor. The following are a few simple meditations, free from religious boundaries, that can help actors to relax.

Before choosing a meditation, however, it's important to remember that in this context it's a training device, not an end in itself. Meditation can help reduce stage fright and certainly helps to train the mind to focus, but it cannot replace good honest hard work. I have heard several stories about actors who discovered meditation and in a misguided attempt to improve their acting went into deep meditative states offstage. One discovered to his horror he'd sat right through his entrance. The other, fearing he'd done likewise, lept from his meditation and bolted onstage three scenes too soon!

Be sensible about meditation. It refines the nervous system, provides insight into the workings of the mind, and has been known to improve a wide number of nerve-related ailments. Plus, meditating in a group enhances the focus and allows for the participants to have a shared experience. Such experiences are useful as a reference point which is always a good thing when building an ensemble. It is not, however, a magic potion that will insure exquisite performances or a suprise call from Steven Spielberg. Therefore, be content with slightly enhanced clarity of thought, more restful and relaxed demeanor, and perhaps a bit more focus.

1. COHERENT HANDS

Sit on the edge of a straight back chair. The feet should be placed directly under the knees and the spine lengthened. Hold both hands up, at the level of the lower ribs, bending at the elbow, palms up, shoulders relaxed. Close the eyes and let the breath settle down into the belly.

Place all the attention in the hands. Now, as though the attention were connected to a meter and you're controlling the intensity of attention, start at a level of four out of a possible ten. Slowly count up to ten, increasing the attention intensity with each number.

At ten, slowly begin to lift the right hand. As you do, allow all attention to shift to the right side of the body. Literally imagine a line splitting the body in half, the right side being activated by the moving right hand. Now slowly bring the hand down as the left hand begins to ascend. Allow the attention to shift to the left side in relation to the level of the left hand.

Do this shifting attention game for at least six passes. Then, without opening the eyes, bring the energy of the body to equilibrium by slowly alternating until the hands feel level. Sometimes the hands will end up in perfect alignment, other times not. What matters is the internal perception of equilibrium.

Sit in stillness, enjoying the simplicity of the energy balance. After three or four minutes, begin to slowly lift both hands. Allow the energy field of the whole body to increase with the smooth trajectory of the hands. Stop at the peak of the energy and let it radiate for a few moments, then begin the descending journey.

The hands should continue past the original point of departure, taking the body's energy lower and lower. Go to the lowest possible energy point and rest there for a few moments. Afterwards, bring the hands upwards to the level which renders the system refreshed and relaxed. Hold for a few moments and then slowly open the eyes.

2. COUNTING THE BREATH

This is a classic and once learned, can be done anywhere, anytime. It is a great stress reliever. It's borrowed from the Buddhist tradition. The ancient Buddhists realized that the essence of meditation was focusing the attention on something. They asked themselves, "What is it that the mind could focus upon, no matter where you were, and it would always be with you?" Their answer: your breath.

Sit on the edge of a chair with the spine lengthened and the head balanced. Both feet should be flat on the floor and the hands folded on the lap. Let the eyelids relax and the gaze fall to the floor at a forty-five-degree angle.

Once settled into this posture begin to place the awareness on the breath. Do not interfere with the breathing, just watch it. At first, the act of observing may alter the natural breath patterns, but usually, within five minutes or so, that aspect dissolves and the breath returns to its normal function.

As you watch the breath you may notice a deep relaxation settling in, possibly a warmth spreading out across the belly, and a sleepy, drifty feeling. The mind may want to wander to more entertaining frontiers, but gently insist that it be satisfied to sit and watch the breath. When you catch your thoughts wandering, don't punish yourself or go off on deliberations of any kind, simply return to the task of watching the breath. Allow yourself to be fascinated by the act of breathing.

Do this for fifteen to twenty minutes, keeping the eyes partially open and relaxed. At the end of the meditation, you'll feel more relaxed and energized.

3. SEAWEED

This is an active visualization meditation. For best results from this exercise, have the leader use the following narration. Soothing music or ocean sounds can be very helpful to maintain the right atmosphere. In soft easy vocal tones, the leader should say the following:

Start lying down on your back with the legs extended and the arms at your sides. Take a few sighs to settle the breath. Imagine you're at the beach in the warm sand with your feet facing the water. Feel the warmth of the sun on your body.

This is a very magical beach. You hear the easy crash of a wave and this blue magical ocean water slowly rolls in and finds its way under both of your feet, supporting them as they float on top of the warm water. After a moment, the tide pulls away and takes with it all the tension stored in the feet.

Another wave crashes and the water rolls in, diving under the feet and rolling up the calf to a spot just behind the knees. The legs are now supported from the knees down as they float gently atop the water. The easy lilt of the water soothes and relaxes the legs. After a moment, the tide pulls away and as it draws down the leg it takes all the tension out of the knees, calfs, ankles, and feet, depositing it into the vast magical ocean.

Another wave rolls in under the feet, the lower leg, and works its way under the thigh to a spot just below the buttocks. Now both legs are floating, suspended and relaxed atop the warm, warm water. Let the legs surrender to the warm buoyancy of the water.

The tide is now receding, pulling away and taking with it all the tension from the thighs, the knees, the calf muscles, the ankles; rolling out the bottom of the feet and into the deep ocean waters.

Another wave crashes and rolls under the feet, the lower legs, the thighs, and dives under the buttocks to the lower back. The lower body from the waist down is now floating, supported by the warm, warm, water. Allow the lower body to surrender, relishing the sensation of floating.

The tide pulls away and takes with it all the tension stored in the lower back, the hips, the buttocks, the thighs, the knees, the calf muscles, and the feet. Sense the warm sunshine on the body, the smell of the salt sea air, the sound of distant seagulls.

Another wave rolls in and under the feet, calves, knees, thighs, buttocks, lower back, and works its way up the back to the shoulders. It also rolls under the hands, wrists, forearms, elbows, upper arm and shoulders. So now, from the shoulders, all the way down to the toes, the body is floating, suspended in the warm water. Buoyant.. .light. ..effortless.

The tide pulls away again, taking the tension out of the shoulders, upper back and chest, upper arms, elbow and waist, forearms and hips, buttocks and hands, thighs, knees, ankles, and finally pours out the bottom of the feet and is dispersed into the vast blue ocean.

A new wave crashes and rolls under the feet, the calves,

the knees, the thighs, the buttocks, the lower back, the arms and upper back, the shoulders, and then fills in under the neck and dives under the head. So that now, the entire body is floating in the warm water, supported, buoyant, safe. Allow the body to surrender to the support of the water. Relish the fun of lightly floating, being carried by a gentle current.

After a few moments, let the current take you to a deeper section of the water. This is very magical water. In a moment you will descend into it, but will have no difficulty breathing and will remain perfectly safe. Staying in this same position, begin to descend. Let the body sink down, down, down until finally coming to rest on the soft cushion of the ocean floor. The water is warm and there are streams of beautiful light flickering everywhere. The sensation is of one of complete safety.

In a moment an undersea wave will roll in and magically support your head, neck and back. It will lift you up and into a sitting position. [This is actually physicalized, not just visualized]. Okay, here comes the wave... whooosh. Let it do all the work of getting you to a sitting position. If the first wave doesn't do the job, allow for a second one to come along and complete the task.

Once sitting, allow for a series of waves to roll along. Each wave should move the body to another position with each position being a step toward standing up. This should be done slowly, with the eyes closed, allowing for approximately ten waves to roll past.

Once standing, imagine you have become a large strand of seaweed. Plant roots into the ocean floor through the bottom of the feet. The rest of the body should remain loose, responsive to every ripple and current surrounding it.

After a few moments, a sudden surge of current will come along and uproot one foot. Here it comes . . . whoooosh. Try not to *do* the uprooting, *let* the sensation produce the effect. Another current comes along and uproots the other foot . . . whooooosh. Current surges will now come along at random. They will push you and your feet must move to maintain balance and to help you travel across the floor. Keep the eyes closed and only respond to the occasional current. If you happen to bump into another seaweed, simply remain connected and respond simultaneously to the next wave impulse. The impulse may separate you or maintain the connection; try not to orchestrate it, let it happen on its own.

Okay now open the bottom of the feet and plant roots down into the ocean floor again. The current has become smooth again. Slowly the water is draining away, downward, like water from a bathtub. The very top of your head is now exposed to the air. Feel the sunshine on the very top of your head.

The water is receding and your forehead is now exposed, now the nose, the mouth, the neck, the collarbone and shoulders, the upper chest, the lower chest and elbows, the hips, the pelvis, the thighs, the knees, the calf muscles, the ankles and finally the feet. You're now standing on the beach, dry, refreshed, relaxed, sensing the warm sunshine on your body. Open your eyes.

VOCAL WORK

There are a number of systems of voice training currently available. All have strengths and weaknesses, all have staunch supporters, and all certainly aspire to the same goal: to train actors to effectively use the vocal instrument for maximum expression with a minimum of effort.

I make no claim to providing anything resembling a program of voice. I am not a voice teacher and don't feel qualified to offer much beyond a beginning level study. I use voice and movement as an integrated part of my teaching, but my primary emphasis is, and remains on the physical. I have worked with singers, including members of the Houston Opera Studio, but only as a specialist using my approaches to help them relax, open up, improve expression and ease of vocal sound.

I would hope that someone in the group or perhaps whomever has been selected to play a leadership role could enhance and improve upon the exercises I have included. If not, work with the following exercises and incorporate others gleaned from the various systems of vocal training currently available.

The following are a few of the exercises that I've found helpful in warming up, activating, and enriching the voice.

1. CRANIAL MANDALA

Working in clusters of five or six people, lie on the back on the floor so that all of the heads point toward a single spot. This will create a circular shape resembling a wheel with the bodies as spokes. The heads should be touching a very important element in this exercise. If there are groups encountering difficulty in achieving this shape, it's best to diminish the groups to four or five people.

Once in position, the groups begin by making a humming sound, working to find a single group tone. Once the tone is established gradually explore pitch, moving upwards and downwards within an octave. The challenge here is in maintaining a consistent group pitch as it moves along the octave.

It's important that everyone work to match the exact note of the pitch, not opting for the octave above or below. In some cases, one or more members of the group will simply produce air and imagine they're producing the note if it is out of their range. This serves a very important function, so resist the temptation to go silent.

Next, the group will repeat the exercise with an open "Ah" sound. Be careful not to allow the volume to get out of control or listening will become impossible and the pitch will suffer.

After about ten minutes, the leader should stop the exercise to introduce the next facet: the groups will now create harmonies with the sustained "Ah" sounds. As you search for the right harmony, take a breath whenever you need and change the group chord whenever it feels appropriate. This usually produces an amazing array of delicious harmonies.

After ten minutes of seeking out pleasant harmonies, shift to the exploration of dissonance. Next, open the exercise to explore rhythms, songs, and free-form sounds. The only strict requirement at this point is to listen to the group and to respond as an ensemble.

By this time, the participants have entered a very special state of mind. The shared resonance produces an enormous amount of vibration in the head and the voice has the opportunity to explore unknown territory. Certain groups will actually take on a particular dramatic characteristic such as exploration of "moaning" or of "calling out in fear." Others may break out in a spontaneous rendition of the theme song from *Gilligan's Island*. No two groups are alike, yet all are equally fascinating.

Allow the free form to continue as long as it seems fruitful. When one or more groups loses steam, continuously falter, giggle, or display any other signs of fatigue, it's time to signal for a halt to the exercise. Tell everyone to stay on the floor and wiggle away from their position in the circle.

Do not get up right away. Many participants will need a few moments to come around from the special meditative state and may even experience momentary disorientation.

Reactions from this exercise will range from being mildly amused to peak experiences. The universal and, ultimately, the most practical result of the exercise is that everyone will have had a good vocal workout, and will have improved blending, matching, and contrasting pitches. In addition, over time, there will occur an enhanced vocal range and vocal confidence. Self-decreed "non-singers" may indeed find they have musical resources they did not know existed.

2. VOICE MASSAGE

One of the impediments to full vocal production is tension. Some people actually rely on tension to create and sustain vocal sounds. Over time, however, this approach debilitates the voice and robs it of the rich nuance it might otherwise have developed. The voice seems particularly sensitive to tensions held in the musculature of the body.

This exercise employs massage to the body while producing sound. The combination releases trapped aspects of the voice and enhances communication between body and voice. When the body and voice are relaxed and when both are engaged in producing sounds, a deeper, more authentic delivery from the actor evolves.

This exercise is tricky. People doing it for the first time, particularly if they don't know one another, find that massaging another person's body itself induces a layer of tension. For groups which might be candidates for this kind of discomfort, it may be necessary to introduce the exercise in gradual stages. Being playful and light-hearted is also helpful in the early stages. Having the freedom to express discomfort through laughter and play will quickly dissipate excess nervous energy.

As the exercise progresses, and people become less selfconscious, the participants can experience more serious explorations. Later, and certainly with groups that have already established a rapport, the exercise can become a wonderfully powerful and deeply satisfying experience.

Select a partner. Decide which will be the active partner and which the passive. The active one will begin by massaging the shoulders and arms of the passive partner. As the muscles of the arms and shoulders get massaged, the passive partner activates the voice and allows the vocal sound to reflect the sensations and the release created by the massage.

The passive partner is only passive in the sense of receiving the massage, but is otherwise quite active in terms of vocal production. As the partner is massaging him, he is to express in vocal (non–verbal) terms, what he's feeling. At first, this produces quite a lot of generic sounds. It may become necessary for a leader to interrupt the exercise and encourage everyone to release deeply and more fully into the experience.

The active partner is not only active in terms of delivering the massage. He too is producing sounds reflective of his feelings, intentions, reactions, and observations. His vocal work can encourage the partner to genuinely open up into the release sensation of the muscles and thereby unlock the vocal potential.

After fifteen minutes, allow the vocal release and the massage to expand to include the neck, face, back, hips, and legs. End the exercise with a full massage of the hands: the voice and hands have a very intimate connection.

Take a short break and begin again with the partners switching roles. Follow the same pattern as described above, Carefully monitoring to avoid going too fast or too slow.

3. TONGUE EXTENSION

This is a silly but effective exercise aimed at stretching and strengthening all of the articulators. It also happens to be a good icebreaker; allowing inhibitions to fall away into a sublime sense of absurdity.

Stand in a circle, open the mouth and fully extend the tongue. Keeping the tongue fully extended, look around the room at each other. This usually gives way to fits of laughter. Allow some freedom to laugh and then redirect the intention back to the exercise.

Keeping the tongue extended, everyone is to count out loud, clearly and distinctly, from one to twenty. Let this happen in a chaotic free-form manner at first. When everyone has reached twenty they're free to return the tongue to the mouth and resalivate.

Having done this once through you'll be warmed up and ready for the next step. Repeat the previous exercise, only this time the participants count to twenty in the following manner: "one, one – two, one – two – three, one – two – three – four, one – two –three – four – five," and so forth, up to twenty.

Take special care to articulate every consonant, speak loudly and clearly, and remember the tongue isn't to retreat even an inch. Only after reaching the final number can you allow yourself to return the tongue. After a brief resalivation, everyone must count to one hundred as quickly as possible, speaking every consonant with complete clarity.

You'll be amazed at the relative speed and accuracy of your speech following this tongue extension. Done on a regular basis, this exercise can do wonders for those people chronically afflicted with "lazy speech."

4. WALKING TONE

This is another exercise that functions on many levels. It's a means to work the breath support. Second, it's a quick way to diagnose if you have poor breath habits or underdeveloped breath capacity. Finally, it's a way to demonstrate the value of connecting even simple exercises with emotional vitality.

The exercise requires a piano and a large open room. The leader begins by having everyone walk in a smooth continuous free-form pattern. After a few moments, the leader should strike a note on the piano and ask that everyone match that note, sustaining it as they walk. Do this several times until all participants have the hang of it.

The next step is for everyone to walk, sustaining a clear unbroken matched tone for as long as they can go *on one breath.* They must stop walking when the breath runs out and the tone stops. Wait until the last person has finished the tone (make sure this person goes the full walk, not stop short out of consideration for the group). Strike a new tone and let the exercise continue like this for at least ten tones.

The final step is to invest the tones with feeling, with a strong image or impulse communicated through the sustained sound. Remind them that they're not to alter the pitch or abruptly alter the volume. Instead, they're being invited to fill the exercise with their inner life.

After a few attempts at this, it usually happens that those people who were weak before discover new reserves of power and expression. Others may find that they tend to overproduce the expression and diminish their breath capacity. The majority of participants will report a much longer breath/walk and a satisfying subjective emotional connection.

5. STRETCH AND YUMMY SOUNDS

This is primarily a vocal "cool down" technique. It's also a good gear-shifting exercise following meditative, emotional, or highly demanding physical sessions.

Everyone will stretch and yawn, rolling on the floor and moving in luxurious ways while making "yummy" sounds. "Yummy" translates as those sighs, hums, smacks, growls, grunts, and squeaks we make while waking up in the morning, enjoying a massage, or settling into delicious experiences of any kind.

The combination of physical stretching and "yummy" vocal expression releases a lot of tension and centers the voice into a warm gentle place in the body. The yawning clears the mind and normalizes the attention.

6. SOUND SCULPTURES

Move freely and in a relaxed manner while making sound. While doing this, seek out and find a position that offers the maximum vocal resonation. Once you've found it, refine the position until it becomes a living sculpture: a relaxed yet dynamic sound resonator. This position will be know as "A."

The same instructions apply as another search begins to find a second position called "B" and a third to be called "C." Explore the three positions making sounds and connecting feelings to each sculpture.

Next, link the three resonator sculptures with sound and movement to create a short abstract piece of theatre: there's a beginning (A), a middle (B), and an end (C). Explore your choices until you've secured a repeatable sequence. Play with the dynamics of time and space by stretching certain elements, or speeding through a section. After a half hour of shaping and refinement, everyone should present their mini-theatre pieces to the group.

7. SECRETS IN SOUND

Take a few moments to think of some deeply repressed secret. The more forbidden the secret, the better. It can be a secret about a real incident, like a childhood experience that nobody knows about, or something else, such as a fantasy about someone that you would never dare reveal.

Focus on this secret and, using no words or revealing gestures, confess this secret to an imaginary partner, not with words but through sound. Keep peeling off layers of anxiety surrounding this secret until you can enjoy the freedom of telling it, albeit in abstract form, to the entire world. Don't be afraid to use the full vocal range.

8. SOUND WEAVING

Start this exercise with partners. Reach across the space toward one another in silence. Once the hands clasp, both emit whatever sounds want naturally to emerge. Keep making vocal sounds, taking a breath whenever necessary, and moving through the space. As you move, reach out to others in the group. If you find another hand, release your original partner and emit a new sound as you move through the space with the new partner. You're attempting to weave through the whole group in this fashion, reaching and changing sounds.

The rule is, however, you may only move and make sounds when hands are clasped. If your hand gets released and you have no partner, you can only reach out silently, in place, attempting to link with someone.

In this way, one partner must reach out for another across the space and only move while still in contact with someone. Let the sounds reflect the inevitable conflicts and surprising situations that will arise. Continue this exercise until everyone has weaved through the group and has again reached his original partner.

Once this first round has been completed, everyone should next shut their eyes. Keeping eyes closed, weave through the crowd in an effort to move and vocalize your way back to your original partner. As before, let the voice register all the nuances of the game.

EMOTION

Most people are afraid of emotions, having been conditioned to repress or hide them when they occur, and they're embarrassed by them when they emerge in public. Actors, of course, must freely express emotion appropriate to the technical demands of the dramatic format.

This dichotomy between emotions and technique has been at the center of controversy regarding actor training. One school of thought strongly guards against engaging true organic expression of emotion, because it can become indulgent, uncontrolled, and ultimately self-serving, robbing the audience of emotional identification.

The other school insists upon emotional truth, advocating an honest biological expression tempered to fit the needs of the text. This latter school of thought has recently gained dominance as a result of the medium of film. On film, an actor cannot afford aesthetic distance. The camera is too revealing.

In answer to the demands placed upon the actors working in today's market, many actors, directors, and educators have delved into the emotional realm. They're trying to discover ways of triggering and controlling emotional responses which need to match the appropriate degree of timing and depth over the course of many performances.

Stanislavski developed "affective memory" as a means to this end and Lee Strasberg joined this line of research in his work with "emotional recall." All the great acting teachers of our age have wrestled with this challenge of how to get the actor's instrument so charged that their work is at once technically fascinating and emotionally powerful.

Within this branch of work there are two further schools of thought which have recently emerged. One claims that the most reliable and sensible way for an actor to fill the emotional demands of a scene is to pursue clearly defined objectives and allow the communication of the other actor to stimulate emotional reality. The other one claims that the actor can have techniques to trigger emotional states which will then match the truth needed for the scene and engage both fellow actors and audiences.

Most people recognize that a rational marriage of the two is the best way to go. Young actors who are afraid of their emotions will avoid being vulnerable at all costs; they will need help to break through emotional barriers. Others, who are emotionally open, need help to find ways of connecting with their objectives and directing their emotional states to fit the aesthetic demands of a particular project.

Below are a few simple exercises which may be of help. These are all quite safe and are designed to avoid triggering the repressed and, consequently, more volatile wellsprings of emotion. Contact with full-blown emotional states should be done, at least in the beginning, within a very special protective environment. (I approach this more specifically in the section called, THRESHOLD WORK.)

1. MOVE UNTIL YOU LAUGH

This exercise is a terrific release one that brings intellectualizers right up against their major obstacle. It is designed to stimulate delight and laughter. It sometimes, however, stimulates the opposite, something which should be allowed but not encouraged.

The directions for this one are quite simple. Everyone is to move around the room in whatever fashion, at whatever pace, and do whatever they must do to *make themselves laugh*. There's an implied double-bind here: on the one hand they're looking to laugh, a relaxed and natural response; on the other, they're TRYING to make themselves laugh, an action which has a degree of tension and artificiality to it.

This split is exactly the dilemma faced by the actor. The only way out is in the doing. Invariably, once you plunge into the exercise, you'll discover some way of moving, not-moving, hopping, rolling, or just being, which triggers a true and delicious laugh. Of course, with laughter being so infectious the exercise gets easier and easier.

As an interesting twist to the exercise, it can be useful for you to move in a manner so intensely serious it provokes laughter. By giving yourself permission to be melodramatic, wildly serious, and ridiculously severe, you'll invariably break out into fits of laughter.

When the laughter finally surges forth, images, flavors, sounds, and all manner of subjective material surfaces. It's useful to have a post-exercise discussion to verbalize these impressions. Occasionally, you'll stumble upon something that strongly continues to trigger the laugh response. If so, you've found a very useful acting tool.

By the way, this exercise is a very useful pre-show warm up for actor's who may be involved in a farce or a high energy comedy. The zanni energy and the release propels the actors into a sharp, spirited mood that tunes their minds and bodies to the right frequency for such work.

2. UNIVERSAL FRAGMENTS

There are a number of phrases universal enough to be endowed with any intrepretations of emotional states. These phrases, or fragments of speech, are convenient lenses through which an actor can project his/her inner life. Because they're free from any circumstances and are essentially "content-less," the actors can concentrate on the experience of penetrating the words with fully expressed emotions without the pressure of expectation.

The ultimate value of such an exploratory exercise is that it can help the beginning actor to develop the appetite for emotional honesty. This exercise will quite vividly expose emotional artifice and reveal areas of easy emotional access.

Start with a random walk maintaining a private circle of concentration. As the walking progresses, the leader needs to have everyone punctuate the walk with an occasional sigh. The sighing breath helps to warm up the emotional center. After a few moments, the leader must stop the group and tell them they're now going to insert a specific word or phrase into the spots of punctuation. The only difference being they'll have a *qualifier* which will inflect the word in one emotional direction or another. They're not to try to show or indicate the emotion. Instead, they're to *experience* the emotion and *allow free expression* of the body.

Giving the body the freedom to express itself naturally while invested in an emotional state creates the much needed link between body and mind, a state that later helps produce fully integrated acting. That is, the outer will indeed reflect the inner.

A good word to start off with is "wow." It has very little contextual identification and is therefore ideal for carrying the charge of various emotional states.

The leader should inform everyone that the word they'll use in place of the sigh is "wow" and that they must say it during each unit of expression. It need not be expressed loudly or even clearly; it's important only that the emotion and breath are connecting with a spoken word.

Next, the leader must inform everyone they'll hear a qualifying statement that will guide them toward expressing their feelings. They're to give total freedom to the body and to let the word (or words) come out as part of the overall expression.

The following is an example of the kind of instructions the leader uses for this exercise:

> Let's begin with an easy walk. Keep your breath stream open and maintain a private circle of concentration. Let the body have its freedom. Allow it to try out a variety of postures, positions, rhythms as you work. Using the word *WOW*, express the feeling of having *compassion for someone else's pain*. Let it take you by surprise. You're walking along and then suddenly the feeling.

> Try it out several times. Do not indicate the emotion, experience it. Try sitting, leaning, or even lying on the floor.

Let them do this one for a while until the mood has clearly changed. Continue with:

> Good. But work the muscle both ways. If you get into an honest emotional state, let the body have its expression and then come back to neutral. Coming back is as important

as going out there.

Once they have the hang of conjuring the feeling, saying "WOW" and letting the body explore various ways of expression, introduce a somewhat less introspective qualifier such as:

Fine. Now explore the WOW of seeing a magnificent sunset. Again, start in neutral; just walking. Let the sunset take you by surprise. Let the breath influence the body and the speaking of the word. Try it several times until you're genuinely there!

By this time, the group should have a handle on the mechanics of the exercise and can begin to explore at a slightly faster pace. Remember to insist upon coming back to neutral. Also remember that memories, images, and associations will often arise during this exercise and the participants need not be attached to them. They are natural occurrences and to the degree they enhance or deepen the experience are useful; otherwise they are harmless or at worst a mild nuisance.

Use some or all of the following qualifiers, inventing more of them as you customize the exercise. These qualifiers are designed to trigger emotional sensations and expressions within a relative safety zone.

Using the phrase,___(FILL IN THE BLANK)_____, express the following:

Sudden illumination, you suddenly get it. It all makes sense!

Relief, having just survived a near fatal accident.

Intimacy, a warm intimate memory surfaces. It could be of a sexual or nonsexual nature.

Indignation, anger at injustice done to you or to others.

Avoidance, use the phrase to erase or brush off a horrible or disturbing image, memory, or thought.

Self recrimination, you tried to help but said the wrong thing. You blew it. You made the situation worse.

Self congratulations, it was a gem. Everything you said came out just right and made the situation wonderful. You did it right!

Hopelessness, exhausted. You see no hope. You haven't the strength even to try.

Self pity, no one understands. You mourn your shortcomings and your pitiful place in the world.

Joy, your ship has come in! The best thing that could happen at this time in your life has just happened! You've made it! Whatever the dream, it's just come true!

After several experiences with the last one, the leader should tell everyone to maintain the feeling and to physically express themselves in the space. This stirs the atmosphere considerably and, as it reaches a fever pitch, get everyone's attention and tell them to maintain all the inner feeling but to suppress the physical expression. Then ask that they sit down in this condition. After a few moments, explain they're to imagine a dear friend has sat down next to them and has just received devastating news. This friend obviously needs someone to talk to.

Let this imaginary scene play out for at least three or four minutes. After returning to neutral, have a discussion about your experience, starting with the last exercise and working back to the first.

This exercise is a means to prime the pump of emotions. It diagnoses quite effectively which emotions are difficult or blocked for the participant and reveals in both subjective and objective ways the great resource of emotions within everyone.

GAMES

Games are a good way to blow off steam, to reconnect to the exhuberance of childhood, and to sensitize the individual to the group and the group to the individual. It's also just plain fun, a quality which can go a long way toward injecting relaxation and joy back into the work.

1. FREEZE TAG

The rules are simple. If tagged by the person designated as "it" you must freeze. Regardless of your posture, you must remain frozen. However, you're allowed to make one adjustment which is to open the legs. This adjustment is made to accommodate the next rule: a frozen person can be unfrozen if someone who is not "it" dives or scoots through the open legs.

Due to this release technique of zipping through the legs, it's wise to designate *two* people as "it." A good "it" team can freeze up the whole group leaving no one to release anyone else. By the same token, if a group is fast and effective, the "its" will never succeed in freezing up the group.

Change the "its" from time to time to provide variety and to give them a rest. By the way, if a person is tagged while in the act of going through someone's legs, he must remain frozen and cannot be unfrozen for the remainder of the game.

2. FRANKENSTEIN

The rules, although simple, take some getting used to. Basically you have a group of "victims" who must keep their hands at their sides while walking around the room *with eyes closed*. One or two people are chosen to be the Frankenstein. These individuals, who also have their eyes closed, are allowed to extend their arms in front while walking around the room.

The Frankensteins will no doubt encounter someone. When they do, they're to lightly grasp the neck of that person. The victim must then let out a bloodcurdling scream. Following the scream, the victim becomes a Frankenstein, lifts the arms and begins to stalk for victims.

Naturally, the scream of a fallen victim alerts people nearby and sends them shuffling away to a safer area. The problem is that there begins to be an increasing number of Franks running around.

Inevitably, two of the Frankensteins will encounter each other. In this case, they scream and become humble victims again.

With this series of screams and transformations it's a game that can go on for some time. It is particularly hilarious if one half of a group is allowed to watch the other half play the game. Then, after a designated time, the groups switch and the previous participants become the new observers.

One cautionary note: discourage screams that are obviously throaty or potentially damaging to the vocal apparatus. Also, there should be a designated leader to ensure people don't fall down or to "create" a new Frankenstein if all have managed to turn into victims.

3. MAGNETS

This is similar to Frankenstein, although much more sedate. Everyone is dispersed in the space with eyes closed.

They must keep moving with their hands at their sides while attending to the object of the game, which is to *avoid touching or being touched by any other player.*

If a touch occurs, those two players are magnetized, connected *at the point of initial contact.* Insist upon the latter point for it will prove to be a wonderful and challenging dimension to the game.

Once magnetized, the players must continue to move about the room with eyes closed in whatever position they can manage. Eventually, however, they'll touch or be touched by another player. Soon their small cluster will begin to act like a single organism. At this point it's useful to remind the organism to remain quiet, so as not to give away its position. The group will then quite naturally become a large stalking magnet.

This exercise is another one that's enhanced by having a set of observers and a set of participants who change roles after playing for a while. No peeking allowed. Peeking only robs you of the sensitivity enhancement of the exercise, not to mention the fun.

The winner is the person (or persons) who never get magntized.

4. KILLER BALL

This is a favorite of students who have attended the National Stage Combat Workshops. The game moves fast and stirs up primal attack and defense instincts within a safe, enjoyable format. It requires a small plastic children's ball about the size of a standard 4-square ball.

Everyone gets into a large circle. Two volunteers get into the middle of the circle. One is the target person; the other is his or her defender. The people in the circle throw the ball in an attempt to hit the target person. The defender spins, deflects, and otherwise defends the target. The target person remains behind the defender, usually with hands on his back, and dodges all attacks while using the defender as a shield.

When the target person is hit, they must quickly rejoin the circle. The person who hit the target person must run in and defend the defender who is now the new target. That is, the previous defender moves into the target position and needs a defender. The new defender is the person who made the successful hit. The members of the circle know, however, that once a target is hit, the defender is fair game and they're allowed to try and hit him even before the new defender has run into the center of the circle.

This last element of hitting the new target before the new defender is in place can result in a very exciting and quick succession of "kills."

If a group is exceptionally large, arrange two concentric circles with the inner circle being the active players and the outer circle providing both a catching net and moral support. Switch the circles from time to time.

Another good way to spice up the game is to use two balls. This doubles the chances of scoring and keeps the game moving at a blistering pace.

THE COOL DOWN

As important as it is to warm up, it's equally important to cool down. This is especially true during the winter months in cold climates. If warm muscles are suddenly exposed to cold temperatures they contract too swiftly. This can result in chronic stiffness, pinched nerves, and muscle cramps. In addition, the strain on the temperature maintenance system of the body can cause undue stress which effects the immune system. Avoid this by following a few cool-down procedures.

The simplest method, especially after cardiovascular work, is the slow walk with a breath count: the person cooling down goes for a walk and inhales with one step and exhales with the next step. Walk and breathe like this for at least ten steps. Then, the person should change the breath to *two* steps, or beats, for the inhale and exhale. Again go for at least ten steps. Follow this with three beats, four, five, and so on until the system equalizes to a comfortable breath pattern.

Another method is to roll on the floor. Start on the back and stretch out the limbs with the arms overhead. Begin a sideways roll in any direction, coordinating the breath with the movement.

Yawn and stretch during the rolls until the body feels relaxed and slightly cooler.

If a shower is handy, it's good to take a medium-hot one and then gradually adjust the temperature to completely cold at the end. This final blast of cold water serves to shut the pores of the skin and to cool down the body in a quick and refreshing manner.

One can do any number of things that will serve as a cool-down. The hard part is actually *remembering* to do a good cool-down. Making it an integral part of any workout will ensure the habit becomes instilled.

WHERE ARE YOU NOW?

The journey so far has warmed your body and warmed the group. The exercises have been largely individual, but done in a group setting; increasing your will power and helping to achieve the first level of trust among your fellows. The exercises have been sequenced either by a selected leader or have followed the suggested sequencing provided at the back of this book. The exercises should not be abandoned as you go forth into the next phase of work. Instead, they can be arranged to serve specific physical demands, to provide a warm-up in a generic sense, and to maintain and deepen the trust among he members of the group.

By now your body should be more supple, your mind more alert, and your emotions more accessible. You have the beginnings of a working vocabulary with fellow actors and have had some shared experiences that have led to new understandings of each other. You have learned postures and movements that have set a strong foundation. You are ripe for more advanced work that builds upon that foundation to guide you toward the experience of ensemble flow.

Like a member of a mountain climbing expedition, keep a sense of adventure and relish the discoveries as they unfold. Maintain a positive attitude, make your contributions when you can, and support each and every person as they pull themselves along. Patience and perseverance are key ingredients. If you manage to weather the climb, I promise you the view will be fantastic!

PHOTO: TOM PALUMBO

Where Are You Now?

PART II

ENSEMBLE AND RITUAL THEATRE

In part I, *The Actor With a Thousand Faces* established the vocabulary and the shared experiences that have prepared you to enter into a more profound and hopefully more satisfying phase of work. With body and voice well lubricated, you can now trust that the foundation work in rhythm, space, rapport, breath, balance, posture, and warm-up techniques have prepared you to delve deeper into the ensemble flow.

Part I has provided the basic techniques. In Part II, you will learn how to apply those techniques to dramatic exercises that will bring out the inner artist in each member and teach the group as a whole to become one entity in the pursuit of an artistic goal. I will introduce the components of ritual theatre, give instructions on how to transform the workspace into a sanctified arena, provide experiences with universal sacred shapes, supply provocative philosophical viewpoints to be wrestled with throughout the text and continue to reveal exercises that greatly improve powers of concentration, creativity, and expression.

After exploring and making discoveries in characterization, visualization, text, mythological thinking, and clowning, Part II will eventually give you the experience and the structures to confidently launch you into creating and performing viable works of ensemble theatre. The shape, size, subject and style of those works will reflect the unique chemistry and work ethic of each and every member. That, however, will in turn reflect the unique chemistry of the ensemble as a whole. There is an ocean of bliss awaiting you, jump in and relish with rigorous grace.

WHAT IS A RITUAL?

By now the group will certainly recognize the sensation and the value of the ensemble flow. How that experience relates to culture, myth, and ritual theatre is the nature of this next investigation. Before the work can begin in earnest, however, some discussion of the word ritual should occur.

The most common notions of what constitute a ritual are the things that have become habituated into our daily routine. Our morning and evening preparations, for example, are considered rituals because of their repetitive nature and because they're actions that accomplish very definite tasks with a minimum of effort. Although these actions can certainly be theatricalized, they're not in themselves relevant to ritual for the theatre.

Rituals are also defined as ceremonies associated with cultural or family customs. These customs are ritual actions that have become adopted by a specific set of people in order to maintain community and reinforce group identity. Rituals of this nature are very close in form and content to ritual theatre; some would even argue they are a form of theatre.

There's another level of ritual associated with the quest to come into accord with the ultimate and mysterious power of the universe – sometimes referred to as religion. Rituals of this order develop according to specific elements most immediately involved with the society. The rituals of early religions were all centered around animal mysteries and the relationship of the hunters to their animal food source. Later, when humans began to cultivate plants as the main food source, the rituals evolved to reflect the agricultural mysteries of the seasons, the sun, the seeds that die yet mysteriously become plants, the rivers that periodically swell out of bounds, and so forth. Gradually, another element of religious ritual evolved that centered around events associated with human development and consciousness.

The need to tell stories and to enact rituals of all kinds, no doubt, led to the development of theatre. Like ritual, there are levels of theatre that deal with the mundane, there are levels that deal with sociological issues and customs, and there are levels of theatre that deal with the quest to come into accord with the mysterious power of the universe. Theatre is most effective when it mangages to weave all three levels into a single event.

An unfortunate component of all ritual is that it can easily lose the core energy that first inspired it. Rituals often suffer from staleness and atrophy as the years erode their power until finally they become empty, impotent gestures, infused with misinterpretations and ignorance. Inevitably, over many years of repetition, even the most carefully guarded rituals drift from their original intentions and become hollow, sometimes absurd versions of the original. In the end, the exact function of the ritual is lost or hopelessly obscured as it drifts through time unmoored.

The Easter egg hunt, for example, is a ritual that continues to be enacted by families in many parts of the western world. There are few people, however, who have any notion why they color and hide hardboiled eggs and even fewer who stop to question it. Yet, if we take a step back, certain questions most certainly arise: This is a Christian ritual. To what, exactly, does the Easter Bunny refer? Are painted eggs related in some way to resurrection, fertility, springtime, anything at all? Who started this custom and what does it accomplish? If these questions are not or cannot be answered and the original function of the ritual has been lost, what need is being met by the continuance of such an ambiguous ritual?

Some ambiguous customs, when confronted with their decay and possible demise, may suddenly give birth to rituals within the ritual in order to perpetuate and revitalize the core ritual (a survival tactic that prevents it withering from sheer neglect). For example: Not long ago I recognized that the New Orleans Mardi Gras festival was a ritual that, although linked to our collective need to express the shadow side of our human psyche, had no specific link to a defining event or purpose. As years wore on, I observed that the vitality of the once robust festival began to wane considerably, threatening to reduce it to little more than a poorly attended tourist attraction.

In recent years, however, a new Mardi Gras ritual has emerged to save the day: women who attract attention by various methods, including exposing their breasts to people stationed on festival parade floats, are rewarded with colorful plastic bead necklaces. During Mardi Gras, the cheap necklaces, which under normal circumstances are virtually worthless, become objects of extremely high value. Consequently, goddess–like status is awarded women who are seen walking about wearing numerous strands of necklaces. What obviously began as a joke, has now become a major revitalizing force and for some, the sole focus of the festival. The ritual within the ritual in this case has succeeded in giving a boost to the event.

There are many places around the globe where cultural rituals are alive with meaning and function with enormous vitality. This is particularly true in India, Bali, Brazil, and much of Asia. Their power is sustained by their ability to fulfill the primary function of all authentic rituals: transition from one state of consciousness to another. The nature of the transition is dependent upon the nature of the ritual, the aim of the participant, and the ultimate merits of the experience.

Stale rituals do not facilitate transitions of consciousness, regardless the aim, and eventually die out. In the final stages of decay, empty of real power, the rituals serve only as a nostalgic data bank, destined to enact the story of the ritual instead of the ritual itself.

How is it possible for vibrant and effective rituals to die out? There are many reasons why rituals decay: cultural upheavals, natural disasters, scientific discoveries, to name a few. It seems to me the most common cause is that humans have a penchant for habituating behaviors. Conscious habits very soon become unconscious habits. There are many reasons for habituating a ritual, and some are no more harmless than a desire to create a reliable system to enhance or perpetuate the ritual. Unfortunately, what may make the rituals more convenient, may also render them ineffective. What results is very much like the difference between talking about riding a bicycle and actually riding a bicycle. True rituals actually travel.

In my experience, two very good ways to insure that rituals do not dry up but instead retain their true power is to continually create new rituals and to re-define, reawaken, and genuinely renew, old rituals. Ensemble theatre is one very effective means of accomplishing both these tasks.

In the beginning, any group dedicated to this idea must spend a lot of time learning about how to get to the simple, pure, undecorated levels of understanding cultural artifacts. This process can be frustrating, especially for the intellect which wants to embellish and complicate everything. However, once the creative process heats up and the ensemble flow has been sharpened by exercises that challenge and energize the group, the participants will be ready to look through to the essence. It's at the essential level where the flame of knowledge can be ignited. Since much of theatre, in both Western and Eastern culture, began on the mythological level, it's fitting that the group take myths as the initial cultural artifacts with which to work.

WHAT IS A MYTH?

This is a subject that could, of course, fill volumes. There are many types of myths and many facets to the interpretation of them. For our purposes, it's only necessary to know that myths are common to all mankind and that they follow very similar patterns all over the world. In addition, although universal in structure, their specific aesthetic elements are keys to revealing the unique inner life of their home.

Myths provide a means by which individuals and groups can penetrate the mysteries of their cultural imagination and our common human experience simultaneously. They teach values, decode dreams, store historical information, and give a culture or tribe a fabric of understanding that includes the whole range of their experiences.

For westerners, the mention of myth conjures up the ancient Greeks and Romans. For most, these sources are little more than curiosities, remnants of cultures long dead that have no relevance to the modern world. While it will become evident that these and other myths do indeed function actively in the modern world, it's important to note that ancient myth is only a part of this continuous and ever-present human dimension. As we'll discover, present-day cultural and personal myths have enormous impact upon art, culture, and politics.

Unfortunately, in recent years the word myth has come to connote something unreal, a fiction. This definition has nearly succeeded in marginalizing myths to the degree of uselessness. It's true myths are often encoded with symbols and meanings related to the culture and times in which they flourished. It's also true, however, that the essential meaning of many of these myths are easily unlocked with universal keys. Forging the keys takes some work, but the effort is rewarded when the myths begin to come alive. With some help from Joseph Campbell in the latter stages of this work, the ensemble will forge some universal keys that will unlock the secrets and partake of the nourishment within the mythological dimension.

THE ENSEMBLE JOURNEY BEGINS

Ensemble ritual theatre has the power to expand the awareness and artistic contribution of the actor. At the end of this century, when much of the world is in need of authentic, effective new myths and new forms of expression, the actor with a thousand faces can help navigate those waters and make a beneficial contribution to humanity.

Once it's been determined that the foundation training has been completed and the group has survived the struggles involved in the first phase of their journey together, the group is ready to consider serious research into myth and ritual. A special meeting of all participants should be arranged in order to clarify goals, discuss options, and to reaffirm commitment to the creative process. The tone of the meeting should be sober, but not laden with mysterious portent. Instead, allow the atmosphere to reflect a sense of adventure, as though about to embark on a fascinating but precarious voyage.

For any group to arrive at this stage means they've been working for a considerable amount of time and have arrived at certain understandings. This investment of time and effort has uniquely prepared them to embark upon this next phase of work together.

THE QUESTION OF LEADERSHIP

If there's not already a teacher or a leader to facilitate the work, the group should select one or more candidates to assume that responsibility. One of the most important functions of the leader, or leaders, is to select and facilitate the exercises and creative voyages of the group.

ADVICE TO THE LEADER

1. Take time to fully express your personal connection to ritual theatre or to ensemble expression of any kind. If you have any pet peeves, be honest and up front about it at the beginning, so as to avoid unnecessary conflict later on.

2. Avoid acting like anyone but yourself. I know this sounds facetious, but when in the role of teacher or leader of something so engaging and mysterious as ritual, it's tempting to assume the persona of an enlightened expert. That's not to say not to occasionally invoke your presence or share your authority when the need arises. Only that the knowledge will emerge more fluidly and fully if filtered through your direct personality. Remind the group and yourself it's not you speaking and leading, but your experience flowing through you.

3. Choose only the exercises you feel genuinely excited about and to which you feel a connection. You may want to incorporate exercises of your own invention or make variations on some of the ones included here in order to align with your personal aims and the aims of the group.

4. Some exercises may work better than others with some groups. That is up to your discretion and a little trial and error will soon define the kinds of exercises most likely to be effective with any single group.

5. Be alert at all times for the wax and wane of the flow of energy in the room. Some days the group will be charged with energy and focus, other days they'll need prodding. Each session will assume a character of its own and will often go through pockets of wasted time and effort. The nature of the work will sometimes require moments of silent reflection. Remember, a crisp wakeful silence is worth all the weighty pauses in the world.

HEMISPHERE RESEARCH

It's useful early on to have a discussion concerning the latest findings in brain hemisphere research. It would certainly be impractical to venture out into this territory too zealously. Nevertheless, it helps some who may be experiencing anxiety to understand how their perceptions work and why many of the ritual theatre exercises may at times seem strange or threatening.

The discussion should begin with a brief description of the two modes of cognition. L-mode or Left Brain is classified as verbal, logical, survival oriented, and highly analytical. It favors clear, sequential thought and finds abstract or ambiguous notions to be irritating or confusing. The R-mode or Right Brain, on the other hand, is nonverbal, spacial, abstract, emotional, and intuitive.

Everybody experiences communication between the two hemispheres via the central brain structure known as the corpus callosum. One hemisphere usually dominates over the other and this domination is, in part, responsible for the individual's personality and learning style.

Traditional education models favor the left brain and often discriminate against the right. Reading this sentence, for example, an activity strongly associated with education, is a left brain activity. The ability to act, dream, sing or dance it, on the other hand, is a right brain activity. The educational mission of ritual theatre, therefore, is to help integrate the two halves and thereby encourage *whole brain* thinking. The experiences of ritual and ensemble awareness usually stimulate and awaken the right brain first. That is why it's necessary to have discussions at the end of class from time to time to help the left brain process the new input. Gradually, this process unifies the two hemispheres.

QUESTIONS FOR DISCUSSION:

1. What do you do that is L-mode? R-mode?

2. Why awaken and stimulate R-mode thinking?

3. What is the value of L-mode thinking?

4. Do you tend to rely on one modality more than another?

LEADER: Somewhere in the discussion it helps to introduce a very simple concept, articulated by Betty Edwards, art teacher and author of the best-selling *Drawing in the Right Side of the Brain and Drawing on the Artist Within.* She states, "The right brain can be activated by simply giving the left brain a task that it does not want to do." Examples of this might be: Drawing something upside down, dancing a sentence, sitting in silence for long periods of time, talking gibberish, etc.

Emotions will become increasingly integral to this work, therefore it's important at this stage to remember that emotions are a right brain function and consequently somewhat confusing and unattractive to the left brain. When and if emotions do surface during ritual work, it's vital to neither worship, nor analyze them to death. As expressions of the right brain, they are of equal value to L-mode expressions as well as other R-mode expressions such as singing or dancing. Make the effort to minimize the left brain's temptation to criticize or prematurely judge emotional expression.

KEEPING A JOURNAL

The leader and all participants will want to keep a journal to record impressions, dreams, ideas, gripes, and nonsense. Bring it to every class in case inspiration strikes during an exercise or if the leader asks you to write for awhile. This need not be a daily diary; it's a creative work journal. No one, except those you have approved, should be allowed to read it. It may seem tedious at times to record things, but my experience has proven it to be of enormous value in later years, when you may get that secondary "Aha" moment related to experiences you had in class.

A journal is also a great resource for ideas and impressions later on in your life. It's not uncommon for a student to read an old journal and come across a bit of information immediately applicable and useful to their lives at the present time.

Remember, the journal need not be limited to words. It is a creative project unto itself, so feel free to draw, doodle, paste pictures, and anything else that strikes your fancy.

As you progress in the experiences of ensemble theatre you will begin to understand the inherent values of friction and conflict within a group. Therefore, in the beginning, observe your reactions and be particularly sensitive to not assign blame to the leader. Leaders, facilitators, teachers, directors, whatever the title, are all human beings. They will make mistakes on occasion and they sometimes be painfully honest in their appraisals. Be secure in the knowledge that a good facilitator is not infallible, and that your growth pains are only natural and need no scapegoat.

Keep in mind that the work of ritual ensemble theatre is supposed to be fun. If you're not having at least some degree of fun, you're not doing it right.

TRANSFORMATION OF THE WORKSPACE

The first task of any group wanting to become an ensemble is to transform the space into a workspace; one that feels activated by the presence of your particular group. A thorough clean-up of the space is a very effective start. A good workspace should be very clean anyway. Cleaning the space gives the actor a chance to invest the workspace with labor and attention, qualities that will sustain everyone.

When the space is cleansed and prepared, a separate space should be arranged for personal belongings. If people need to keep their belongings in the space, put them in a single place where they'll be most inconspicuous. Ideally, however, the space should remain free of personal items.

Beginning exercises for transforming the space:

1. Put the hands together, rub the palms back and forth vigorously until they heat up from the friction. Maintain rubbing, and move them along the perimeter of your body, warming up the space around you. Next, move through the space, travelling to all areas, warming up the entire chamber.

2. Fill the space with sound: Each participant travels across the space and emits sounds as if painting until the space is resonating.

3. Count every brick, every panel, every window, every light socket or anything else that is patterned to help create the space. Verify these details and record them. Give the walls and the various directions names that relate to the numbers discovered.

4. Move objects and furniture and anything that can be moved into a continuous array of shapes. Try putting everything in the middle, or in rows, or upside down near the far wall, or anything else..Eventually arrive at or go back to a configuration that resonates with the group.

LEADER: You must orient yourself in the space where you can see the entire group at all times. Find a spot where you retain focus, but don't invade the playing space. From here you can lead the exercises and be available to give feedback, suggestions, and to respond to any questions.

THEATRE IS WHERE YOU FIND IT

Walk around the workspace being sensitive to places where you're uncomfortable, places of power, places of intrigue, and so on. After several minutes of this, find a niche somewhere; a place that interests you. Once you've settled in, study your immediate vicinity. You might be nestled in near a window ledge, the top of a chair, a corner of a mirror, an open area on the floor, and so forth.

Next, in a playful way, imagine you're a giant, looking upon a theatre space. However absurd or unusual it may seem, convince yourself you're looking at a theatre and that, in a moment, a show of some sort will begin. Your little niche will begin to take on more vibrancy as you delight in making this perceptual leap.

Continuing to view your niche as a real stage setting, assume that the performers who will work in that space don't know you're watching. Begin to observe various scenes as they unfold from your imagination. Do this for at least ten minutes. After the alloted time, let the scene come to an end. Begin again, with a different show or the same one, and this time imagine the performers know you, the giant, are there watching them. In fact, the show is designed expressly for you. Free your imagination again and watch whatever unfolds for the next ten minutes. Let the performers be funny, let them be exquisite and charming, let them move you in some way.

Next, when the leader gives the signal, switch your perspective and become one of the performers on that stage. You can close your eyes if you need to. Let your mind play with what you're are doing, how you feel, what your task is and how you feel in that unique space.

After about five minutes, the leader should gently tell the group to take a deep breath and return to their normal perceptions of the space before them. A short discussion should follow. Questions to consider:

1. What do you think is the most valuable part of the exercise?

2. Were you able to allow your imagination to play with scale?

3. What kind of theatre event unfolded in your space?

4. What did it feel like to scale down and become one of the performers?

LEADER – This exercise invites the imagination to participate in the free association of images and ideas. It also teaches a very important esoteric idea: "The model is the thing itself." That is to say, like a totem or an amulet or any other ritual object, the power and effectiveness of the object depends upon the individual's ability to "enter" it and to extract something of meaning.

While this isn't an essential component in the creation of ritual theatre, it is extremely important in demonstrating to each individual the potential of their imaginations. Advanced groups may want to discuss the symbolism of the giant and how it applies to ritual theatre.

SEALING THE SPACE

For outside-world distractions to dissolve and for a group of people to focus together properly, the work space needs to be sealed. This is a concept readily accepted when a director announces "closed" rehearsals. It's not usually referred to as sealing the space, but indeed that's what's happening. By calling "closed" rehearsals, the director is insuring that attention cannot escape or be invaded.

A simple way to demonstrate this is to have everyone simply sense the difference between the workspace when the door is open and when the door is closed. This isn't a game of preference, but is to recognize that there is indeed a shift of atmosphere. Closing the door is just the first step in truly sealing the space. Suggested exercises for thoroughly sealing the space (after all doors are securely shut) are:

1. Ring a bell, gong, or any other device that produces a bright sound vibration.

2. Have the group do an opening warm-up, one that's vigorous, quickly accomplished, and ends in a moment of silence.

3. Start with silence and wait, listening and sensing until the space feels sealed and ready for work.

4. Have everyone who crosses the threshold into the room assume the mental posture of having crossed beyond the veil and into the next dimension.

5. Invent or borrow a "Four Directions" ritual that honors the directions of North, South, East, and West. These rituals almost always end with a recognition of Earth below and Sky above. This ritual places the participant squarely at the center of his or her universe and helps impress upon everyone the need for personal commitment.

The Circle
(ABOVE AND RIGHT)

PHOTOS: TOM PALUMBO

The Square
(LEFT)

SHAPES AND SCULPTURAL DYNAMICS

The warm up is over; the space has been prepared and sealed; the imagination has been liberated. Now, the work begins. I offer this exercise as an ideal starting point. It is an experiental investigation into "sacred shapes." As a simple, but profound experience, it teaches the difference between information and experiental knowledge, a concept that will form the basis for all future investigations. In addition, it establishes the first contact with a universal aesthetic, setting the stage for understanding how to sense the "essence" of a thing, person, idea or event.

The arrangement of space and the atmospheres created by that arrangement has long been an important part of human culture. This is especially true of mythical or religious cultures where life and the mystery of life and death are inextricably woven. Ancient caves, Greek theatres, Persian temples, European cathedrals, Mayan ritual sites, Native American kivas, and the aesthetic or communal structures of virtually all peoples on the globe throughout history have this in common: coded into the design of their ritual structures, however grand or humble, are the symbolic attributes of the shapes that comprise the structure.

In other words, choices were made in accordance with the subjective feeling and consequent meaning associated with particular shapes. Through this process they became "symbologized" or "made sacred." Throughout recorded time, there are five basic shapes that, by their very nature, have proven to be almost universally accepted as "sacred" by the priests, shamans, artists, philosophers, and laymen who design, build, and use these various structures. Those shapes are: the circle, the square, the triangle, the rectangle, and the spiral.

This exercise invites the participants to use the body to experience and intuit for themselves, the meaning and qualities associated with each shape. All responses to the exercise must be valued and contradictory experiences are not necessarily mutually exclusive. What the group hopes to find is a true visceral response to these shapes. The memory of this experience will then inform and guide much of the work to follow.

THE CIRCLE

The leader should begin by inviting the group to move about the space noticing circles. As a participant, draw energy from every circle you see. See the door knobs, the round heads of nails or screws, the circular shape of someone's eyes, and so on. Avoid going back to the same circles you noticed before. Press onward with increasing energy as you discover more and more circles around you. (5–10 min.)

With no break, the leader should instruct each member of the group to individually create circles in the space. Draw circles with your nose, create circles with your arms, legs, fingers. Roll on the floor, curl up like a doughnut, challenge yourself to create more circles than you thought possible. (5 min.)

Again, without a break in the momentum, the individual group members should be instructed to find a partner nearby and begin to create circles together. If there's an odd number, allow a group of three to form. Participants should keep discussion to a minimum and should press onward finding more and more ways to create circular shapes together. (5 min.) [Warning: This phase of the exercise can become very funny, and if allowed, will descend into silliness. It is important that everyone, especially the leader, remain serious – not heavy – just intent upon sincere exploration.]

After ample exploration time and before the group momentum is lost, the leader instructs everyone to expand their peripheral vision to include the entire group. As a group, AND WITHOUT TALKING, they must now create circles together. Breaking off into sub-groups is not allowed. (5 min., or as long as needed)

The leader must observe the group and encourage them to keep going if they reach an impasse. Usually, the group is so in tune with the circle by this time they easily create a number of shapes. If this is the case, the leader need only remind them to keep evolving the shapes, to keep exploring. When it nears time to finish, the leader need only say, "Okay. Find a closure together. Bring it to an end."

The results of this last exercise are always delightful and occasionally astonishing. Let the resonance of the closure set in for a while. The leader should then call a break, allowing people to get a drink of water and write in their journals.

THE SQUARE

It's effective to follow the circle exercise with the square. Substituting the square shape for the circle, the leader should follow the work sequence described for the circle. It starts with observing the shape, experiencing the shape subjectively, experiencing the shape with another, expanding the work to include the entire group.

Don't stop between phases. There's no pressure to be clever or to create anything of immediate value. Instead, observe the shape of the square as rendered by the human body. No talking or, at least, very little talking is allowed, to enhance concentration and observation.

End the first session on sacred shapes with a discussion. The leader should be familiar with the subjective experiences of each shape and be attuned to the objective qualities observed as the group worked. In other words, the leader should have some understanding of the shapes, in terms of the most common subjective responses to them as well as some idea of their historical use in terms of sacred architecture, art, folklore, or cultural custom. If the leader isn't knowledgable in these areas, he or she can simply relate their own experience with the shapes and draw conclusions based on that, and what was observed during the exercise.

DISCUSSION TOPICS:

1. What did the Circle *feel* like?

2. What did the Square *feel* like?

3. What is the difference between the two shapes?

4. What was your communication like with each shape?

5. Does anyone know the image called "The circle in the square?" (If anyone has seen the logo for New York's Circle in the Square Theatre, then they know the image.) What does it signify?

6. Leader should facilitate a discussion of the ancient symbology of the circle. It represents, among other things, eternity, the spirit, the heavens, the cosmos, timelessness, recurrence or reincarnation, the wheel of fortune, etc. (A look at ancient artifacts and the religious iconography of nearly all world religions will reveal the use of the circle as a fundamental symbol through the ages.)

7. The leader should next facilitate a discussion of the ancient symbology of the square. (Here a study of artifacts will reveal the use of a square to represent the four corners of our world. It's often used as the symbol for matter, the earth, time, limitation, rational mind etc. Game boards are often decorated with squares, symbolic of the steps we take in life. The square is a more earth-bound shape, engaging more earthly concerns. Think of the "town square" and "square dancing" and getting things "squared away.")

8. The leader should next facilitate a new discussion on the subject of the "Circle in the Square." (With more data and a cultural context, the discussion should come around to the ancient idea regarding the merging of heaven and earth; the Hermetic formula: "As above, so below" and the reconciliation of opposites.)

THE TRIANGLE

The group can do the same exploration with the triangle. Like all shapes, this one has its own dynamics and limitations. The leader may want to remind the group to seek out true triangular shapes, particularly when working as a group. Finding straight lines and the appropriate angles of the triangle are a work in itself.

When it becomes apparent the group has exhausted the triangle, move on to the next shape.

The Rectangle

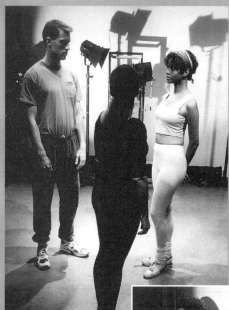

The Triangle

PHOTOS: TOM PALUMBO

The Spiral

THE RECTANGLE

Approach this shape in precisely the same way as the others. However, the leader may want to remind people to insist upon rectangular shapes and not squares. When the shape has been explored by the group, move on to the next.

THE SPIRAL

The only differences in the exploration of this shape relate to safety and internal mood. Spiral shapes can trigger sudden bursts of movement and velocity and because of this everyone needs to be slightly more aware of the others working around them. Spirals can also trigger emotional states, memories, or moods. Although it's interesting to note these as they occur, it's best not to indulge in them.

DISCUSSION TOPICS:

1. What did the triangle *feel* like?

2. What did the rectangle *feel* like?

3. What did the spiral *feel* like?

4. How did each shape affect your ability to communicate with others, both in teams and in a group?

5. The leader should facilitate a discussion of triangle energy as it relates to the ancient idea of Trinity. The Triangle shape is traditionally used to represent focused energy, the reconciliation of opposites, the perspective of faith, the existence of the ancient "observer" who sees the duality in life, and much more.

6. The leader should facilitate a discussion of the rectangle's energy. Be content at first to gather subjective data about how it felt, how difficult or easy it was to explore, where rectangles were found in the space, and so forth. The group

should take note of the wide use of rectangles in architecture, books, computer screens, picture frames, etc. The leader can then lead the group into a discussion of the ancient "golden rectangle" widely used in Greek art and architecture. (The golden rectangle is also a shape that represents the idea of creation as an infinite display of modular proportions.) This discussion is important because it will link up with the discussion of the spiral.

7. The leader should facilitate a discussion of the spiral's energy. Discuss whether or not feelings were triggered. Talk about the sensations of spiraling down as opposed to spiraling upwards. Discuss the spiral as it relates to things in the world such as old watch springs, heating coils, coiled snakes, turbans, sea shells, etc. It's then very effective to discuss the spiral as it relates to the golden rectangle. Unless you have experience with this idea, the relationship may not at first be evident. Lawrence Blair's book Rhythms of Vision is an excellent resource to understand this relationship. There is a well-known drawing of a nautilus shell and how its proportions relate directly to the proportions of the golden mean. (See Parabola magazine, "The Golden Mean", Vol. XVI:4.)

8. End the unit on sacred shapes with an open discussion of what new data has been secured through contact with the shapes. Remember that this data must remain active in order to integrate future experiences in this work. Although not absolutely necessary, it can be useful at this stage to remind the group that nearly all of science and art and music grew out of the various ancient mystery schools, including those created by the great Greek mathematician Pythagoras. The group's work with the sacred shapes, is a modern echo of those schools.

THE WAY UP AND THE WAY DOWN ARE THE SAME

The Greek Philosopher Heraclitus is credited with saying, "The way up and the way down are the same." This is a paradoxical statement, typical of mystic formulations that seek to unhinge left–brain logic and liberate right-brain thinking. This is an opportune time for the leader to introduce this phrase and then allow it to simmer for several weeks before bringing it into discussion.

The discussion is one that reveals how such a potent, yet paradoxical phrase works like a key to unlock parts of the mental process that may have been dormant or on hiatus. Use the statement as a probing device, deepening your understandings and expanding your conceptual horizons.

THE QUESTING

A genuine ensemble doesn't simply follow the wishes of a director and act out parts. A genuine ensemble struggles to refine individual aims and to deal with issues too large to tackle alone.

Finding an individual aim, classically known as "the quest" takes a lot of inner work. In fact, most great sages agree that the act of searching is itself the pearl of wisdom. The value of such a pearl is determined by the sincerity of the search.

One of my teachers was known for his ability to quickly lead a student into a confrontation with the quest. Simply by asking, "Who has a question?", he would instill a state known as "holy dread." Every student was challenged to dig within to formulate a question that would be a "real question" and not an "American question." American questions are those formulated out of idle curiosity, not genuinely connected to a real inner need.

Sitting in these atmospheres of "holy dread" can be excruciating. It can also be incredibly exhilarating when a real question manages to eek, blurt, or spill out of someone. A real question charges the atmosphere and leads to deeply felt understandings available to all.

While it's silly and ultimately destructive for a leader to assume sage-like authority, there's one question that can safely be put to the group that will effectively recreate "holy dread" and stir the embers of personal responsibility regarding one's education. The leader should ask the group, "If you were in the presence of someone who really did know, without a doubt, the answer to your question, what would you ask?"

Sense the change in atmosphere as this question sinks into everyone's consciousness. The leader should remind the group that this is a question to weigh, to mull, to consider until an answer (the question) arises. Knowing the question is, of course, halfway toward knowing the answer.

At this point it's important everyone knows they must seek to understand, but also have the courage to live without answers.

LIFE MASKS

A life mask is a neutral rendition of one's face that can be worn as a tool to eliminate habitual facial obligations and thereby liberate more universal expressions of the self. The life mask tends to inspire essential, full-bodied behavior undistorted by cultural or personal idiosyncracies. This allows for encounters between participants that transcend the ordinary boundaries, invoking deeply felt sensations normally obscured by personality.

The availability of plaster bandage has made the creation of life masks a relatively easy process. Although the purpose of the process is to have a mask, the construction of the mask is an experience unto itself. That is why I place emphasis on the two phases, separating the creation of the mask from the process of playing the mask.

INNER JOURNEY, MAKING THE MASK.

LIST OF SUPPLIES (FOR GROUP OF TEN):

1. One box of quick-setting plaster bandage (2' or 4" strips. Usually 20 rolls to a box)

2. Several jars of vaseline petroleum jelly.

3. Newspapers, towels, facial soaps and creams.

4. Five pairs of scissors.

5. Wide plastic bowls (not too deep).

6. Secure open space, with bathrooms nearby.

7. CD or cassette player plus music.

8. 1/2" to 1' white elastic strips.

9. Several jars of gesso (artist's sizing compound).

10. X-acto knives or single-edged razors.

Set aside a full two hours to complete the molding of the masks. Everyone should wear clothes that they do not mind getting a little dirty. Plaster dust, newsprint, and water spills are the inevitable reality of this process.

The participants should work in teams. Each team should find a spot in the room where they can work without bumping into anyone else. Next, they need to cut a roll of plaster bandage into a variety of strips. (Put down newspaper to catch the plaster dust as it falls during the cutting process.) The sizes of strips will vary slightly depending upon the width of the bandage and shape and size of the individual faces. Generally speaking, the strips should be cut as follows:

10 large strips, approx. 3 X 5 inches.
15-20 medium strips, approx. 2 X 3 inches.
8-10 long strips, approx. 1 1/2 - 2 X 6 inches.
Several 1 X 1 squares to use for reinforcement.
Several odd sized strips
Several very small strips for around the nostrils
Two specially cut "nose strips."

Once the strips have been cut and organized according to size,

EXPLORING LIFE MASKS

the plastic container needs to be half–filled with **warm** water. Lay additional paper down where the passive participant will place his or her head. This partner will lay on the floor on his back, facing the ceiling. Place the plaster strips on one side of their head and the water dish on the other. This is to prevent water from accidentally dripping or spilling onto the strips during the mask–making process. Keep a towel handy for cleaning up during and after the mask–making.

The partner on the floor should relax, breathe gently, and await the experience, making sure they are comfortable and ready to start. It's good to have some soothing music playing during this process. While the active partner will be concerned with quickly and effectively applying the plaster bandage, the passive partner will be surrendering to a whole host of experiences, including a mind journey. Soothing New Age or Classical music accommodates the journey and helps keep the mask–makers working smoothly and calmly.

The mask–makers need to situate themselves near the head, usually starting in the upside down perspective. They need to take a good look at the nose, particularly the long strip of tissue separating the nostrils and cut two or three nose strips to accommodate the size.

Begin by coating the entire face with gobs of vaseline. Put extra vaseline on all areas of facial hair. (I sometimes ask bearded participants to shave beforehand if they're willing. They will get a better mask and it will prevent the possibility of a painful mask removal process.) Extra coating on eyebrows, eyelashes, and around the hair line will prevent the hair from being incorporated into the mask. Make sure the vaseline goes on every portion of the face, below the chin and even onto the neckline.

Once a thorough coating of vaseline is on the face, the strips of plaster can be applied. Start with the large surfaces of the face. Take a large strip, dip it quickly and smoothly into the water, allowing it to drag the edge of the bowl slightly as it is lifted out. This drains off excess water.

Place the strip evenly on the forehead and go quickly to the next large strip, dip, surface, drag on the edge, and place on the cheeks. Do this same process over the eyes and the mouth, keeping these features in the center of the strip. This will prevent them from being distorted by the seams formed by the edges of the strips.

Next, pick up some medium strips and begin to fill in the bridge of the nose, the chin, temples, jawline, and anywhere else that appears in need of covering. Work quickly and surely. The plaster drys fast and the mask needs a minimum of two layers of plaster bandage to be effective. Put on the nose strips and use tiny strips to round out around the nostrils. Take precautions not to drip water into the nostrils or make the opening too small for the partner to breathe. On the other hand, do not leave the nostril openings too open or the mask will appear distorted.

Place the long strips along the edges of the mask to serve as additional reinforcement. The one–inch squares need to be placed at the temples, just above the ear where the elastic will attach.

Return quickly to the large strips on the forehead and cheeks and work fast to complete a second layer of bandage. Often it's necessary to work out of sequence, especially if one section of the mask is drying faster than another. Keep in mind that once the plaster is dry, it will no longer accommodate new strips.

The last layer should be smoothed out a bit by gently rubbing each strip before moving to the next. When the entire mask is complete, take several strips, dip them, and paint over the mask, adding additional plaster to the external surface.

Next, simply wait for it to dry. Most masks take between ten and fifteen minutes to dry enough to be removed from the face. A mask in the process of setting feels warm to the touch. A dry mask, one that is ready to be removed, feels cool.

At all times during this experience, it's essential that the atmosphere in the room remain calm, serious, and supportive. Silly or raucous behavior can ruin the experience for the person on the floor. View this experience like a meditation and keep in mind that because so much of the face is covered, disturbances of any kind can trigger panic responses in certain individuals.

Once the mask is cool, stand or crouch over the partner, grab the mask at the edges near the jawline and gently pull up on the mask. At the same time, ask the person to blow through their mouth. If there are no hairs attached and if the mask has dried correctly, it should come right off. Place it gently to the side, resting on the cheek and not on the edges.

If hair has become enmeshed in the bandage, remove that section by holding the center of the hair with one hand and gently pulling the mask with the other. The hair usually separates from the mask easily. Fortunately, I have never had a situation where the hair was seriously attached. If faced with that problem, however, I would suggest using vaseline to work into the area where the hair is tangled into the mask. If that fails, cut the mask around he area and then the hair can be coaxed out easier with soap and water. There should never be any need to cut the hair. A new mask can be constructed in short order.

When the mask is removed, tell the partner to keep their eyes closed, hand them a towel and soap and lead them to the nearest sink to wash the face and to remove any plaster granules that might be left around the eyes or the nose.

While their clean up is in process, clean up the work area, replace newspaper if necessary, cut new strips, get new water, and lay down on the floor. Repeat the process as described above. When all the masks are completed, allow them to stay in one spot overnight so they may fully dry. The next day they should be wiped out with a paper towel to remove excess vaseline, the edges should be trimmed and the eye opening drawn with pencil.

The eyes should be larger than life, but not too large or they will look cartoony. A simple almond shape is best. Using an X-acto knife, carefully cut out the eyeholes. Very carefully place the mask on and look in a mirror to see if the eyes are even and if they are big enough. Make any necessary adjustments to the eyes.

Do not be overly concerned by the frayed edges. They can be smoothed out later with gesso.

The edge of the mask should follow the facial lines, dipping underneath the chin by an inch or two. With the mask on, put a mark on the spot above the ear where the elastic will be placed.

The mask should fit snug against the face, secure yet comfortable. There are several ways to place the elastic onto the mask. The most secure method is to use a strong needle and simply sew it onto the mask. If that method is not practical, go in 3/4 of an inch on the mask and force a small hole with a knife or with the blade of a scissors. Feed the elastic through the hole, double back and sew the elastic to itself. Be careful to measure the elastic first.

Once the elastic is secured. Paint the mask with several layers of gesso, allowing for ample drying time between layers. Be sure to dab gesso around the eyes and around the edges and on any frayed areas. The gesso acts as a sealant and will dry to a white semi-hard consistency.

The mask is now complete and ready for use. Be aware that these masks are fragile and must be stored, transported, and handled carefully. Repairs are impossible since the plaster has already set, so treat them with special care.

THREE REALMS JOURNEY

During the days when the masks are drying and being prepared, a few sessions can be devoted to visualization exercises. Everyone should lay on the back on the floor with knees up and feet on the floor in alignment with the hips, or with the legs straight out. It might be helpful to dim the lights, but not to total darkness.

In this exercise, the leader will guide the participants into a visualization journey very similar to those experienced by ancient and modern Shamans. This is called the three-realms journey, because it occurs in three parts and each part accesses a different level of experience. To a Shaman, these realms are actual domains where activities and entities encountered can have impact upon the outer world in which we live. Others might view these experiences as dream states triggered by hypnotic suggestion. I think both answers are equally true and equally false. The best approach for believers and skeptics alike, is to experience the journeys and then draw conclusions based on that individual experience.The mind responds readily to archetypical imagery such as mountains, paths, towers, tunnels, caves, animals, and so forth. This exercise uses the archetypal imagery of tunneling below earth, travelling on earth, and flying above earth to liberate visions that are at once highly personal and powerfully universal.

The purpose of the exercise is two-fold: to expand the imagination in a way that gives the participant access to new creative resources and to allow the participant to have a brief experience of one of the simpler techniques used by Shamans and Sages throughout history.

The leader should adhere to the wording of the following inductions to prevent confusion and to insure for enjoyable journeys.

Notebooks should be kept nearby to record the journeys immediately afterwards. These visualizations are safe, non-invasive, and easily brought to a halt or re-directed should a problem arise.

LEADER (speaking to the group:)

Take a few breaths to settle into the floor. Inhale deeply and let all the air out. Good. Do this again. Very good. Now place your attention on the backs of the eyelids. Watch the play of shadows or flickers of light or texture. Now in a moment when I clap my hands, open the eyes and then shut them quickly again; like you have taken a snap shot. (Wait a moment or two and clap)

Good. Observe any afterimages on the backs of the eyelids. Take another picture. (clap) Watch how the image, the shape of light, slowly dissolves, sometimes changing colors as it disappears. Take another picture. (clap) Try to keep the image intact. Don't let it drift away. Use just a little bit of effort to keep the image on the palette of the eyelids. One more picture. (clap) Keep the light there, hold the image as long as you can. (Wait a few moments).

Now place your attention on the inner screen of your imagination. Put yourself in your favorite spot in nature. If you do not know of one specifically, invent a scene that pleases you. (Give a few moments to establish this) Now look around you and notice an entrance leading down into the earth. This could be a door, stairway, a cave, hole in the ground, or whatever your imagination wants it to be. Go to this entrance and descend into the earth. You may have to crawl, jump, wiggle, . . . whatever. (Give them a moment) Now allow for your travel to be easy as you descend deeper and deeper into the earth.

Feel the gentle pull of gravity as you journey downwards. If it's too dark, arrange for a bit of light to help you as you descend down, down, down, into the earth. (moment) Your path now levels off and takes you to the right, turning right and travelling along this deep underground pathway. Now your path takes you to the left. Come to a stop at the edge of a cliff. There is a bridge crossing a very deep chasm. Go to the bridge and cross over to the other side.

On the other side, find a path that leads to a clearing. At the center of the clearing there is a ceremonial structure with a bench nearby. Go to the bench. Call out for an animal guide to come to this place and greet you. This is your power animal. (moment)

If there are several animals or your animal keeps changing shapes, insist that one single animal come to you at the bench. Do not try to alter the shape of the animal. A power animal can come in many shapes and none is any more auspicious that another.

Once the animal has arrived, play together. (a few moments)

Let the play come to an end. Your animal will now take you on a journey through his realm. Allow the animal to place you where you will be secure and safe and can see everything. (moment) Now take off together. Your animal will now show you around this world.

(Let a minute go by)

Come back to the bench at the clearing. You must say goodbye to your animal now. Assure your animal that you'll meet again. Thank the animal. Before leaving, your animal is going to give you a gift. Let the animal place the gift into your body somewhere.

Now say one last goodbye and watch as the animal runs off and disappears out of the clearing.

Cross the bridge to the other side of the cliff. Travel along the path until it takes you to the right. Keep travelling until you need to turn left. Soon you encounter the incline leading up and out of the earth. Finding it easy to ascend, move upwards, up, up, up, continuing upwards at a fast but comfortable speed until finally you resurface at your nature spot. Bask a moment in sunlight and breathe in fresh air.

Take a few breaths as you allow your awareness to come to the backs of your eyelids. Sense your body on the floor. Stretch and yawn and slowly come out of it. As soon as you're ready, go to your notebooks and write down everything you can recall about this journey. (Allow at least ten minutes for this and then take a break)

After the break, invite everyone to settle in again onto the floor. They can stretch and shake-out beforehand if the need arises. Start in the same manner as before: the leader instructs everyone to breathe deeply, to watch the scene on the backs of the eyelids, to take several "snapshots" and attempt to hold the afterimage in their sight. Move to the inner screen of the imagination and the leader should say the following:

LEADER:

Place yourself in your nature scene again. Look around you and enjoy the security, serenity, and beauty of your surroundings.

Follow a path as it travels through your special spot, leading gradually away from your scene and taking you into a soft rolling meadow. Continue on the path past the meadow until you see the edge of a beautiful pine forest. Follow the path into the forest.

Go deeper and deeper into the forest. It's a beautiful, magical forest. Friendly and safe. Travel past huge trees, waterfalls, and small clearings. (Allow a moment to pass) The path leads you to a large clearing and in the center of the clearing is a theatre.

Observe this theatre and sense that you are about to witness a show. Find a seat. You hear some introductory sounds, and then the show begins. Watch and enjoy this show in your magical theatre in the forest. (Wait at least a full minute)

Allow the show to come to an end. Show your appreciation to the cast and all who helped create this event for you. (moment)

Say your goodbyes giving assurances you'll return and step onto the path heading back away from the clearing. Come back past the small clearings, waterfalls, and huge trees. Move swiftly past the greenery to the edge of the meadow. Walk along the path through the meadow until you notice you're entering your special area. Follow the path until you return to where you began. Take a last look around, enjoying the scene, and then return to this room.

Place your attention on the backs of the eyelids, sense your body on the floor, stretch like a cat as you slowly come out of it.

When you're ready, go to your notebooks and record everything you can recall about this last journey. (After ten minutes or so, announce another break)

By this time, everyone knows the routine and after the break can quickly get into position for the last journey in this sequence. The leader should repeat the same instruction as before. Upon moving to the inner screen of their imagination the leader says:

LEADER:

Visualize yourself in this room as you lay on the floor.

Sense yourself from the inside and at the same time, visualize what you look like from the outside. Allow the rigid reality of the room to unlock slightly and see yourself floating up and out the window (or whatever is appropriate to the specific workspace). See the building from the outside as you continue to float upwards away from the earth.

You're safe and secure, warm and relaxed as you float higher still. See the land receding as you notice the first few puffs of clouds. Go through this layer of clouds until you're floating above them. Enjoy the soft beauty of the cloudscape before you.

Keep travelling upwards until the atmosphere disappears. Observe everything around you as you continue on your upward journey. Travel now out into space, seeing the planet Earth drifting away from you. Continue travelling upward past the Moon, past Mars, Jupiter, Saturn, Uranus, Neptune, Pluto, and out into open space watching the Solar system get smaller and smaller as you drift ever upward. (wait a moment)

Encounter a resistance, like an invisible ceiling. Transform yourself into something enabling you to continue through this resistance. Once on the other side, observe everything around you. Keep floating up until you encounter another invisible ceiling. Another transformation and you can make your way into the next level. Pay attention to everything. Find a stairway that leads up to a door with a sign on it. The sign reads: "Higher Self. Please Knock."

Go up to the door and knock the appropriate knock. (moment) The door opens and you enter a room. Look all around. You encounter someone there who looks into your eyes and you embrace your higher self. The higher self wishes to tell you something, listen very carefully. (moment) You must now return. Leave reassurances that you'll return. (moment)

Return to the door and come down the stairway to the level below. Transform in order to return from this level down to the level below. Feel yourself dropping down. Another transformation and you drop down to the first level you passed into. A final transformation and you are below the threshold of the first level of resistance.

See the solar system coming into view as you float downward, returning past Pluto, Neptune, Uranus, Saturn Jupiter, Mars, the Moon, and entering the delicate upper atmosphere of the Earth.

Continue downward until the light gets brighter and you see the rolling tops of clouds. Drift down through the clouds, down until you sight land, down until you can see the building, down until you sense yourself reentering the room from the window. Return all the way to your body and lay in exactly the same position as you are now. See the flickers of activity on the backs of your eyelids, sense your body on the floor, stretch and come out of it. When you're ready, go to your notebooks and record as much of this journey as you can remember.

After about ten minutes or so, take another break. Upon returning from the break, sit together with notebooks nearby and rest in a few moments of silence. When it feels appropriate, begin a discussion to share experiences and express ideas about the three realms.

SUGGESTED TOPICS FOR DISCUSSION:

1. What was the sensation of going down, staying level, and travelling upwards? Were any of them harder, easier?

2. Did one level liberate more creative activity than another?

3. Were you surprised by anything along the way?

4. How can this technique be used in a practical way?

5. Share experiences and discuss the elements that might be universal or at least similar to other elements.

6. What is the "higher self?" Does it really exist?

7. Do you intend to return to any of these levels? If so what would be your aim?

LIFE MASK EXPLORATIONS

THE HUMAN DILEMMA

Once the completed masks have been adjusted to fit comfortably, the group is ready to explore the unique and timeless mystery of the mask. Start by sitting in a circle facing away from the center. Place the mask on the floor with the expression facing upwards. Place your attention on the mask, observing every detail of its construction.

After a minute or two, stop observing detail, hold the mask in your hands, and simply look at the expression. Continue looking until you begin to have the sensation that the mask is looking back at you. Allow only minimal movement of the mask in hand. After several minutes of this, close your eyes and feel along the contours of the mask. As you do this, sense where on your own face this touch is located. Link the two sensations so that wherever you touch the mask, you feel the imagined sensation on your own face.

After several minutes, and while keeping the eyes closed, place the mask on your face. Secure the elastic, arrange the hair and make any and all final adjustments necessary so that you'll no longer have to touch the mask. On the signal given by the leader, begin very slowly, again with the eyes closed, to come to a standing position. Take your time and stay connected to the presence of the mask throughout the entire process of standing.

Once standing, open your eyes and look out at an imaginary

horizon line. Look far, far in the distance, expanding your inner energy and presence to fill the space. Maintaining this expanded awareness, turn slowly over your left shoulder and encounter the other masks. No sound is allowed. In silence and only with the movements and gestures of the body, begin to explore the other mask beings. See them as if for the first time. Allow yourself to communicate pure, simple, essential expressions.

Leader, this first encounter may take one minute or it may take thirty minutes. Each group is different. If need be, encourage everyone to meet at least the presence of every other mask in the room. Once it appears that the masked characters are beginning to seek out silly entertainments for themselves, deepen the experience by taking them through the following:

LEADER (*speaking*):

At this point, imagine you're all strangers who have suddenly realized you are alive on this planet. This room is the extent of your world. Ask yourself, "What's going on here? What is there to be done? Why are we here?" Work together to find answers to these questions.

At various intervals, the leader may want to say something to the group as a reminder. The phrase, "What is there to be done?" is very effective. Each group will wrestle with the challenge of this exercise in a different manner. I have observed groups trying to create human ladders to ascend upwards in an attempt to do something of value. Other groups will separate and eye each other suspiciously; some factions will band together or the occasional cynic will sit down and mock the entire effort. Regardless, it never fails to be riveting and deeply moving.

Once the group has reached a plateau or it is apparent that they need a breather from the masks, end the exercise. After a short break, sit together and discuss what occurred. For some, the mask-work will have been liberating, for others it will have been restrictive and unnerving. All reactions are valid and need to be discussed in terms of the practical and philosophical elements of this first encounter

The Human Dilemma

PHOTOS: TOM PALUMBO

with mask–work.

Here is a letter given to me by a Anthony Irons, a graduate student at Penn State University, shortly after experiencing this exercise:

Dear Mark,

On March 25, 1997, we (the first year M.F.A. class) partook of an exercise of exploration with our life masks. This exercise is my most memorable studio project to date at Penn State. The experience of the exercise is obviously personal and the journey towards any discoveries about myself or even this world still invades my thoughts. However, I feel compelled to share part of that journey with you. The following is an attempt to express the latter part of that exploration:

Stand. Stand. Staaand! I'm almost there. I have begun such a long time ago. So long, in fact, I have forgotten the reason for standing at all. All I remember is that I must. After knowing I wanted to stop trying several times along the way, and now realizing I am almost there brings such ecstacy that I lose myself in joyful anticipation. But the excitement is mistook as my discomfort and my breath give in to that anticipation and you offer a gesture of gentle release from the mask.

Finally I stand. I stand still. I indulge in that stillness, content with its ever so peaceful, restful state; a sweet reward for the long trying journey. But my excitement subsides. My contentment trickles down and fades away into the earth, along with the excitement I brought up with me. I realize there may be more. I decide to see if there is more.

My eyes, I ask them to open. They do, slowly. There is more. There is much more. There is so much more it scares me. But I still find comfort in my stillness and do not move. As long as I do not move I will be okay, but okay to do what? All I knew before was to stand and that is now done. Now confusion and fear begin to set in and there is excitement of another kind. I feel lost and afraid and bereft of purpose.

As I stand trying to hold onto (as best I can) stillness, my hand is touched. Every ounce of my being is jolted. The touch is warm. It is soft. It slowly moves across my fingers and I know my hand is terrified and looks to me for instruction. But I have none.

All I am sure of is standing. All I am sure of trusting is stillness. So, I ask my hand to trust the stillness also and maybe the touch will leave. It does. The touch goes away. But now I have been touched. I have seen more and I have now felt more. Now, I am compelled to do more, to do something more than standing. The stillness must be abandoned along with my old purpose. I ask my legs to move me. They do. They, slowly, take me forward three steps. I then ask my legs to turn me around so I may see more. They do. They slowly turn me around. They are cautious and unsure and do not know why they are doing this, but they trust me. I am carefully made to face another direction.

What my eyes next witness is so overwhelming I question the decision to turn around. I question any decision I made after standing. I question the decision to ask my eyes to open in the first place. I even question the journey to stand at all. There are so many figures moving in space, moving, touching. They are fast, sporadic and intimidating. "How can they do that?" I wonder. "How can they move so fast and trust? How can they ask their hands to touch? Why are they moving and touching in the first place?" I wonder if they know something I don't. I don't dare ask myself to move and touch like them. I don't feel safe with them. I am fearful. But as long as I don't move and touch like them, I don't think they will notice me.

Suddenly, one of the figures moves past me (Jim). It is familiar. I can trust this one. I dare not ask my mouth to make a sound. The other figures would notice me. But if I ask my arm to move towards the familiar figure the others may not notice. My arm agrees and moves. But it moves too slowly. It is too cautious. The familiar one is already gone and my arm has only just left my side.

I want to close my eyes again. I wish I could go back to how it was. I want to go back to even before the stillness, before the purpose. I realize I don't remember what was before the purpose, but it could not have been as threatening as what I feel now. I can't remember. I can't remember what came before and I can't remember how to get back. I don't even know if I am able to get back. I feel myself losing trust in myself.

They know I have no more instruction. They feel my fear, my desperation to do something and my ignorance of not knowing what to do. My arm continues up without my consent. I have nothing to tell it. It wants to leave to find a new purpose. It is lost in desperation. It reaches up in hopes that one of the fugures will find it and share their purpose. I surrender to the action, drowning in fear and hopelessness. I want to close my eyes. I want to go back.

As you can see, the exercise has the potential to evoke deep feelings and create a lasting impression. Each experience is completely unique, yet all report a magnified sensitivity to each unfolding moment, to the atmosphere of the room, to their senses, and to the inner workings of their mind and body.

QUESTIONS FOR DISCUSSION:

1. Did anyone have the sensation of the mask looking back at them?

2. Did anyone sense the connection between touching the mask and their own face?

3. What was the sensation of standing? Looking out onto the horizon line?

4. What happened when you encountered other mask beings?

5. What was your experience dealing with the questions of why you were here and what was to be done?

6. What is the larger significance of those questions?

WHO'S ON FIRST?

(This exercise works best if there is a large mirror available in the workspace). Begin again in a large circle, standing this time. Observe the convention of turning away to place the mask on. Once the mask is secured, turn back toward the circle and wait until everyone has turned.

Break up the circle by moving in a random pattern. As you weave through the space at a slow easy pace, observe the others around you. Observe their walk, their posture, their rhythms. Next, find a partner and begin to mirror one another. Explore as much detail as possible.

At the signal from the leader, remove your mask and trade with your partner. The masks will no longer fit, of course. This should not be a serious problem unless someone has a mask where the elastic is pulled dangerously tight. If that problem arises, switch partners.

With your partner's mask on, begin to move around the room, impersonating their walk, their posture, and their rhythms.

Stop on occasion by the mirror to see if your rendering is convincing. Relate to the others as this character. Try out a number of sitting postures, reclining postures, everything.

After about fifteen minutes of this, find your partner again, (you will have to recognize yourself in them) and let them show you their version of yourself. Do the same for them. Finally, after the two impersonations have been witnessed by each partner, remove the masks and exchange them. (You should have your mask back.)

Have a brief discussion about the experience, allowing any questions to arise naturally.

RECONFIGURATION

This is a fun mask exercise and a good antidote to the heavier, more existential ones experienced up to now. In small groups of three, four, or five, explore what happens if the mask is worn anywhere but on the face. This could mean wearing the masks on the top of the head, back of the head, the feet, the buttocks, the elbow, virtually anywhere the mask can be safely secured.

After some initial exploration, settle on the new placement of the mask for the whole group. Now begin to create a short piece using the masks in these new configurations. The masks can dance, tell a story, create a comedy show, fall in love, any number of things. The only restriction is that the work must support and even justify the placement of the mask.

NOTE: The elastic need not be the only means of supporting the mask. Some groups in the past have held it in their hands, or managed to prop them up in their T-shirts. Be careful, however, not to harm the masks. Many an overzealous group has ended up with damaged or destroyed masks. Be creative, but be sensible.

Leader, watch the groups as they explore and develop their pieces. Try to avoid two groups doing the same one. If two groups are both using the masks on the knees, for example, suggest to one that they consider the feet, or the elbows.

Allow approximately fifteen minutes for this exploration then begin a countdown. Tell them they have ten minutes to put together something to show. Inform them when five minutes have gone by, three minutes, two minutes, and let the final minute be flexible enough to allow the straggler group a little extra time.

Quickly assign the order in which the groups will be seen. Let each group present their piece from where they were working and have the room gather around to watch their presentation. Give brief feedback or suggestions and move on to watch the next group.

VARIATIONS ON THE EXERCISE:

1. Allow exploration and then ask them to put together a piece using three different placements of the mask. They must also work out a suitable transition from one to the other. This will take a full fifteen minutes, possibly more.

2. Employ sound, words, dialogue, or music.

3. Have the masks start out on the face, get dislodged, and then wander from position to position, reacting to their absurd fate and struggling to normalize. Let the piece end as each group sees fit.

THRESHOLD WORK

Acting can be very transformative. Through the process of portraying characters, the actor has the opportunity to expand his or her own individual character. Indeed, much of actor training is geared toward providing the kinds of experiences which will unlock, expand, and refine the individual's resources. This is usually a very long and unpredictable process.

Through exercises I call THRESHOLDS, however, the process is quickened, and the results are measurable. Behind every personal quest, be it a climb up Mt. Everest or a bicycle trip to Canada, a dip in the pool of meditative consciousness or an aerobic workout, the person is hoping for some measure of change. They hope for small or in some cases complete transformations.

Spend three weeks in another culture and I guarantee there will be transformations. The range of which depends completely upon the individual and the impact of the experience, but the experience itself will produce change. And that's the reasoning behind these few THRESHOLD exercises. They're not meant as entertainment or novelty. Instead, they provide the actor with an inner experience of great personal challenge, a mountain to climb if you will. And like a voyage to another land, transformations great or small will occur.

Each exercise is designed to illicit a certain spectrum of possible change. The measure of that change is verified in both subjective and objective ways. And the aim, regardless of the effects within the exercise, is to enhance the actor's palette of experience, which is very often nothing more than reintroducing something forgotten or repressed. It's a safe encounter with deeper facets of being.

Please follow the instructions for each exercise completely. They've been refined over the course of many years to accommodate nearly all contingencies; any divergence will most likely disrupt or weaken the results. The exercises are meant to be attainable challenges where the level of risk and endurance are in the control of the participant. At no time should a leader push anyone to exceed their own pace.

Since each exercise is a powerful experience in itself, no two exercises should occur in the same week. Participants will need at least that long to assimilate the impact of their experience and to begin to find ways of applying it to their craft.

TIME TRAVELING

Due to the length and pace of this exercise, I suggest providing some very subtle and soothing background music. I've found the harp music of Georgia Kelly to be ideal.

This exercise is best done on a wooden floor. Carpeted surfaces often cover concrete which can be too unforgiving to the muscles and bones and "carpet burns" are a definite hazard.

Everyone should be dressed in loose fitting clothes. Remove all jewelry, hair pins, or pocket stuff. This is for comfort as well as safety.

The facilitator of this exercise should take care that the room is well ventilated and secure from curious visitors. Find out if anyone is dealing with a structural injury or is on any medication for blood-pressure or related conditions. If so, allow them only to observe the exercise. Also, if there are more than ten participants, the facilitator should have an assistant to help keep an eye on everyone.

To begin (following a restroom reminder and short warm-up) everyone will lie down on the floor on his or her back, leaving ample room between each other. The group should take a few deep breaths to settle the system and to focus the mind.

Although directions were explained beforehand, the facilitator should now reiterate whats about to transpire: to go from a prone position to a standing position in a **slow** and **continuous** manner. The slow is extremely slow, **the slowest they have ever moved!** Even the eye, tongue, and facial movements should be smooth and slow. For the first go at this exercise, allow only 90 minutes; encourage the participants to use all their time.

If it happens, during the exercise, and it often does, that they find themselves in a bind, they must solve the problem with the same slow movement. (It can be helpful, just prior to the exercise, to allow the participants to try out several patterns of standing so they may settle on the one they believe is best suited to them.) Once in a while someone will get themselves in a position where a T-shirt is obstructing the mouth or they're in danger of falling over. In these extreme cases, the facilitator or assistant is allowed to help them get back on track in a safe and simple way. Otherwise, let them encounter and solve their own obstacles.

The leader should sprinkle the event with the following phrases – hearing these statements helps the participant maintain the throughline intention of the exercise:

"Resist the temptation to go fast."

"Stay slow, you have plenty of time."

"Keep your focus here in the room – going from this position to a stand."

"Don't forget to breathe."

"If you get in a bind, reverse at the same slow pace and try another solution."

The facilitator should also inform the group where they are in the process. If it's a 90 minute session, at approximately 22 minutes into it, the group should receive an announcement they're 1/4 of the way there. At 45 minutes they hear they're 1/2 of the journey and so forth. They need this occasional help with time. This exercise is called TIME TRAVELLING, in part, because it eliminates all normal perception of time.

When the group members get to a final stand and as the head lifts, the leader or assistant should whisper to them to take a few slow steps and then gradually find a chair and sit down. There should be some cups of water readily available and some Kleenex for those who are releasing emotionally. (There are occasions when a participant needs a Kleenex during the work, and I have as the leader simply held the Kleenex to the nose and done the honors without too much fuss.)

The after–effects of the exercise may vary widely. Some participants burst into tears, others feel a deep peace, others feel powerful, like they could run a marathon, while others feel pooped. All, however, report having a profound new awareness of themselves and a renewed confidence in their abilities.

Objectively, they'll appear grounded, real, sincere, mature and even sage–like. They will at the same time be vulnerable, funny, and compassionate. Although, the after–glow of the exercise rubs off fairly quickly, the new and deeper relationship to time lasts forever.

As an added challenge, the time-travel should be longer, if only by five minutes, each time a participant does it. This is very demanding work and each time it's attempted it must be treated with the utmost care and respect.

EMPTY TO BE FILLED

The core idea behind this exercise is that, for many people, emotional charges have been lodged in the body's physical structure in the form of chronic tension and illness. Once the emotional charge is accessed and released, true relaxation can occur. One reason why these emotional barriers are never released in the course of ordinary life is that most people are afraid of their deep powerful emotions. And even if they aren't, there is no socially sanctioned outlet for these feelings.

This exercise is a close relative to those developed in the Rebirthing movement of the early 1980's, the Spriritual Emergency work of Stanislov Grof as practiced at the Esalen Gestalt center in California, and Wu-Ji, a breathing practice developed by modern Chinese Taoists. The therapeutic results are similar to these methods, yet the aim in this exercise remains linked to the work of the actor.

It's essential to have a safe, secure, preferably soundproof room to do this exercise. This is because, more than any other exercise, this one depends upon the privacy of the workspace. Permission to release emotion is, in this case, directly related to the degree of safety and privacy sensed by the participant.

Assuming that a suitable space has been secured, the participants should be instructed to arrive with the following items: Two blankets (or one blanket and a mat to lay on), a pillow, a box of Kleenex, a notebook, and a fruit juice if they so desire. They should be dressed in loose fitting clothes.

The facilitator should bring a portable tape player, tapes of rock music which have steady commanding beats, (avoid music which is slow, sentimental, or ominous sounding), extra blankets, water, Kleenex, and a watch.

Arrange the space so everyone can lay on their back on a blanket or mat. Allow them to be close to one another, but with a respectful distance. Leave pathways for the leader to comfortably get to everyone without having to step over anyone.

Their instructions are to lay on the floor, maintain a rigorous breath rhythm, and allow themselves to release *any and all emotions* that bubble up. They can cry, yell, scream, moan, and move within a limited range while remaining on their mat. They are not allowed to leave their blanket area, engage anyone else in their journey, or to fall asleep. This latter rule sounds silly except that one very powerful defense against release of emotions is sleep.

To the uninitiated, the idea of laying down and breathing and emoting sounds like a ridiculous proposition. To those people who are most resistant to the idea, it is best to ask them to suspend prejudgement and to enjoy the cleansing benefits of the breathing.

Invariably, however, it takes just under three minutes for people to be experiencing all kinds of emotional release once the exercise gets underway.

Make sure everyone has gone to the restroom just before starting the exercise. Due to the high level of ventilation, the cleansing functions of the kidneys will be working in high gear and will fill the bladder at a more rapid pace.

Also, make sure nobody is wearing contacts. Even the lightest versions will irritate and hinder the process. As in all threshold exercises, make sure nobody is on any medication and that they're not wearing necklaces or sharp jewelry. Absolutely no gum chewing!

Inform them that the music is provided to help them maintain the rhythmic quality of the breath. It also provides a loud audio cushion to the room which enhances the overall privacy of the exercise. Also advise those people who may find themselves intellectualizing the experience to simply empathize with someone next to them and try to get into their emotional state. This usually gets the ball rolling again and re-launches them into their own journey.

I often refer to this experience as a journey. This is because, for the participants, it will sometimes be experienced as one. Memories surface that may have long been repressed, old injuries may be re-experienced, fantastic visions and various hallucinatory phenomenon may be experienced, along with moments of extreme bliss.

The participants will sometimes experience extreme changes of temperature. It's not unusual to see a participant throw off a blanket only to grasp for it minutes later. Some shiver and sweat at the same time, while others bask as if enjoying warm sunshine.

There are, of course, amazing displays of emotional release which cover the whole gamut of possible emotions. There's hysterical laughter, profound sobbing, angry screaming, frozen terror, infant-like bliss, tender sorrow, bitter frustration, flashes of maniacal joy, and on and on ad infinitum. Many participants report feeling sexually aroused at times or just deeply sensual. What is most important for the facilitator and the participants to honor is that all manifestations, regardless of their origins or expression, are allowed.

Everyone is working with the understanding that emotions are being ex-*pressed* and re-experienced and that's all. I often tell a group that they are, in essence, taking an emotional dump.

The participants should be aware that they may experience numbness in the face and limbs. They may at times feel deep pain in an area of old injury. They may experience many thoughts which will frighten them. The only advice is to work through those tough spots by expressing the emotion associated with it. They can raise their hand at anytime if they feel in trouble.

With the lights dimmed to a comfortable glow, have everyone start a very fast, deep inhale and exhale rhythm. They should take the air in and out through the mouth. The abdomen should expand with the inhale and contract with the exhale. *Make sure the abdomen is moving.* Turn on the music and yelling over the sounds, tell everyone to use the rhythm of the music to help maintain the breath.

It's important that the participants feel free to vocally express the sensations they feel. Therefore, encourage them to let it out vocally and not hold back. Because the breath rhythm is so intense in the beginning, nearly everyone experiences some degree of cramping pain. Encourage them to express this pain vocally. Others may be suddenly afraid and need to express fear while still others will launch full blast into a release which has been waiting at the floodgates.

Although it may seem impossible to the uninitiated, this process continues in this manner, uninterrupted, for at least an hour and a half. The breathing actually becomes quite easy and fully integrated into the various emotional experiences. In some cases, the abdominal breathing is not working to release emotions or is in some way restrictive. The facilitator at that time should kneel nearby and instruct the participant to reverse the breathing; expanding the upper chest with the inhale and expanding the abdomen with the exhale. Allow this reverse breath for awhile and see what happens.

The facilitator must work the room, so to speak. He or she must be alert to people who appear to be falling asleep and get them into the breath rhythm again. It is primarily a job of reassurance to those people who are afraid that their face will never again thaw out or that because their hand has frozen into a cramped position they will never again be able to use it. They need reassurance so they can re-enter the exercise and commit once again to their release.

Sometimes a person begins to cough up junk from deep in the lungs. Hand them plenty of Kneenex and encourage them to go all out in their efforts to cleanse.

In my experience, unless someone is turning blue, all complaints and fears and discomforts are derived from naturally occurring responses to the exercise and are nothing to be alarmed about. Everything thaws out, all pains dissolve, and even the most fearsome states of release soothe to a sweet, blissful relaxation at the end of the session.

With regards to the music, the ideal situation is to have a special tape made to accommodate an uninterrupted flow of rhythm and sound. If that is not possible, make all tape changes as brief as possible.

The group should also be informed of where they are in the process. Tell them when they are 1/4, 1/2, 3/4 of the way and when 5 minutes is left.

At the end of the session, turn the volume down on the music very slowly and announce time is up. Tell them it's best to end on a laugh, so they should now laugh. That in and of itself is sometimes absurd enough to get them laughing. If that doesn't work, tell them to think of the absurdity of their own life. If that again doesn't work, tell them to think of the absurdity of the life of someone else in the room. That last one usually gets them going. If not, don't worry about it. It's not crucial.

Give them time to stretch and come out of it. *Do not allow anyone to stand up for a few minutes.* Everyone will feel a little light-headed and it's unwise to let anyone stand or walk for a few moments. Just let everyone come around naturally.

After a few minutes, invite them to take a restroom break and to have some juice. When everyone has settled back in the room after about ten minutes, instruct them to spend a few moments writing in their notebooks. Then, after about fifteen minutes, bring everyone together and let them talk about their experience.

This latter step is important. It helps them to assimilate the experience and to honor the humanity of the entire event. The facilitator is there to keep things organized and to listen; making sure the experience has a sense of closure. The participants should be made aware that they're now very vulnerable and should not jump right into activity. They certainly shouldn't have any alcohol or stimulants or any kind.

It will be a day or so before their metabolism returns to its previous state. What will remain, however, is a newly acquired relaxation, and a lightness with regards to emotions. Profound emotions will no longer seem so scary that they need to be locked away. And for the actor, both of these results are most beneficial.

FROZEN FIRE

Some students like to refer to this one as "freeze tag from hell." This, like all threshold exercises, brings participants right up against their will center. Each person encounters a personal threshold; the place where they are ready to pack it in. They are also in the unique position to observe how the will can nudge the threshold further away.

This whole process provides a very close look at the inner workings of the mind and its connection to the body. Participants come to understand how powerful thoughts are in relation to the feedback loop from the nervous system. They also come to learn about how resourceful the body is in coping with challenges.

Start with a fluid free flow of movement around the room. The leader calls "freeze" at random intervals, holding for different lengths of time over the course of about five minutes. Somewhere in there, and preferably when not predicted by the participants, the leader calls freeze. As they hold, the leader informs them this is the "big freeze" and they must stay frozen in whatever position they're in for as long as humanly possible. This could mean ten minutes, an hour, two hours, or more, depending upon the individual and the posture.

Leader, tell them that they're safe and that when they reach their absolute threshold, they can melt down to the floor and rest on their backs. Remind everyone to open the breath stream and to relax into the posture as much as possible. Be alert to anyone who is trying to go too far or who's in a posture that's going to severely cut off circulation or breath.

Some unfortunates will have chosen postures painfully awkward or off-center. These folks will have the hardest job and although many are consequently forced to bail out early, I've seen some people, in outrageous postures, outlast virtually everyone.

On the other hand, some participants will have easy postures to rely on. In these cases, their struggle becomes more mental than physical; which is often the more difficult of the two. The leader must encourage everyone to stay frozen, to fight against the temptation to move, to avoid blinking and to settle the breath to a deep, silent place.

Early stages of the work are quite euphoric and are often charged with a heroic atmosphere. Everyone is at first preoccupied with all the exotic sensations occurring in stillness. This soon shifts to an appreciation for the more subtle feelings revealed. Before long, however, the reality of the situation sinks in and the participant begins to work on a variety of mental and physical strategies to sustain the position.

With everyone well acquainted with the first portion of the exercise, the second becomes much easier to instill. This second portion should not occur in the same day as the first as it may be too exhausting. At the appropiate time, introduce phase two of FROZEN FIRE.

The second part isn't elaborate, but it is very unusual and sometimes very difficult. The difference between the first portion and this section is that, in this one, the group members are asked to initiate the freeze on their own. The difficult part of this task is that *they are asked to take themselves by surprise.* They are not to predict, plan, or anticipate when the freeze will happen.

It may take a few trys to allow people an opportunity to explore this new approach. Once everyone has a sense of how to do this (it's difficult and everyone should not be expected to be able to accomplish this each and every time), introduce the element of *social interaction*.

This is when the exercise takes on a very bizarre atmosphere. Each participant is asked to engage in conversation with someone else or with a small group of people. Let the conversation flow smoothly and naturally. At some unpredictable point, however, they are to surprise themselves and freeze in whatever position and mood in which they happen to be. If it's in mid–conversation, the other interlocutors are asked to honor this and let the conversation veer onto another tack.

It's often the case that one person freezing suddenly prompts all the others in a group or the opposite partner to freeze as well. Encourage everyone to resist the temptation to fall into the other person's freeze moment and to freeze only when they themselves truly initiate the surprise.

It will take a few minutes for everyone to get over the awkwardness of making small talk while the surprise freeze game is being played. They are allowed, by the way, to talk about anything, including FROZEN FIRE. It can be delicious to catch oneself in mid–reaction to the game itself, in mid–laugh, as one is reaching for a book or turning to answer a question from across the room. These liminal or "in between" positions are very revealing, very expressive, and ultimately very useful for the actor looking for ways to improve the skills of behavioral observation.

After a while, people will probably be releasing themselves from their freeze positions for two primary reasons: discomfort or consideration. When this occurs, stop the exercise and point up the fact that people are breaking out of the freeze when it feels convenient or because they are afraid of frightening someone else in the group. Ask them now to remain in the freeze until they sense the first impulse to stop. Then ask them to go beyond this first impulse, the second, and all the others that may emerge. Let them run right up against their personal limitations.

Some people will break concentration early either by accident or design. Don't allow them to feel defeated. Some actors have a natural affinity for stillness while others must struggle mightily to sustain even the simplest freeze. Help them realize the greater lessons learned from their actions. If time permits, allow them the opportunity to go in again. In fact, if at anytime a person breaks the freeze, they're allowed to re-initiate a conversation and a new freeze posture.

The next layer of risk here is to invite them to go beyond even the socially acceptable limit; to own the exercise for themselves and not to halt their work out of classroom etiquitte. Of course, this must be done with a degree of common sense. They mustn't be allowed to hurt themselves or break the law. Yet, within a certain parameter, this latter condition can often cure a student of "studentitus" and awaken within him or her a new, more powerful self-authority which extends beyond the polite considerations of classmates or teachers.

At the appropriate time, signal the end of the exercise and ask that everyone melt down and rest on the floor. After a rest, invite them to write in their journal or to simply sit in silence. This is not a competition and people enduring until the end should not be rewarded any more that those who left the postures early. It is a personal education, not a test.

One word of warning: Leaders, be on the lookout for people who may have low blood sugar. This particular exercise can cause them to go off into the ozone and if they start to look pale or dizzy, halt the exercise for them and let them lay on the floor.

Also beware of people in positions which may cut off their circulation in one or more limbs. Allow these folks the luxury of one adjustment which will prevent them from the intense discomfort of blocked circulation.

This threshold is called FROZEN FIRE because the freeze posture generates a great deal of internal heat. The body, although frozen in time and space, will feel at times as if it's literally engulfed in flames. This heat is the fire which tempers the steel of the inner character.

SAMURAI SQUAT

This exercise borrows heavily from martial arts and everyone must be forewarned that afterwards, their legs will be sore for a few days. The exercise helps to develop mental focus, cleans the body, and gets the participant in contact with deeper, more primal energies.

Stand in a wide second position, feet well apart, and turn the toes inward so the blades of the feet become parallel. Sit down in this position about halfway, until the thighs are straight enough to sit plates on them. Make sure the knees are over the feet and not extended beyond the toes. The spine should be straight.

In the beginning, place the arms in front of the body as if holding a hula-hoop. The elbows are rounded and the shoulders are dropped.

Stay in this position without bobbing up and down and breathe deeply. The goal is to remain in this squat for as long as possible. When the arms get tired place them on the hips.

Do not hold the breath at any time.

At first there is a great deal of discomfort. This gives way to heavy breathing and expressions of anger or fear. Before long, however, the bottom of the feet will feel like they've opened up and after that, the squat becomes easier. Through most of the exercise there will be shaking in the legs. In fact, there may be moments when the whole body seems like a major earthquake. Heat builds up and a sweat will begin to pour out of the body.

Everyone will be tempted to raise up from the squat. It's the job of the leader to remind people to stay low and to focus their minds away from the discomfort.

Each person has a different threshold for this exercise. So, do not compete with others. Go as long as is necessary to sense your own moment of inner struggle. Resolve the struggle, THEN stand when the decision is made consciously and not as a reaction to the effects of the exercise.

Leader, when group members decide that they must finish, help them to a stand and guide them to a place where they may lay down and rest. You must also be alert to see if anyone looks like they might fall down or pass out. People at risk like this should be helped out of the squat and guided to a rest place. As a general rule, don't allow anyone to go beyond 20 minutes on a first experience.

TRAMPOLINE

This one is a lot of fun because it engages the imagination. After a warm up, everyone is to imagine that the floor surface is, in actuality, a huge trampoline. Make sure that everyone is wearing shoes and that the space is free of obstacles. Everyone must participate fully or the exercise won't work properly.

Start out in a private circle of concentration, jumping and working to believe in the image. After establishing the imagined reality for yourself, begin to expand the circle of concentration to include others nearby. After some time linking up with several people jumping, bouncing, and rollicking on this huge trampoline, expand your awareness to include the entire group.

In the first ten minutes, the fun of the exercise sustains the enthusiasm and keeps the energy fully charged. The notion of a threshold is in explaining that they're to continue on this trampoline for a full hour.

To make it through, it helps to change the manner of jumping from time to time, engage others in silliness, songs, competitions, etc., and occasionally to fall to the floor, where you can use the arms to give the legs a bit of a rest.

The leader should announce the half-hour and 3/4 hour marks and then give the one-minute call and the last ten-second countdown.

At the end, the leader should instruct everyone to lay on the floor and roll around gently, breathing deeply, and stretching like a cat.

The body will retain the sensation of the bouncing, in much the same way it will after playing for a few hours in an ocean shorebreak. After rolling around and stretching, when the participants get to a stand and begin to walk around, they'll still be haunted by the echo of the trampoline bouncing.

This exercise can unleash many childhood memories, it can lower one's center of gravity, and it creates a shared experience full of hilarity and physical challenge.

ACTIVE IMAGINATION

The group has experienced visualization in a passive mode, where they lay on the floor and watch as the scenes unfold in their inner screens. The imagination can also engage just as effectively in a more active mode, using the whole body and interacting with others in the group. Begin with a few of the following imagination exercises:

1. There are two big buckets of water in front of you. One is filled with cold water and the other with hot. Place your hand in one, experience it fully. Place your hand in the other, again experience the water. Lift the hands and sense/see the water drip down the arm. Shake off the water.

2. Take an imaginary mallet and strike an imaginary bell. Listen to the ring. Hear the exact pitch of the bell, see the exact shape of the objects, sense the vibrations caused by striking the bell.

3. Watch as a tiny seedling grows at time-lapse speed through the floor, its vine-like stem and wide green leaves expanding and growing upwards into the room toward the ceiling, becoming Jack's beanstalk to the clouds.

4. You have suddenly forgotten how to walk and you must invent a way of moving your body through space.

5. Pick a partner and believe you're long lost friends, out of touch for ten years. Catch up on your lives, telling fantastic tales in a convincing manner.

CHAMBER IMPROVISATIONS

We can now expand the imaginary circumstances into what I like to call "chamber improvs." These are imaginary situations that use the real workspace as a location, changing only certain elements or conditions within the chamber itself.

Start with everyone on the floor, eyes closed. When the leader gives the signal, the participants open their eyes and find themselves in this strange room. They're to pretend not to know one another and through the course of this exercise, they discover that the only thing all of them have in common is they were all travelling by bus. The room is locked and theories abound as to how they came to be in this chamber.

The leader is invisible to everyone, interjecting occasionally to heighten the stakes and alter the conditions within the room.

Let this improvisational reality set in for at least ten minutes.

LEADER (speaking):

(After a few minutes, call "freeze!"). Stay frozen everyone. Pick up where you were, except that gradually you begin to notice that the room is getting hotter and hotter. (Observe this until the group has reached a peak. Call "freeze" again.) The heat subsides but after a short period of comfort, you begin to notice the room is now getting colder and colder. (Remind them to use their imaginations to make this situation as real to them and those around them, as possible).

(When they've reached a peak with the cold, interject, speaking right over the improv): The temperature's returning to normal.

Let the temperature normalize. Discuss among your-selves what your reaction to all of this is. (After a moment or two of discussion): Begin to notice things about the room that seem strange to you. What's going on? Perhaps this is some kind of experiment aboard an alien spacecraft. (Observe them as they try to solve the riddle of their situation. Find a logical place to stop this scenario with a "freeze" command and move on to the next conditional intensifier): The atmosphere is becoming increasingly dense. You must press against the space to move. The dense air is pressing you to the floor and walls of the space. Struggle against this. Try to find a way out of this predicament.

The exercise will have a life of its own and a good leader will guide the imaginary scenarios only if guidance is needed. The leader should interject another set of circumstances only if the scenario starts to dissolve or the dynamic reaches an impasse. The changing circumstances reignite the imagination and provide enough variety to insure that everyone has at least one experience where the imaginary world seemed remarkably real.

SUGGESTIONS FOR ADDITIONAL INTENSIFIERS:

1.   The group realizes that someone has played a joke on them. They all wanted to go to their high school reunion and were told it was at this location.

2.   Someone smells smoke outside the walls of the room and it becomes apparent the building is on fire.

3.   The group are winners of a national art contest who must now compete as a team and create, in one hour, a full ad campaign, (slogans, songs, dances, TV, and radio spots), They are competing against another group in another contest.

4.   They're a group of hostages, recently captured, placed in this room in an unknown location. They're locked in and cannot escape. Their captors have left them there all day.

5.   The group realizes they're all recently deceased and are trying to figure out what they're expected to do. Is this heaven, hell, someplace else?

THE RELISHING

This exercise, perhaps more than any other, can awaken the senses in a manner that dramatically revitalizes our innate, but often occluded ability to genuinely relish being alive. Within a short amount of time almost any group will have arrived at a sublime and warmly intimate appreciation of themselves and the others around them.

The leader will guide the group through the following exercise.

LEADER:
Lay down on your backs, lengthen the spine, relax the limbs, inhale deeply, and exhale with a long luxurious sigh. Do this again. Good. Let the voice participate in the sigh. Try a few more on your own. Good.

Now come to a complete, but relaxed stillness. Imagine you're in a deep trance–like slumber. You've been sleeping for some time and there's danger you'll never wake up. Suddenly, you awaken within this sleeping body, but soon realize you cannot move anything. You cannot even open your eyes. You have thoughts, but you can't communicate them.

Gradually, after much effort, you manage to contact one finger. One finger of one hand. This one finger is you now, wanting to awaken the rest of the body. Let this finger work hard to awaken the other fingers. They're totally asleep. See if your finger can awaken the other fingers.

(After a minute) Now one other finger awakens. You celebrate together and vow to awaken the others. The other fingers gradually awaken one by one until the entire hand is awake. Let the hand celebrate being awake and free of that heavy slumber.

The hand now knows what it must do. It must work to awaken the arm. Try every means possible to awaken it, shake, dance, stroke, flop, anything. (After a minute) Gradually the arm awakens and it's extremely happy to be alive. Let the arm dance and celebrate the joy of being able to awake and move.

Then the arm begins to explore this limp, sleeping body. It tries to awaken the body. When it become apparent the body will not awaken, let it focus on waking up the other arm. Maybe two arms will be able to wake up this sleeping giant.

(After a minute or two) Let the arms celebrate together. Good. Now go to work on a leg. Maybe the two arms can awaken a single leg. (After a few minutes) It's working, the leg is beginning to awaken. That's great, no time to lose, wake up the other leg.

(After the other leg is awake) Celebrate together arms and legs and feet. You are awake! (After a minute) Now work to awaken the pelvis. (Wait a minute) That's good, its working. Now, the abdomen, stomach, and chest. That's right. Let them come alive and celebrate being awakened.

Now the head. Try to awaken the ears, the nose, the tongue, the voice, the eyes, everything. Work carefully, but effectively to get the senses to engage. One by one, let them awaken and let them take time to relish the awakening. (Several minutes) Once awakened, let the whole body celebrate together the joy of being alive.

Now turn to someone near you and admire them. Communicate with your awakened eyes, toes, arms, abdomens, voices, everything. Let yourself appreciate the miracle of their awakening.

(Usually there are some very fine moments of play mixed with expressions of joy, love, respect and mutual appreciation. Let this continue as long as it needs to, then instruct them to go to the next phase):

Now take in the whole group. Relish them. Look at their faces, their feet, their arms. everything. Take a few moments to relish and awaken each other as a whole.

(There's no predicting what the group will do at this stage. Anything is possible. Let the scene unfold naturally. This section has the potential for some truly amazing moments, moments that defy explanation. After a few minutes, when it appears appropriate, halt the exercise and invite everyone to assemble for a brief discussion.)

SUGGESTED TOPICS FOR DISCUSSION:

1 .What was unique about this experience?

2. What part of the body felt the least inclined to awaken?

3. What is the value of relishing?

4. How do you feel now compared to before the exercise?

TABLEAUX

T hese fun exercises combine sculptural aesthetics and stage movement to create visual compositions. They attempt to communicate a variety of assigned feelings, ideas, moods, and situations. They are introduced at this point in part because they are a relief from the more intense and demanding threshold exercises.

It's also a valuable tool for the theatre, enabling everyone to experience how delicate the relationship is between the visual composition of bodies onstage and the conscious or unconscious meaning encoded therein.

STILL PHOTOS

The still picture is the best place to start. Nearly everyone can relate to taking snapshots of one kind or another. First, agree upon or create a frame size. A space roughly ten feet long, four feet deep, and eight feet high is a suitable starting size. Then within the frames, groups of three, four, or five will work to develop compositions that match the assigned qualities.

The beauty and challenge of this exercise is that talking is not allowed. The groups must communicate silently among themselves as they work to create pictures. This may sound difficult, but by this time the group is so in tune with one another that the compositions seem to flow out of them with very little effort.

After each composition study, each group should present their three tableaux. This provides a sense of purpose and stimulates a great deal of creativity.

COMPOSITION #1: TENSION

Create three tableaux where the dynamics of the composition evoke tension. These aren't necessarily pictures depicting things ABOUT tension, although that certainly can be included. Instead, they're studies in visual and emotional tension through group composition.

COMPOSITION #2: AMBIGUITY

Create three tableaux where the dynamics of the composition evoke ambiguity. The viewer should be forced to consider questions such as: Are we seeing what we think we're seeing? Are the characters really angry or just playing? Is that three or four people?

COMPOSITION #3: THE EDGES

Create three tableaux where the dynamics of the composition engage the edges of the frame as integral to the appreciation and under-standing of the whole. The primary character, object, or point of focus need not be in the center, but might be seen just at the edge. Perhaps we see only parts of things at the edge and they're clues to the whole arrangement.

COMPOSITION #4: AESTHETIC BEAUTY

Create three tableaux where the composition arrives at a balanced, harmonious, and beautiful picture. Incorporate elements of the ear-lier studies, but they must be gracefully arranged so as to please the eye and evoke a sense of peace and beauty.

WORD CREATION

In this exercise the leader prepares a list of words to be used as springboards of creativity. Participants separate into two or three large groups and stand in a huddle, concentrating, ready to spring into action. The leader then goes to each group and quietly, but clearly, says a word from the list.

Upon hearing the word, the group must instantly forge a tableau inspired by whatever impulses were triggered by the word. They hold this shape until the leader returns with a new word whereupon they will again instantly forge a new tableau.

The leader must travel quickly from group to group completing at least three words for each. At the end of the cycle of words, the group is asked to demonstrate their tableaux in the order the words were given. (*That's one of the reasons for only doing three or four words*)

SUGGESTED WORDS FOR THE LIST:

Forest	Space	Funeral	Clock
Murder	Fortune	Drunk	Machine
Escape	Birth	Waterfall	Dance

Variations on the exercise:

1. Have each group create a sound/chant to go with each tableau.

2. Have the group decide on the transition qualities from another word list consisting of words such as: Melt, float, flip, stomp, run, explode, strobe, fall, inflate, fold, spin, fizzle, sweep, grind, shimmy, hop, etc. Using this variation, it would be possible to see a group inflate into a tableau based on the word, "forest," melt into the "dance" tableau and shimmy into "murder."

3. Combine the groups and add a word here and there to create a sentence that can be performed as a sequence of tableaux.

CLASSIC COMPOSITIONS

This research-oriented exercise needs to be assigned at least a week in advance. Inform each group they're to go to the library and find three classical paintings that have groupings of four or five people. They're to decide upon three paintings and then work, outside of class, on creating three distinct tableaux based on the works of art. Bring the books or prints to class to show to the entire ensemble. When everyone has demonstrated their classic compositions a discussion should follow.

SUGGESTED TOPICS FOR DISCUSSION:

1. What is it about the composition that attracted you?

2. What is the artist trying to convey by this grouping of people?

3. What was the sensation of being in the compositions?

4. What was challenging about reproducing the artist's painting?

5. Which artists lend themselves to classical compositions?

ANTI-CLASSIC COMPOSITIONS

This is just like the previous exercise except the participants are invited to seek out works of art from contemporary sources that don't adhere to rules of harmony and picturization. Groups are even allowed to use paintings that are abstract and may not depict the human figure at all.

The same rules apply to the exercise in terms of demonstration.

Show the tableaux and then afterwards the ensemble can view the work that inspired the tableaux. A discussion should follow.

SUGGESTED TOPICS FOR DISCUSSION:

1. What attracted you to the artwork?

2. What is each artist conveying and how did you translate that into a tableau?

3. How did this sensation differ from classical compositions?

4. What was the challenge this time?

5. Was it liberating or more difficult using abstract work as a springboard?

VIDEO SPRINGBOARD: KOYAANISQATSI

A gymnastic springboard is an apparatus that gives the gymnast the ability to vault higher, soar longer, and translate the additional energy into more creative and effective moves. A creative springboard is a metaphorical apparatus that functions in much the same way. For the artist, almost anything can be used as a springboard providing it fuels the leaps of the imagination and propels the artist into more creative and effective work.

From time to time it's useful to provide such springboards in the form of video tapes. There are many tapes that provide high quality inspiration to a group seeking to explore ensemble theatre.

One of my favorites is the tape of a film entitled *KOYAANISQATSI.*

This film, created by director Godfrey Reggio, composer Philip Glass, cinematographer Ron Fricke and presented by Francis Ford Coppola, is a breathtaking montage of music and visual images so powerful they defy verbal description.

The title, *KOYAANISQATSI*, is a Hopi Indian word meaning "life out of balance." The meaning of the title becomes increasingly clear as the film moves from depicting the grace and power of nature on the macro and micro levels to the depiction of how the human species creates disintegration through our ignorance of natural laws.

I have shown this tape to no less that five different groups and it never fails to evoke the same mood in all. The groups are inevitably filled with a powerful mix of silent astonishment and profound melancholy. Without using a single word, the film manages to tell volumes about the relationship of decay to growth, clouds to ocean waves, cities and microchips, abandoned tenements to people on the street, and countless other images that escape us in our everyday perceptions. To see ourselves as a species out of balance is bitter but necessary medicine. When the embers of our collective conscience become stirred through such a work, it can be a vital springboard, a resonating motivator with the power to propel the viewers into formidable action.

I recommend the following sequence for this creative springboard:

SESSION I:

1. Several days prior to the video showing, the leader should tell participants to bring sketchpads of various sizes and a variety of drawing utinsils, (i.e. crayon, pastels, colored markers, etc.) to the workspace on the appointed day.

2. After a brief warm-up and focusing exercise to help the group be present in the room, The leader gathers the group in chairs or an equally comfortable sitting arrangement. Make sure everyone has a clear view of the television screens. Begin the tape.

3. At the end of the tape, the leader should instruct the group to go immediately to their sketchpads and begin to draw whatever images emerge. Assure those participants who are timid about their drawing talents that their raw, untutored

expressions are often the most powerful. The important thing is to avoid engaging in conversation or analysis. Go directly to the paper and begin to draw. Inform the group they have only fifteen minutes in which to express their impressions. At fourteen minutes give a one-minute warning and insist that everyone stop work immediately at the command "stop."

4. Take a five-minute break. During the break everyone is free to talk, but not about the video.

5. After the break they're to return to their drawings where they can create new work or refine the original for the next fifteen minutes.

6. End the session with this second drawing phase.
The participants will need time to digest the images over the next few days. Gather up all the sketches and keep them in a safe place until the next session.

SESSION II:

1. Spread the drawings out on the floor, leaving room for participants to walk around them, weaving their way as though walking through a museum. The group should then, in silence, walk around the room and take in all the artwork.

2. Once the group has had the chance to look at everyone's work, invite the individuals to gravitate toward a work that seems to call to them. It doesn't matter if it's their own work or not. Several people may end up looking at the same picture. Ask that they begin to fall into the picture, letting their minds roam freely through the colors, the lines, the images, and the ideas that might be percolating.

3. After about twenty minutes, the leader should ask the participants to go to their sketchpads and begin to draw images that are evoked from the previous picture they were just exploring.

4. After fifteen minutes, take a five-minute break to rest the mind and to adjust to a new phase.

5. Following the break everyone should sit in a circle with their new drawings in hand. The leader should facilitate the sharing of each drawing. The participants are free to seek out other works as they speak in order to show how their ideas developed or are linked to another work. The images on the page can be discussed in terms of the images on the video and the sounds associated with both. Usually a lively discussion ensues along with an appreciation for the unique artistic flavor of each participant.

6. The facilitator should help the group perceive any thematic elements that recur from sketch to sketch and to help guide the discussion toward those things that reinforce the positive contributions of everyone. Finally, and this is the most challenging, the group needs to review their experiences up to this point and the drawings they've made and seen and then create a single MASTER SKETCH. The sketch should not be an attempt to include every element because that would be a mess. Instead, think of the sketch as a distillation of those compositions that most inspired the group into an agreed-upon aesthetic image. The group is not allowed to disband until the master sketch is completed.

SESSION III:

1. Using the Master Sketch, and remaining silent, the participants are to begin to move their bodies in the space in ways suggested by the master sketch. Start close to the sketch and then move away, freeing the body to evolve whatever movements want to emerge. If the movements lose their liveliness or if a participant feels stuck in a rut, they can return to the sketch at any time for more inspiration.

2. After a half hour of exploration of this nature, invite

the group to connect their movements in shapes and rhythmic patterns suggested by the sketch. If there are musicians in the group, allow them to select instruments to support and augment the movement patterns as they evolve. Gradually, and there is no set time measurement for this, the group will have evolved a ritual dance. Let the dance take shape and build to whatever closure might naturally occur. If it looks as though the dance is going to maintain a loop until everyone drops from exhaustion, the leader should help bring the dance to a stop. Everyone should take a ten-minute break. Following the break, the group should engage in a discussion about the experience.

SUGGESTED TOPICS FOR DISCUSSION:

a) What is the potential for further development of the ritual dance?

b) What existed in the final experience that was linked-to the original video?

c) How might this experience be related to the ceremonialdances of indigenous cultures?

e) What other ideas, notions, images, sounds, or thoughts have surfaced as a result of the video?

f) In what way could the film, the artwork, or the dance reflect the mythological dimension?

APPLIED ALCHEMY

Most people associate alchemy with the image of a Medieval wizard working furiously in a darkened chamber, surrounded by flasks and beakers and bubbling potions, greedily hoping to discover a means to turn lumps of worthless lead into shiny new gold. Although that cliche image has survived, no doubt perpetrated by the pre-Renaissance Church who felt at the time threatened by the resurgence of Gnostic pursuits, it doesn't do justice to the reality of alchemical practices.

Turning lead into gold is a metaphor for transforming the base qualities in man into ones that are more refined. Western alchemists were probably influenced by the Eastern alchemists, who had developed a variety of yogic systems aimed at extracting the "higher" spiritual essences out of the "lower" essences of the body.

No doubt, a few notorious alchemists, misinterpreting the Eastern way of thinking, became obsessed with efforts to turn actual lead into actual gold. And indeed, it may have become a myth, spread by the alchemists themselves to heighten their popularity and strengthen the mystique they enjoyed. Regardless of the reality, any research into this area soon reveals that the search for gold had very little to do with the greater body of work concerning alchemists.

Early alchemists were the forefathers of modern scientists. They were inventors and seekers. Their early experiments may well have appeared magical to illiterate townsfolk and were certainly considered diabolical in the eyes of the church. Nevertheless, they endured ridicule, oppression, and even outright persecution for many years, until the Renaissance when some of their pursuits became legitimized.

With legitimization came demands for empirical data and practical, socially beneficial results. Soon, the original emphasis on inner development gave way to the more popular wonders of external science. However, those western alchemists who remained dedicated to the inner path didn't simply disappear. They formed brotherhoods and mystery schools where their investigations into the nature of our inner reality could proceed. They continue even today in similar fashion meeting in small gnostic groups to pursue their spiritual evolution.

Eastern alchemy too is still very much alive today, touting a wide array of specialized yogic disciplines. Ironically, the largest component of inner alchemical work is done by people who are not aware their process is fundamentally alchemical. I refer here to the many traditional and non–traditional religions operating globally. Unconscious alchemical processes, however, are notoriously unreliable and usually achieve tepid results, if any.

The following are several exercises and discussions that focus on the alchemical process and help bring the participants to an understanding of alchemy in its historical and contemporary context. It's important to realize that, although esoteric and seemingly exotic, the alchemical process is essentially the process of becoming an artist.

The actual field of alchemical endeavor is secondary to the artistry and excellence to be achieved. In this way, it's easy to see how culture, and indeed all of civilization is the result of the alchemical process.

THE FIVE ELEMENTS

Alchemy starts with the essential composition of the human body. The ancient Chinese and Greeks and numerous other cultures came to recognize that we're composed of basic elements. Some use a system of four elements to describe this composition, some five, some six. Regardless of the system of categorizing, it doesn't take long to realize that the ancients were fundamentally correct. If we use the Chinese system of five elements, we can easily observe that within us there is water, earth, air, fire, and metal. The integration and cooperation of these elements determines our health, personality, and preoccupations in life.

Here are some brief descriptions of the five elements as they relate to their natural state, their metaphorical reality, and their reflection in the human being:

WATER: We are made up almost entirely of water. The liquids of our body flow and surge and regulate most of the biochemical processes responsible for keeping us alive. By studying the character of water one can further understand the role it plays in our essential being and our personality.

Qualities of water: Water is reflective. It seeks equilibrium and will flow naturally to deep earthy places. Water can douse a flame. Although a lot of fire can transform water into steam. Steam can exist in the air as a cloud, and there conduct fire in its form as lightning. An excess of steam will cause the water to fall to the earth. Water can assist the destruction of metal by the air (oxidation) and assist the transformation and transportation of metals in glacial movements, rivers, oceans, etc.

Watery people are usually slow. It takes a lot to get them, excuse the pun, "steamed up." They like to flow with moment-to- moment reality. They're usually sensuous people, reflective, poetic, and have moods that gravitate downwards. Stable watery people have enormous depth and create things that reflect that depth.

EARTH: We eat the food of the earth, gaining much of our direct nutrition from its vitamin and mineral resources. The old adage, "From dust to dust," speaks of our ultimate earthly composition. In a very real sense, we really are what we eat.

The earth is primarily still and solid. Movement is possible through the powers of wind, water, and pressure. The earth stores metals and transforms itself gradually over time through sediment, occasional volcanic eruptions, and metamorphic processes.

Earthy people are solid individuals. They love to protect and nurture people, plants, and animals. They love food and drink and have enormous patience. They are practical people, somewhat set in their ways and resistant to sudden change. When change occurs, however, they adjust quickly. Earthly concerns are usually focused on basic survival needs and the cycles of growth and decay.

AIR: We breathe air, utilize its life supporting elements, and expel the unused portions. Our bodies can live for a time without water and without food. We cannot live very long without air.

PHOTO: JIM CALDWELL

The Element of Fire in Performance

Too much air or a rarified mixture can affect our equilibrium, making us dizzy, or "light headed."

Air is very changeable. It is light and comforting in its form as a breeze yet terrible and swift in its form as a tornado. The primary quality of air is movement. It must move to be effective, enjoyable, or intense. Air travels far across great expanses of the earth and drifts in stratified layers upward into space.

Air increases fire, although a large enough gust can blow the fire out. Air and water do not mix unless water transforms into steam or air transforms into bubbles. The earth is sculpted by the air, in the form of winds, and the sea is disturbed by the air if the winds stir the water strongly enough.

Air people are good communicators, swift and refreshing in their thoughts. They will fan the flames of a fire person, and gradually sculpt the ideas of earthy folk. The air person is sometimes accused of being an "air head," indecisive and forgetful. They make up for this by being witty, inventive, and creative. Air people love to defy gravity in music, art, and dance forms. They like open spaces, windows, and love to travel.

FIRE: We are electromagnetic beings, with a neural network that conducts electrical impulses throughout the body. This electrical activity is our link to the element of fire. Our brains are aflame with the millions of thoughts and images, impressions and decisions being computed there. The fire energy travels to all parts of out body and returns with equal speed to the brain to process an enormous amount of sensory data. Fire changes the form of water, melting the ice or producing steam. It can melt metals and even turn the earth to a molten state. It can also heat the air, redirecting it upwards.

Fire needs friction to bring it to life. Once ignited, it feeds on the air and consumes dry or semi–dry organic material. Fire is fast and stimulates all it contacts. Fire is quick to consume and quick to die out. Fire transforms.

The fire person is temperamental. They think a lot and feed off of their own thoughts at times. They have little patience and enjoy making quick precise decisions. They don't like to be around water people for very long; especially if outnumbered. Fire people cannot help but want to affect change. They try to quicken and steam up water people. They are in awe of earthy patience, but have no desire to adopt it as a lifestyle. Fire people love metal people, because once heated up they are malleable. Fire people enjoy the company of air people, because air folks fan their flames and make them burn brighter.

METAL: We must have a trace of metals in our bodies to properly maintain the nervous system and to provide bonding agents for certain nutrients. These metals must be maintained in a delicate balance with the other elements. Too much of some kind of metals is highly toxic while not enough of others is equally damaging.

Metal conducts electricity and regulates temperature. It gives strength and character to the land. Metal is a mysterious element. Embedded in the earth's crust, it lays dormant providing only the slightest contribution to organic life until liberated by the hands of man.

Metal needs fire and friction to refine it. Repeated firings temper the metal and give it flexible strength. Metal can also be brittle, snapping when under pressure that's either too stressful or misdirected. When refined or polished, metal is reflective, bold, valuable, and highly useful. Unrefined, metal may have strength, but the qualities are smothered by its earthy, unrefined quality.

Metal people are good in a crisis. They can handle the heat in the kitchen. In fact, if the heat and pressure of their lives is regulated, metal characters transform into people of admirable courage. They literally "test their metal." However, some metal people, untested and poorly tempered, are slow, brittle, and bitter. They've avoided the heat of confrontation in their life and consequently, they have little warmth and a lot of cheap brittle armor.

Metal people have difficulty relating to Air and Water

people. They find comfort and security in earthy people and bond most successfully with fire people.

At this point, it should be recognized that there is no such thing as the people mentioned above. These categories are generalizations aimed at helping to understanding dominant human traits. The reality is that we are unique combinations of all five elements and the composition is always in flux. We may have a general propensity toward one or more of the elements, but they're always subject to environment, age, and personal direction.

The true alchemist seeks to find a healthy equilibrium of all five and then orchestrates the energies consciously to forge his or her soul. Nearly all early work in alchemy is directed toward mastery of each of these elements. The following are exercises to explore the five elements and to provide a taste of how they might be mastered.

Walking The Water Basin:
Stand anywhere in the room. Visualize a waterfall falling from within the top of the head and landing on the bottom of the feet. Let this waterfall relax and sooth the body. Gradually sense the water gathering in the legs, filling up until it stops, levelling off at the top of a basin; the edge of which is at an imaginary line just below the hips.

Walk around the space carefully, without splashing the water out of the basin. Try to sit, spin, greet others, and even run keeping the water from splashing out. Sit on a chair, focus on allowing the water to settle until it's perfectly still, a deep silent reflecting pond.

Planting Roots into the Earth:
Stand on a patch of ground. If this isn't practical, use the imagination to visualize the studio floor as a soft earthy floor. As you stand with the feet firmly planted on the ground, imagine that the bottom of the feet merge with the earth and in part become the earth. Let the feet feel cool and welcome the chance to transform temporarily into soil. After the initial image has been established imagine that the bottom of the feet open up to allow roots to emerge. Sense these roots burrowing into the ground, spreading out and stabilizing you.

Smell the earth and sense its deep, primal power. Walk around the space uprooting and rooting the feet one at a time until the walk becomes smooth. Sit on a chair, relax the belly, and become a mountain. Allow your mind to have very solid, practical thoughts.

Playing in the Clouds:
Stand tall and visualize yourself floating up above the rooftops and into the clouds. Walk on the clouds, push the clouds away, stack them, nestle with them, shape them, play catch with them. Take five deep Yogic breaths of this rarefied air. As you do this, raise your center of gravity so you feel like a balloon suspended on two strings called legs. Float around the room and as you do, let your thoughts drift and shift and float.

Go to a chair and lightly touch down into a sitting position. Let your thoughts soar, dream, envision, skip merrily from thought to thought.

Becoming the Flame:
Sense a small candle flame burning at the center of your chest. Let the flame flicker, glow, and pulse. Gradually become that flame. Imagine your body is the flame and your feet are connected to the wick of a long taper candle. Stay controlled as a candle flame until at some point you leap to another flame or to a nearby tree. Become the flame of a forest fire, raging through the forest.

Let the fire internalize until it is only the image of a forest fire in the mind. Walk around the room with the mind on fire, talking, relating, coming up with ideas, debating issues, getting involved. Convince someone else of something and then let an idea take fire so that you might feed off another point of view until the room is on fire with discussion and ideas.

Internalizing the Metal:
Imagine you're dressed in a full suit of armour. Walk around the room in this metal suit. Gradually let the metal become internalized until it becomes an inner shield, a core strength protecting the pure heart. Become mercury, rolling, collecting with others then beading off alone, finding the lowest level in the room. Become gold, valued, soft, beautiful. Try silver, valued, reflective, slightly malleable, beautiful. Become iron, stable, valued but not dainty, reliable, useful,

practical. Become a finely tempered sword, a razor blade, a sledge-hammer.

THE APPLAUSE DISCUSSION:

It may seem odd at first to have a discussion about applause while in the midst of a unit on alchemy. It's precisely that curious juxta-position, however, that helps to dust off old expectations and brings new life to the understanding of alchemy.

Start by applauding. Applaud each other, the sun, the architect of the workspace, anything that comes to mind. The leader should then ask: "What are we doing?" Invariably someone will answer, "applauding" or "clapping" or "honoring" etc. The leader then points out that yes, it is all of these things, but these are just names for the action.

Again the leader asks, "What are we doing?" Wait a moment and if no answer arrives provide the simplest description: "We're pounding two hands together aren't we?"

A discussion should ensue that marvels at how almost all humans accept this action as a sign of approval. Why? The discus-sion can involve ideas about the two hemispheres of the brain are oscillating in unison, the palms universally used to sooth pain and heal, producing a sound that is an extension of that energy, the col-lision of electromagnetic fields emitting a wash of charged sonic energy bursts that connect to a deep memory of the sound. Or, per-haps, it's just one of those customs that started as a joke and through the ages became the accepted form of showing approval.

All of the ideas relative to applause are right, because no one knows why humans choose to bang their hands together to show approval. If all of them are equally right, then all of them are equal-ly meaningless. But that is not the point. The point is to demon-strate that something as common as applause remains an unresolved mystery to us. It's only one of myriad customs and cultural habits we blindly accept through conditioning.

The alchemical path strives to peal away the blinders and to see the essence of our behaviors. It then works to eliminate unconscious actions in favor of conscious ones full of meaning and purpose.

The point need not be labored. It's enough to stimulate the awareness that there are countless rituals and conventions of behavior that have become unconscious and therefore dead. The alchemist seeks to awaken life.

THE FRICTION DISCUSSION:

The alchemist knows that transformation requires heat. And like the scientist in the lab who may want heat to create a chemical transformation, the heat must be the right kind of heat. There are numerous choices for the scientist to consider. Is it best to use low steady heat, a laser beam, a flash of heat, a pottery kiln, bunsen burner, outdoor grill, sunshine? Similar choices must be considered by the inner alchemist.

The kind of heat and the manner of application defines the gamut of alchemical paths. Some use faster methods with intense pressurized heat; risking a few failed experiments, but getting dramatic results when transformation occurs. Some use slower methods with gentle heat that may in the long run be more reliable, but there's a risk that a few subjects will lose interest, fall asleep, or die before completion of the work. Other methods exist somewhere along the spectrum between the two extremes.

Regardless of the path, there are certain constants that apply to all and relate to the simple laws of physics. We know that heat is necessary, but what produces heat? Fire or various forms of the same element. What produces fire? Friction.

Friction, therefore, is a fundamental component of the alchemical process. And like all friction, it is produced by the resistance to relative motion by two or more surfaces in contact. In other words, by some kind of conflict. An example from life is where two people connected in some way have opposite opinions and tastes. Their natural motion will create a center of resistance and the friction will emit various forms of heat.

Conflict can also be an inner source caused by the contact between desire for an ideal imagined future and the recognition of a less than ideal current reality. The collision of opposing values where temptation meets intention is another particularly effective source of friction.

The entire process of learning is saturated with frictions on large and small scales; encouraging growth through measured encounters with frustration, challenge, competition, and reward.

The creative process is also filled with similar frictions. The purpose of which is to generate the quality and quantity of heat necessary to cause a transformation. Some transformations are mapped out and have a degree of certainty about them. Others are transformations into the unknown. Those involved in these endeavors are hoping their transformative efforts lead to successful creations.

The group by this time has experienced a great deal of friction in many forms. Nevertheless, it's useful and important to understand how friction plays a constructive role in the developing human and how the group can capitalize on this awareness.

The following several key exercises explore friction from an alchemical point of view:

1. Umbilical Day: Team up in groups of three. The three should be people who don't normally gather together.

With a piece of inexpensive rope, they're to tie themselves together, leaving a six-foot length between them. (A two-person group is allowable. Three is ideal because there's more natural friction with three.) They must stay tied together for a full 24-hour period. (Please use common sense and take extra precaustions, carting around a rope between you could not only be difficult, but dangerous.) Afterwards, meet and discuss the element of friction in the exercise.

2. Give yourself an hour to write a haiku about friction.

3. Listen to the kind of music you know you dislike.

4. Commit to doing everything with your opposite hand for two full days.

5. Publicly declare your opposition to something.

6. Go to your favorite ice-cream shop and only look.

Any one of the exercises above will give a definite taste of the kind of heat generated by friction. There are many time-tested ways that alchemical friction is created and all have been used by artists and religious groups at one time or another since the dawn of time. Most are not appropriate within the context of this work, but I'll list a few to demonstrate my point:

1. Forced awareness of mortality
2. Deep massage
3. Fasting
4. Auditory overload
5. Sustained danger
6. Exposure to a foreign culture
7. Long periods of voluntary silence
8. Continual change in the environment
9. Trance states
10. Alterations in breath control

Another thing to consider is that heat in all forms has a tendency to either escape and travel upwards or to ignite other things near it. That's why passionate people tend to generate passion in those around them.

Interestingly enough, most of the meditation forms of mystic religions not only work to create friction, but also work to seal the heat in the body so it won't dissipate and hinder the transformation process. Many of the esoteric yogic postures and meditations, for example, are designed to "lock" the body in such a way as to prevent "leakage" of the energy.

So it's not only important to generate friction to product the proper energy or heat, but it's equally important to make sure the energy doesn't dissipate and thereby render the efforts useless.

THE LAW–OF–NECESSITY DISCUSSION:

Most of us, by now, are aware of "Murphy's Law" which states that if it's possible for something to go wrong, it will and at the worst possible time. I have no doubts that we have all had days that seemed entirely ruled by Murphy's Law. There is another law, similar to Murphy's Law in its placement outside the rational rules of classical physics, that rules much of the alchemical path. This law is known as, The Law of Necessity. The law states that certain aims can only be achieved through the power of real necessity. Real necessity differs from being down on one's luck.

Real necessity is a conscious situation that places the person at a strategic risk.

In the theatre, for example, real necessity is created by the deadline of an opening night. "The show must go on" is a statement born out of the recognition of the power of real necessity. The greater the risk, the more power is generated to fulfill whatever task is at hand.

Sometimes the conditions for real necessity are brought on accidentally. Many people have witnessed or experienced first hand extraordinary feats of strength and endurance, brought on by the simple fact that they did what was necessary. The famous story of the woman who lifted a bus to save her child is a prime example. Life is spiced with these incidences, albeit usually not as dramatic, where necessity draws out extraordinary resources.

The conscious application of this law can create a true and valuable experience. Unfortunate as it may seem, most people do their best living only after they've been informed by the medical establishment they're going to die. Both individuals and groups must be willing to risk, to put themselves on the line, to confront their fears and get to the pure, uncluttered state of necessity. When that occurs, there's the kind of coherency that gets results. It's as if the universe receives a signal through all the static and readily responds.

Good teachers try to create environments where real necessity can emerge. In Martial Arts training for example, there are instances where the sensei (teacher) will arrange for a "guest" to visit the dojo.

The guest will be given the task of putting an advanced student to a test so severe, the student feels they must fight for their life. When the power of necessity engages within the student, the "guest" halts the attack, bows to the teacher and quietly leaves. The student is at a new level of understanding.

A question all good students and alchemists must continue to ask is, "How can I create real necessity?" The answer must be sensible with a risk factor commensurate to the level of achievement. It would be unproductive, for example, for a martial arts "guest" to try and produce that kind of necessity in anyone other than an advanced student.

ALCHEMY AND PHYSICS DISCUSSION:

Science departed from alchemy in its early days in order to satisfy humanity's need for empirical data. Isaac Newton, almost single-handedly, launched mankind into a whole new awareness of his universe. Most astonishing was the fact that life on earth was ruled by very definite laws. Laws that could be put to the test and could produce visible results. It was as if man was coming out of a stupor.

At the same time, alchemy had begun to rely increasingly on fantastic and convoluted explanations of the universe. Alchemists were disliked by the church and some were drawn to the study as a means to rebel against Papal authority. Their work could undermine the world view of the church, but could not supply a cogent replacement. Science, on the other hand, had very palpable gifts to lavish upon civilization and didn't disturb people with questions about the nature of the soul.

The sincere alchemists, mystics and religious seekers, watched in amazement as their work stepped out of time with the new march of science. For centuries it looked as though science and religion were on separate paths destined never to see eye to eye. Then, early in this century, and to everyone's astonishment, science came to a new understanding of the nature of light and before they knew it, quantum physics was born.

Today, science can comfortably make statements that once were considered the ravings of daydreaming mystics. It's acceptable, for example, to view all matter as vibration at a certain frequency; a statement often made by ancient mystics. Einstein's theories, particularly the theory of relativity, shook the foundations of classical Newtonian physics and placed science precariously close to alchemy once again.

I mention this now because the world of art, music, dance, theatre, and virtually all of civilization is currently being affected by the new developments in physics. To put actions into appropriate perspectives, it will be important to integrate these new ideas and contribute to a positive application of them.

VIDEO SPRINGBOARD: MEETINGS WITH REMARKABLE MEN

To proceed with this segment, it's necessary to find a video copy of Peter Brook's film entitled, *Meetings With Remarkable Men*. Several New Age book stores in the larger cities carry it and it can often be ordered through video catalogues. The film, which was produced in 1978, is an autobiographical account of the early life and seekings of the Armenian mystic, G.I. Gurdjieff. While the film remains somewhat flawed as a cinematic effort, it's nevertheless a powerful account of the process of seeking a true ensemble and eventually finding it. Starring Terence Stamp, Athol Fugard, and Dragan Makismovic as Gurdjieff, it's an excellent example of the Hero's Journey; a standard motif in mythology. It also gives credence to the idea of the existence of Mystery Schools, special monasteries dedicated to spiritual development.

The film should be seen by the group and then a discussion should follow either immediately or at the next meeting. Suggested topics for discussion:

1. What was going on at the opening ceremony of the singing mountain? How did that event affect young Gurdjieff?

2. How did books and experiments fail to lead the seekers toward their goal?

3. How did the law of necessity play a role in guiding the young Gurdjieff?

4. Is there any significance to the desert sandstorm and their manner of dealing with it?

5. How does the way Gurdjieff handles himself when his friend, the Prince, is scooped up by this mysterious man contribute to the completion of his search?

6. What is the significance of the long footbridge leading across the gorge?

7. What is meant by Holy Affirming, Holy Denial, Holy
Reconciling? What symbols represent this meaning?

8. What is the purpose of the special movement work
in the mystery school?

VIDEO SPRINGBOARD: MEETINGS WITH JOSEPH CAMPBELL

In 1988, Mystic Fire video and Parabola Magazine sponsored a six-
part conversation with teacher, writer, and noted authority on
mythology, Joseph Campbell. In 1985 and 1986, he and Bill Moyers
met at George Lucas' Skywalker Ranch and later at the Museum of
Natural History in New York to film their conversations. Their meetings which amounted to over 24 hours of film, was then edited and
assembled to become the popular PBS special entitled, *THE POWER OF
MYTH*. At this writing, the series has yet to decline in popularity and
shows signs of becoming a classic.

The enduring quality of the series is due not only to the
insightful questions of Mr. Moyers and the remarkably lucid
explainations of Mr. Campbell, but also to the high quality production values which make use of a wide variety of additional footage
from across the globe. The additional footage, music, and artwork
weaved into the fascinating conversation, creates an engaging and
enormously effective program.

Although the series tackles a multitude of complex mult-cul-
tural myths, it's a testament to the whole project that it stands accessible to nearly everyone who watches it. The subject matter, the
engaging graphic treatment, and its extraordinary accessibility make
it an ideal springboard for ritual theatre.

I prefer to show one tape from *The Power of Myth* at a time, allowing discussion, investigation, artistic reflection, and digestion to occur

before the next one is offered. I allow notes to be taken if participants feel so inclined. It's best to allow the group to go to their notebooks and sketchbooks immediately after the program. This allows
them to express any personal insights, or to jot down ideas, questions, and impressions. When appropriate, the group should sit in a
circle and hold a discussion. I suggest that the leader prepare a list
of questions to help stimulate a lively discussion.

Using the first tape in the series, "The Hero's Adventure," I offer
the following questions as examples:

1. According to Mr. Campbell, the Labyrinth is thoroughly known. What do you think is meant by the labyrinth
and what, according to Campbell, must we do to navigate it?

2. What is a hero?

3. There are many types of heroes. What are some of
the ways that a hero begins his or her adventure?

4. In what way was Moses a hero figure?

5. What are the three temptations of Christ and the three
temptations of the Buddha?

6. How does George Lucas' Star Wars trilogy use standard mythological structures?

7. What is the significance of the "belly of the whale"
motif?

8. What is the first stage of the Hero's adventure?

9. What do myths have to offer?

10. What does Campbell mean by "The influence of a
vital person vitalizes.?"

11. What is the Gaia principle?

12. According to Campbell, what new mythology needs to be developed?

13. How does "The Hero's Adventure" relate to the process of ensemble theatre?

Questions like these should be put forth to the group for each tape in the series. Discussions can range over a wide area, but should be anchored to the particular subject of the video.

After all the tapes have been seen and discussed, the group should agree to a theatrical investigation of the various themes introduced by Campbell. This is an important step for the group. They must now work to decide upon how to narrow a field as vast as myth into a manageable framework. It's impossible for any group to create a piece that addresses all of what's been learned. Limits must be set and it's usually in this area that a group will encounter conflict.

There's no formula for this next phase because it depends entirely upon the chemistry of the group itself. However, the leader can help by suggesting the limitation of a simple three- frame format. The group must limit their work by constructing three distinct frames of reference. The group might choose, for example, to limit their investigation to three myths from a single culture, or three myths from three seperate cultures, or three themes such as The Hero, The Goddess, Eternity, three interpretations of the same myth, etc.

Once the frames of reference have been selected the group can begin to explore and to launch themselves into the process of making a piece of theatre. Many of the exercises and experiences of the group up to this point have prepared the participants to absorb the Campbell material at a meaningful level, which usually makes for very exciting and often very innovative work. Some groups choose to create purely visual collages, some create entire scenarios, some use a mix of narration, symbolic action, song, dance, and poetry. The materials and the exact style will depend upon the needs of the group.

After an initial theatre piece has been completed and there is a sense of completion. The next step is to seperate out those elements in the investigation that are theatrically viable and either refine that piece that exists or select a new theme that can be developed and can become the "thread" by which the group continues to delve into increasingly profound areas of research.

The Power Of Myth video series is available in six one-hour VHS or Beta cassettes. For information write: Mystic Fire Video, P.O. Box 30969, Dept. DL, New York, NY 10011 or call 1–800–727–8433. The six titles in order are: THE HERO'S ADVENTURE, THE MESSAGE OF THE MYTH, THE FIRST STORYTELLERS, SACRIFICE AND BLISS, LOVE AND THE GODDESS, MASKS OF ETERNITY.

HONORING GENDER

Nearly all of the work described thus far assumes an equitable mix of male and female participants. That is the working assumption so that the exercises will apply evenly, regardless of gender. The following exercises, however, depart from that assumption and purposefully separate the genders into their respective groups.

As an experiment one day, I invited only the men to my ritual theatre class and then asked only the women to come to the next class. I had no clear agenda for these classes, only the hope that the separation would reap new and useful data. I knew, of course, that the change in gender composition would refresh the work by virtue of the contrast. I had no idea that the change would be as revealing and as poignant as it was.

The results of these gender separations were astonishing and so obviously valuable to both groups of students that I've incorporated it into my class plan ever since. One young man, for example, had been openly gay for several years, but his involvement in his craft was relatively unfocused and withdrawn. Following his experienced of being honored and accepted by his fellow male peers, his entire energy field transformed. He became involved in gay rights issues in the community, his work in all of his classes improved immensely, and he very soon became the most active and successful student director the community had seen in years.

A young female student had a personal epiphany regarding her identity. She became avidly interested in themes that blossomed into the creation of a one-woman show that went on to New York City and Los Angeles productions. Another young man boldly faced his inner conflict surrounding his relationship with his father and in so doing brought greater maturity and freedom to his acting.

What transpires during such sessions and the consequent results are always slightly different and show varying degrees of benefit depending upon the group. What remains constant, however, is that each group comes away from the experience with a new respect for both genders, a recognition of how gender compositions effect atmosphere, and a powerful understanding of the social conditioning that shape contemporary as well as historical notions of gender.

The following are a few of the exercises that evolved during the experiments. They're designed to challenge, to reveal, and to provoke the participants in a way that stimulates their artistic lives and hopefully encourages the kind of compassion that transcends gender.

NOTE: To cover all the material suggested in these exercises would take more time than is practical for a single session. Therefore, select only a few exercises that seem immediately appropriate to the chemistry of the group, and if time permits, introduce others at later dates. Allow the exercises to take different shapes and for new exercises to emerge spontaneously as the session develops.

HONORING THE FEMALE

This class is focused on the female. It's designed to facilitate the appreciation of women as a gender, strengthen and recognize the special bond women share, clarify perspectives regarding men, and to confront both the feminine and masculine energies within the female.

This is not a class on feminism in the sociological or political sense, although feminist issues and principles unavoidably surface in discussion. The focus is simply to renew the appreciation for the feminine principle and to expand the awareness of the women in the class.

Admittedly, it might be more conducive for a woman to facilitate this unit of study, or a man to facilitate the mens class. I have nevertheless designed the class in such a way that the gender of the leaders of either the male or female groups need not be a factor.

PLAYGROUND

After all the women have gathered in the room, begin to warm up physically and vocally; to take the space fully and to respond to the different atmosphere. When the warm–up is nearing completion, the leader should call out a "freeze" command. While the group remains frozen, the leader says the following:

> LEADER: In a moment you will continue warming up. As you do so, I will count slowly from one to ten. Let yourself grow younger and younger with each count. Let your warm–up transform with the increased feeling of youthfulness. When I get to number ten, allow yourself to be in a grade school playing on the playground. You'll be classmates, somewhere close to seven or eight years old.

As the leader counts, everyone should begin to breathe younger, move and react with more abandon. When the counting finishes, there might be a moment or two of awkwardness, but this usually gives way to a delightful round of playground games. The leader should remain aloof for awhile, allowing the experience to unfold naturally.

What generally happens at this point is a great burst of shared enthusiasm, shared songs, shared stories, teasing, laughter, and affection. Even women who do not share the same cultural base, tend to allow each other to express themselves and to be included in the games. Let this communication continue for as long as it needs to (usually for about twenty minutes) or until there are signs that the imagined reality is dissolving. The leader should then start the count at ten and gradually return to one.

THE HONOR RITUAL

Directly following the previous exercise, the leader should ask the women to take a deep breath and go for an easy stroll around the room. They're to that they're walking in a special place of their own creation. A sacred space where men aren't allowed. Participants should engage their senses fully, saturating themselves in this imag–

ined environment. The leader might urge them to pay attention to the quality of light, the smells, the colors, the textures, and any other structural elements around them. Everyone should slow down and allow the imagination to create this environment.

After several minutes, when the atmosphere has indicated that everyone has established her environment, the women are to silent-ly greet one another, honoring themselves, their mothers, their grandmothers, their great grandmothers, and ultimately the entire ancestral lineage of women. Let this silent ritual unfold in whatever manner it will. The leader should only suggest they begin and then let the event take its own shape.

The results are usually quite astonishing. Many women will reveal their great love and admiration for one another, giving each other permission to elevate their communication beyond the ordi-nary. The ritual itself ranges from simple looks, nods, hugs, and ges-tures to full-blown dance events. Silence deepens the contact and prevents them from having to search for the "right words."

If after a time the ritual appears to be losing steam or looks as if it will not find its own closure, the leader should help by saying, "Very good, now find a closure. Bring the ritual to an end."

At the end, everyone should lay on her back and breathe deeply, reviewing what she has experienced.

YIN AND YANG

After the break, start out on the floor again. Take a few breaths to settle in and the leader will proceed by speaking the following:

Consider the fact that we are born of male and female. Regardless of our biological sex, we are the result of male and female components that have combined to create a being. It stands to reason, therefore, that within you there are female and male energies.

Let's explore these two energies and simply observe the results. See this as a fact finding mission. Just because it seems like a logical assumption that there are both energies, doesn't make it true. And even if you are certain of this hypothesis, use the following exercise to gain additional data.

We'll start with feminine energies, what the Oriental philosophies call Yin. Yin has a number of qualities associated with it. It is passive, receiving, soft, cool, sad, retreating, patient, vulnerable, the moon, the night, the inside; to name only a few.

The front of the body is generally considered the yin side. Sense the yin of the inside portion of the arms, the inside portion of the legs, the vulnerable softness of the belly, the bottom of the feet, the throat. Fully immerse yourself in all that is feminine in the body.

Enjoy being soft, vulnerable, and open. Feel free to change your position on the floor as you search to experience pure yin energy. Allow the female energies to flow through you. (After a few moments) What are the sensations? What are the images or thoughts that attend the yin sensations? Does the yin energy localize anywhere in the body?

(After a few minutes) Now leave the yin and we will explore the yang, or masculine energies. Yang energy is considered to be active, advancing, guarded, hard, quick, angry, hot, impatient, the sun, the day, the outside, and so forth.

The back of the body is considered to be yang. Sense the backs of the arms, the outside of the legs, the tops of the feet, the protection afforded along the back and spine. You may change your position on the floor to help you in your search to experience pure yang energy. Allow the masculine energies to flow through you.

(After a few moments) What are the sensations? What are the images or thoughts that attend the yang sensations? Does the yang energy localize anywhere in the body?

(After a few moments) Now leave the yang energy.

Reposition yourself on the floor if you've moved. Take a clearing breath and then, while sensing the flow of energy in the body, consider the interplay of the two energies, how they each depend upon one another and can be stimulated to take dominance if the need arises.

Take a moment to consider your own nature and ask yourself if you favor one energy over the other. In other words, are you a female of predominantly yin or yang energies? Avoid making any judgements on yourself. Everyone will have a unique mix of energies and each one is capable of adopting various energy modes.

At this point, the leader should invite everyone to sit up and to write in her journals for a few minutes. When the group has had a chance to jot down a few ideas or impressions, the leader should bring the group together for a discussion.

SUGGESTED TOPICS FOR DISCUSSION:

1. Did the space feel different without the men in it? If so, what was the difference?

2. What was your experience as your younger selves on the playground?

3. What was your experience creating your special space where men weren't allowed?

4. What do you recall about the ritual of honoring each other and your mothers?

5. While exploring Yin energy, did you have any specific sensations, ideas, or impressions?

6. What was it like to explore Yang energy? Any specific sensations, ideas, or impressions?

7.   Any thoughts about the blend of Yin and Yang in yourself or in others?

FREE FORM DISCUSSION

Following the discussions regarding the class experiences, the leader needs to guide the discussion in a more philosophic direction. Start by reminding the group that ancient civilizations often worshipped female deities. This was most often the moon goddess. Many early civilizations were matriarchal in structure and women priestesses were considered to be the highest link to the spiritual realms.

The mysterious connection women have to the earth and to the moon were at one time a source of reverence and wonder. The mysteries of female fertility were considered closely linked to the fertility of the land. It became apparent to the ancients that the female menstrual cycle and the cycles of the harvest were both closely connected to the cycles of the moon. This mysterious and wonderful connection became one of many reasons to respect and honor the female of ancient times.

Today, medical science has demystified and reduced the menstrual cycle to a biological function. Its connection to the cycle of the moon, however, still remains a mystery. A mystery so deep, in fact, that it's all but ignored. Let's face it, not many researchers are looking into lunar forces and how it effects menstruation.

These cyclical conditions and the mysterious role as the fertile vessel and the milk–giving nurturer has sustained the feminine mystique throughout history. It's obvious that biologically, women are inextricably linked to the earth and to the forces of nature. They are the vessels of life and we are all children of women.

Perhaps because of the connection with natural forces, women are often considered to be more consciously connected to what psychologist Carl Jung interprets as the power of Eros. Jung uses the term not only as it relates to the erotic, but as it relates to the entire feminine principle, the entire range of instinctual and emotional vitality.

BRIEF DISCUSSION

1. What is it to be female?

2. What is it to be a woman?

3. Why is it that female roommates or co-workers begin to synchronize their menstrual cycle?

4. What other things on earth are affected by the moon?

5. What is meant by the connection to Eros?

6. What is instinct? Emotional vitality?

At this time in history, civilizations all over the globe are forced to reevaluate and to redefine the answers to the above questions. The demise of the goddess cults and the rise of patriarchal societies ushered in centuries of repression and second-rank status for women. Since then, women's mysteries, rather than being a source of reverence and respect, have been ignored, rejected, and even openly attacked.

Today the priestesses have all but vanished and the priests rule. It's predominantly men who have the power in both religious and secular arenas and they've held this dominance for centuries. Women, on the other hand, have had to fight for their rights to have equal medical care, equal pay for equal work, equal consideration in educational and leadership opportunities. And in some cultures, they struggle just to be considered at all.

If there are any doubts as to the state of women in the world, one need only look at television, the most powerful medium of exchange on the planet, and take note of how many programs thrive off the theme of women as victims. And that is just the imagery produced by so-called "developed" nations.

Before getting steamed up about the questions that arise when one confronts the issue, let's back up a bit and look at the way people develop, regardless of gender. Naturally, the first impressions in infancy carry a great deal of importance, setting the foundation for later childhood where conscious and unconscious behavior modeling occurs. Throughout most of childhood, the overwhelming majority of these impressions and behaviors occur in the home. Clearly we tend to repeat the dynamics established in the family or in surrogate families.

The process of socialization occurs next. The child explores and adjusts to the behavior of other children, usually under situations of guidance, and the behaviors are adjusted to achieve perceived goals and win friendship. Next, after years of conscious and unconscious learned behavior, the child enters adolescence and begins to perceive the discrepancies between the model construct of childhood and the realities of the adult world. Caught between the two, the adolescent seeks to bond with peers and to define personal and social identity around those bonds.

Gradually, the process of maturity demands greater and greater levels of responsibility until the adult, as a parent, unconsciously relies on the parental reflex behaviors of earlier learned behavior. The cycle continues, bending in odd directions now and again, but usually holding fairly close to the early parental models, for generations.

This is an oversimplification of the developmental process. Nonetheless, it serves to depict the cyclical nature of human behaviors and explain why so many experts insist that some destructive cycles need powerful intervention techniques to be redirected toward constructive ends.

Leaving this reminder of childhood development for a moment, let's look at the current dynamic of patriarchal domination. Perhaps, as Esther Harding suggests in her book *Woman's Mysteries*, patriarchal societies came into being when men discovered they could use their physical strength to secure personal, as opposed to strictly communal, possessions. Physical dominance and territorial imperative have often accompanied the urge to accumulate possessions. This would explain why women themselves came to be considered as possessions to use and discard at will.

But if women were possessions, why the threat? Why the repression of priestesses? Why the overwhelming shift from female or non-gender gods to male god figures? Why the historical demonization of women as wicked creatures who must take the blame for the fall of man? If men wanted possessions and could take them by force, why the need to dominate women? These questions are worth pondering and considering carefully, by both men and women. For if an answer is found, then the future of women and their place on earth will look considerably brighter.

Let us return to our developmental cycle, to the earliest days in our development. If we look at the obvious, usually discarded as obvious and therefore not subject to scrutiny, we might come upon a useful perspective. Let us consider that, obviously, we're created and sustained within the body of a female. Her glands, her food, her womb becomes dedicated to the service of allowing a tender, fragile creature to develop.

Then, in infancy, we are completely and utterly dependant upon the mother for care and nourishment. Because of our pre-natal connection with the mother and because of her own love, much of the truly comforting early impressions upon an infant are established by the mother.

Imagine being a tiny baby, being held by our mother that to us is a giant, comforting, God-like female creature. Imagine hearing the heartbeat of this huge being that gave you life, seeing this huge face that is nearly as big as your whole body as it breathes and coos and smiles. And then imagine sucking life sustaining nutrients either from the breast or from a bottle supplied by this same wonderful giant. If we carefully consider this compilation of impressions, we can begin to comprehend how powerful the feminine principle is to all of us, especially on a primal subconscious level. To an infant, the mother must truly be a powerful loving Goddess, our first deity.

Could it be that both sexes, as they mature, remain somewhat afraid of that all powerful deity? Could it be that men sense deep down that the female has the power to reach past all of his adult constructs and disturb the deep subconscious memories stored in the distant recesses of the brain? Could it be that if men prove women to be weak, they'll have vanquished that early goddess, and have conquered the frustrating helplessness of infancy? Could it be that the repression of women could stem from something so simple and obvious as the misguided expression of male independence?

Or, if we stay with Jung's interpretation, considering women associated with Eros, we must then consider men to be more closely associated with Logos. (Logos being reason, intellect, logic.) Men strive toward these attrubutes and work to fulfill themselves in the pursuit of Logos, often sacrificing their emotional and spiritual lives in the process. However, since we are made of Yin *and* Yang energies, the interesting thing to note is that the standard associations of Eros and Logos are only the outer representations. A fascinating twist to this Jungian view tells us that inwardly, the female has a core essence of Logos and men have a core essence of Eros. This dichotomy, somewhat poeticically, also presents a dilemma for us all.

Could it be that we're afraid of our inner core? Are some men perhaps confused or even ashamed of their emotions, their instincts, their feminine aspects? Could this be because the outer biological equipment, the Yang mask so to speak, does not seem to support their deeper inner life? In their effort to define themselves in con-trast to women, is it possible that men feel ashamed and somehow dysfunctional if they contact the inner resources?

And aren't some women equally confused by their inner strengths? Some women have demonstrated amazing courage in times of crisis, or display an uncanny gift for logic and detailed mem-ory. Some women sense an inner urge toward Yangness, toward out-ward aggressive adventure in the world. These and many similar impulses seem to contradict much of their life that tends to be ruled by emotions, instinct, and the feminine principle. These contradic-tions can be disturbing and if left unreconciled can lead to fear and confusion.

According to the ancient Taoists, the most powerful force in the universe was Yin. Still, Yin needs Yang in order to exist, and Yang needs Yin to exist. They are interdependent in a dynamic union. According to the observations of the Taoist sages, the qualities of patience, flexibility, softness, and other similar Yin qualities are far superior to the more forceful energies of Yang. The Taoists observed that in nature, the bending reed will survive the strong winds while the brittle unbending one will break.

The power of Yin, then, so naturally resilient, might very well be seen as a threat. Perhaps men subconsciously recognize the brittle fragility of Yangness and fear the power of Yin in women as they fear contacting the Yin within themselves. Perhaps, to maintain a semblance of equilibrium, some men feel compelled to repress women as a means to repress the feminine within themselves.

War is certainly one of man's most effective tools of repression. Women and their children are always the victims of men who use brute cruel force to battle for territories or possessions. War reasserts masculine principles, albeit destructive ones, and thereby negates the values of true masculinity as well as the feminine. But as we've seen time and time again throughout history, the patient ones, the flexible ones, the Yin ones, always win in the end.

There are, of course, some women who have a lot of Yang in them and others with a lot of Yin. Just as there are men with a lot of Yin and others with a lot of Yang. Each individual chemistry is different and subject to change under certain conditions such as aging, external conditioning, and voluntary transformation. According to the Taoists, Yin and Yang are just energies. They need to be balanced within each individual in accordance with the individual nature of the person and the greater forces of natural law.

Unfortunately, most of the world sees only the social definitions of male and female. Women have weaker bodies so they have been relegated to roles deemed appropriate by male-dominated cultures. Self definition, therefore, is rigid and consequently repressive. For the modern female, the liberation of women is an important issue to consider.

Most of the perspectives that incorporate the goddess aspects of the feminine principle come from a view that sees women as sensual, mysterious, emotional, instinctual, vital creatures with a strong rational core. They become, in essence, the goddess.

There's another perspective that considers the goddess imagery and the whole notion of the feminine principle to be a male invention. It's as if men have molded and created a creature to fit their imaginary image. The molding occurs through control, through art, fashion, and advertising. In short, through mythmaking.

The body of woman becomes the projection screen for male fantasies and "woman" doesn't really exists aside from the creation supplied by man. Because of this, females have become fetish objects created and maintained throughout history by a continuous global art campaign that extends as far back as the Greeks.

The advertising world is changing somewhat, but historically, as in today's world, men have created the image of what is "female." Some of their creations seem harmless and agreeable to women. Some fashion inventions, however, appear somewhat dubious at closer inspection. After all, it was men who created foot binding, corseting, hair dying, high heels, cosmetic surgery, and a whole host of other questionable items of enhancement.

Does this support the notion that men have usurped the other gender and recast it as an object to be dressed, shaped, and transformed according to their latest whim? Have women encouraged these things as they hoped to expand their limited avenues of self-expression and self-definition? Perhaps women through the ages were aware of their goddess powers and used art as a means to allow men to worship their image and thereby reduce male anxieties regarding the need to reconcile the feminine principle within themselves.

Then again, it may be as simple as Yin owes its very existence to the existence of Yang, and visa versa. One would perish without the other. Without darkness there is no light and, of course, without light there's no darkness. One quality makes possible the other. Perhaps this dependency, this binding familiarity breeds a kind of contempt responsible for the undeclared war between the sexes.

We're flawed beings, no doubt about it. We're still "in process," wrestling with our place in the universe. Perhaps by honoring the female and working to understand the male, women can diffuse the perceived threat they pose to men and still continue to make their contributions to the world through whatever means they choose.

Suggested topics for discussion:

1. Is there an undeclared war between the sexes? If so, how does it manifest?

2. Are women dominated by men?

3. Are men afraid of the power of women? If so, why?

4. Is the goddess image a true reflection of the female principle or a creation of male fantasy?

5. Are both sexes struggling with their gender identity?

6. Do you agree with those who think that the inner core of a woman is masculine?

7. What men attract you? What men repel you? In what way is attraction and non–attraction related to your inner self?

HONORING THE MALE

This is a class exclusively created for the men of the group. It's designed to facilitate the appreciation of men as a gender, to strengthen and recognize the special bond men share, to clarify perspectives regarding women and to confront both the masculine and feminine energies within the male.

Playing together

Start with a vigorous warm–up, taking in the whole space. Notice any internal differences that might exist in the new environment. When the warm–up is nearing an end, the leader should call a "freeze." With everyone frozen the leader should say the following:

LEADER: In a moment you'll continue warming up. As you do so, I will count slowly from one to ten. Let yourself grow younger and younger with each count. Let your warm–up transform with the increased feeling of youthfulness.

When I get to number ten, allow yourself to be in a grade
school playing on the playground.   You'll be classmates,
somewhere close to seven or eight years old.

As the leader counts, everyone should begin to breathe younger
and to move and react with more abandon. When the counting finishes, there might be a moment or two of awkwardness, but this usually gives way to a delightful round of playground games. The leader
should remain aloof for awhile, allowing the experience to unfold
naturally.

What generally happens at this point is a great burst of shared
energy. The group usually breaks up into teams or into smaller
groups wanting to play a variety of games. The games are usually
competitive and are designed to demonstrate skill and endurance. If
someone's feelings get hurt, there may be teasing but it's usually
mixed with a healthy dose of genuine concern.

Some youngsters are shy and withdrawn. Others are clearly not
shy and work hard to engage their favorite friends in some fun.
Some youngsters get mean, and the leader must be on the lookout
for a scene that might cross the line and become abusive or injuri-
ous.

Let the play unfold naturally until the group shows signs that
the imagined reality is dissolving. The leader should then start the
count at ten and gradually return to one.

THE HONOR RITUAL

Directly following the previous exercise, the leader should ask the
men to take a deep breath and go for an easy stroll around the room.
They're to imagine they're walking in a special place of their own creation, a sacred space where women are not allowed. Only men are
free to come into this space.

Participants should engage their senses fully, saturating themselves in this imagined environment. The leader might urge them to
pay attention to the quality of light, the smells, the colors, the textures, and any other structural elements around. Everyone should
slow down and allow the imagination to bask in this environment.

After several minutes, when the atmosphere of the room indicates everyone has established their environment, the men are to silently greet one another, honoring themselves, their fathers, their grandfathers, their great grandfathers, and ultimately the entire ancestral lineage of men. Let this silent ritual unfold in whatever manner it will. The leader should only suggest they begin and then let the event take its own shape. The results are usually quite astonishing. Many men will reveal their great love and admiration for one another; giving each other permission to elevate their communication beyond the ordinary. The ritual itself ranges from simple looks, nods, hugs, and salutations to full blown dance events. Silence deepens the contact and prevents them from having to search for the "right words."

If after a time the ritual appears to be losing steam or it looks as if it won't find its own closure, the leader should help by saying, "Very good, now find a closure. Bring the ritual to an end."

At the end, everyone should lay on his back and breathe deeply, reviewing what they have experienced. After four or five minutes, the leader should announce a ten minute break.

YIN AND YANG

After the break, start out on the floor again. Take a few breaths to settle in and the leader will proceed with the following:

> LEADER:
> Consider the fact that we are born of male and female. Regardless of our biological sex, we're the result of male and female components that have combined to create a being. It stands to reason, therefore, that within you there are female and male energies.
>
> Lets explore these two energies and simply observe the results. See this as a fact-finding mission. Just because it seems like a logical assumption that there are both energies, doesn't make it true. And even if you're certain of this hypothesis, use the following exercise to gain additional data.

We will first explore what the oriental philosophies call Yang, or masculine energies. Yang energy is considered to be active, advancing, guarded, hard, quick, angry, hot, impatient, the sun, the day, the outside, and so forth.

In terms of the body, the back is considered to be Yang. Sense the backs of the arms, the outside of the legs, the tops of the feet, the Yang–like protection afforded along the back and spine. You may change your position on the floor to help you in your search to experience pure Yang energy. Allow the masculine energies to flow through you. Place all of your attention on the masculine energies of the body.

(After a few moments) What are the sensations? What are the images or thoughts that attend the Yang sensations? Does the Yang energy localize anywhere in the body?

Next, we'll explore feminine energies, what the Oriental philosophies call Yin. Yin has a number of qualities associated with it. It's passive, receiving, soft, cool, sad, retreating, patient, vulnerable, the moon, the night, the inside, to name only a few.

The front of the body is generally considered the yin side. Sense the yin of the inside portion of the arms, the inside portion of the legs, the vulnerable softness of the belly, the bottom of the feet, the throat. Fully immerse yourself in all that is feminine in the body. Enjoy being soft, vulnerable, and open. Feel free to change your position on the floor as you search to experience pure yin energy. Allow the female energies to flow through you.

(After a few moments) What are the sensations? What are the images or thoughts that attend the Yin sensations? Does the Yin energy localize anywhere in the body?

(After a few moments) Now leave the Yin energy. Reposition yourself on the floor if you have moved. Take a clearing breath and then, while sensing the flow of energy in the body, consider the interplay of the two energies, how they each depend upon one another and can be stimulated to take dominance if the need arises.

Take a moment to consider your own nature and ask yourself if you favor one energy over the other. In other words, are you a male of predominantly Yin or Yang energies? Avoid making any judgements. This isn't a quantifier of sexual preference or a contest over who is more macho. Every being has a unique mix of energies and each is capable of shifting energy modes at any time.

At this point, the leader should invite everyone to sit up and write in his journal for a few minutes. When the group has had a chance to jot down a few ideas or impressions, the leader should bring the group together to facilitate a discussion.

SUGGESTED TOPICS FOR DISCUSSION:

1. Did the space feel different without the women in it? If so, what was the difference?

2. What was your experience as your younger selves on the playground?

3. What was your experience creating your special space where women were not allowed?

4. What do you recall about the ritual of honoring each other and your fathers?

5. While exploring Yang energy, did you have any specific sensations, ideas, or impressions?

6. What was it like to explore Yin energy? Any specific sensations, ideas, or impressions?

7. Any thoughts about the blend of Yin and Yang in

yourself or in others?

FREE–FORM DISCUSSION

After these questions have been addressed, the leader should guide the discussion in a more philosophic direction. The following is a list of questions and generalizations about men. They're augmented with brief elaborations aimed at stimulating discussion. The leader should facilitate the discussion, skipping over or including any and all questions and statements useful in provoking an understanding.

What does it mean to be a man?

Men have a multitude of role models from which to choose. The history of the world, by and large, is the history of men and their adventures. Men today, however, are faced with a redefinition of what it is to be a man.

Who are your male role models?

Most men have inadequate role models or discover during this discussion that their models were actually borrowed from fantasy and not genuinely grounded in reality.

What is the Yin within?

Consider the possibility that although men are composed of primarily masculine qualities, they have within themselves a core femininity. It's this inner core that men hope to match in the finding of the ideal mate. The inner core seems to be in direct contrasting ratio to the outer psyche. The cliche of the burly man wanting to marry a dainty little lady is an example of this general inclination. Just as men in touch with their feelings and their artistic qualities often surround themselves with strong- willed masculine women.

What happens when women become moms? Is there any way to untie this knot?

Women, of course, present a formidable problem for men. Because of the powerful influence of "Mommy," men instinctively want to rebel against that power and to define themselves with the father. At the same time, they long for the same comforts and services supplied by a mother and often encourage the very maternal care they're rebelling against. This situation becomes a self–fulfilling double bind.

Are men scattered or just curious?

Another generalization about men (keep in mind that is all these quick observations are) is that unlike women, who have the ability to assume constancy in their focus, men tend to wander from one thing to the next. They're forever skipping along from one object of desire to another, from one pursuit to another, from one philosophy to another; a source of great consternation to a woman who hopes to focus her lover's attentions on her. Discuss the validity of this generalization.

What is the mystery of the male?

Men are thought to be known and women to be mysterious, but any man will tell you that he's as much a mystery as a woman. He has extraordinary dreams, desires, and deeply mysterious qualities. Discuss men's mysteries and then approach the question of women's mysteries.

Have women been repressed by men throughout history?

This usually sparks some very interesting and heated conversations that range from the expressed notion that women have never really been repressed, to the opposite extreme where certain men feel ready to make great sacrifices in order to make up for the past sins.

Why is it that men rarely talk to one another?

Men are at best wary of one another. They seek deep comradeship and the comfort of like minds, but their communication usually remains shallow and brusk. Men seem to lack a context for developing deep friendship.

Women, by comparison, seem to make friends easily in almost any context. To men, women seem to all have a special bonding ability allowing them to make friends with other women within a matter of minutes. While they admire and envy that trait, men are often shocked to see how equally quick women can withdraw from friendships.

Men value loyalty, action, and the kind of friendship that stands the test of time, conflict, and great adventures. Unlike women who have the ability to use conversation as a conduit toward friendship, men bond by *doing* things together. The most lasting male friendships usually develop through shared adventures of one kind or another. There are exceptions to this, of course, and these too should be discussed.

Are men threatened by women?

Based on the historical interplay between the sexes, it would appear that men are often threatened by women. Why is that?

Why must women fight for equal rights? Why are women victims of rape? Borrowing from the earlier discussion (Honoring the Female) about human development, it seems fairly obvious that the first deity was a woman. Yet, western culture has adopted predominantly male oriented religions. Is there a connection?

Is it necessary for a man to break away from and reduce the "Mother Goddess" in order to become a man?

Women are initiated by the forces of nature. Their bodies assume adulthood with the onset of menstruation and they find at least some biological fulfillment in serving as a vehicle for new life. Men, on the other hand, have no natural initiations that compare. Yes there is the hormonal changes associated with puberty, but there is no biological sign that signifies arrival into manhood.

Men have to initiate themselves. In healthy societies, the adult males create rituals to psychologically induct the young men into the adult world. A rite of passage, in the form of an initiation, is created to bridge the step from early adolescence to early manhood. If these initiations are not upheld or get distorted or disrupted, men may flounder for decades looking to create for themselves this psychological step. They may try to find it in their relationships to women, a pursuit that usually produces disastrous results. Only a man deeply rooted in himself can achieve real constancy and coherent focus in life.

How can a man become deeply rooted in himself?

The universe is a swirling play of opposites within opposites.

Today, more than ever, men are faced with the challenge to redefine themselves and to consider what might be their relationship to other men and to women in the future.

Why does it seem that there's an undeclared war between the sexes? Perhaps the dependency on one another breeds contempt. If this were true, the contempt needs to be replaced with respect. How?

We, all of us men and women, are flawed beings. We are still "in process" as they say, wrestling with our place in the ever expanding universe. Perhaps by honoring the male, contacting fellow men, and helping to facilitate understanding between men and women, men can diffuse their compulsion to dominate, end their reliance on war as a means to settle disputes, and continue to make their posititve contributions to the world.

THE TEXT AS CONTEXT AND SPRINGBOARD

Words can have enormous power. And like anything powerful, the effective use of words can be dulled or distorted by overuse or misuse. We all have a tendency to talk too much, to abuse the language, to waste our words in needless chatter. Consequently, our daily language loses its power to shape, reveal, and inspire us.

These exercises aim to reawaken the impact inherent in everyday language, to recharge our relationship to text, to reveal the importance of context in verbal communication, and to remove the boundaries normally imposed by words.

THE CIRCLE SPEAKS

The first exercise is a simple one that many people have experienced before. To begin, stand in a circle facing the center. One person says a word and the person directly to the left, says another word, any word, whatever wants to pop out at the time.

At first it's stressful and somewhat comical as the wo rds tumble out in random sequences, making odd associations and evoking unusual images. Gradually, with a little effort on everyone's part, the words will come out more easily and begin to adopt somewhat of a structure. The sentences formed, regardless how banal, will be poetic by virtue of the very nature of how they were formed. What's most interesting is to listen to the ideas move from individual words, to short phrases, to longer and longer phrases, until a definite theme begins to emerge. At that point, it's not unusual to have the sensation that the entire circle is speaking.

After several satisfying rounds in this one direction, try the same exercise in the other direction. Is there a difference between the two?

SUBLIMINAL FABRIC

The assignment is for everyone to come in with at least five comments that they overheard. These comments, statements, slogans, whatever, must be things that normally they wouldn't have consciously heard. In a restaurant, for example, it is often convenient to tune out the conversations that might be drifting over from nearby tables. This exercise asks that you tune in and select some sentences. Do this in a variety of situations.

On one level, the exercise heightens your awareness to the barrage of verbal input that must be subliminally processed all the time. Just because we consciously tune it out, doesn't mean a part of our awareness isn't dealing with whatever is heard. It also will reveal how random words can link up with associations to create new and creative contexts.

Write down and number each comment (or "line" as we'll call them). Then, in separate piles, put the number one's, the two's, and so forth. Once all the lines have been collected, break into five groups and each group take a stack of lines.

Everyone will have one of their lines as part of the total collected in their group. Don't mention the situation or source of your line. Instead, treat them all as "found text," and therefore open to creative interpretation. All previous associations they have will only be inter-

Dream Theatre — The Journal Comes to Life

PHOTOS: MORRIS LAMONT

esting in retrospect.

Once an order has been devised, everyone will have fifteen minutes to arrive at a presentation of the text. Explore the text through a variety of means: Chanting, singing, whispering, growling, different characters, different situations, movement or dance, telephone calls, radio announcer, and so forth. The first ten minutes should be devoted to the free-form exploration, the last five minutes should be used to solidify the transitions, the timing, the flow of the sequence, and everything relative to the presentation of the selected associations.

When the fifteen minutes is up, the leader can announce an order or the group can choose an order. Then, one by one, each group should enact their presentation for the group. After everyone's finished, take a moment to review the text of each group and ask the participants to reveal where their phrase actually came from.

It can be very illuminating to observe how close or how far an exploration can go from the original context of the words. What's interesting to recognize is that the subliminal data we don't consciously regard gets implanted nevertheless in the subconscious. Discuss the general nature of these subliminal comments and how they're processed by the subconscious.

CREATING THEATRICAL/PERSONAL METAPHORS AND MYTHS

DREAM THEATRE

Dreams can be a source of great inspiration and revelation. They've been a mystery and a delight to mankind since the dawn of time. Many of man's most valued inventions were concocted in the dream state. And dreams unite us as a species. Nearly all of us can relate to the fears of a nightmare or flying dreams or dreams that seem so real, waking reality pales by comparison.

Understandably, dreams were of great interest to early psychiatrists attempting to map the human psyche. Freud considered them useful, but diminished their importance as primarily "wish fulfill-ment." Carl Jung, the contemporary of Freud and a major contribu-tor to the field of psychology, considered dreams to be much more than mere wish fulfillment. He saw them as a major key to unlock-ing the secrets of humanity's innermost nature. He considered the dreamscape reality to be one of great universal as well as personal significance. Through dreams, Jung found it was possible to chart the course of therapeutic treatment.

Unlike therapy situations where dreams are psychological tools, this class uses the dreamscape as a portal into theatrical creativity. It's not uncommon that the characters, situations, and locations of the dreams provide understandings that were previously masked. The emphasis, nevertheless, is on the unusual perspectives and ideas afforded us by creative freedom of dreams.

As preparation for this class, participants should be asked to keep a dream journal in order to write down their dreams. If some report they don't remember their dreams, encourage them to keep a notebook by the bed and to start jotting down even small bits of dreams. The presence of the book usually stimulates the memory and soon the person may become inundated with remembered dreams.

Everyone should bring the dream journals to class. Even if they know they're not going to use it that day. It often happens that someone else's dream triggers a dream memory and having the jour-nal handy insures it won't be forgotten.

The class starts off simple enough. Everyone enters the space, does a brief warm up and sits down in a circle. Participants wait patiently while the group gathers at a slow and silent pace. Finally, the facilitator asks the group, "Does anybody have a dream?"

The person or persons who have a dream (the dream can be a recent one, a recurring one, or one from the past) to share with the group, should raise their hands. The dream need not be an entire one with a convenient beginning, middle, and end. Dream fragments are often more potent than entire epics.

The facilitator must choose from the raised hands. The person selected then proceeds to describe the dream experience to the group. It's important that the person describing it does so in a first-person present tense. That is to say, while describing the dream they should re-live it, as if narrating it as it happens. An example of this is:

"I am swimming underwater and notice that it's a huge swimming pool. In the distance, swimming towards me is a small umbrella. I'm afraid of the umbrella and as it gets near me, I sing this weird song: (*singing*) Elbow Bilbo whoooosh–whoooosh. As I sing, a beautiful cloud sprouts from my thigh and floats upwards and out of the water."

The group should listen intently, empathizing and enjoying and visualizing as the dream is being described. The facilitator should make sure that the person sharing the dream doesn't distance him or herself from it by making unnecessary commentary or attempting to entertain the listeners.

When the dream description is finished, the dreamer is allowed to cast his or her dream from the people present. The dreamer can play him or herself or another part or even stand outside the enactment. Since this is a dream, people need not be cast in normal ways. Using the dream narrative above, for example, someone could be cast as the umbrella or the whole group used to recreate the pool, or the dreamer could take the role of the cloud. There are no limits so take the lead from the dreamscape and be unconventional.

Once everyone's cast, the dreamer should direct the participants in their roles. They should be allowed a few moments to rehearse their parts and then, after a few minutes, the dream is enacted. Afterwards discuss which parts of the enactment seem most provocative. Take those parts and recast or redirect the action to get a different angle on the scene. Allow for improvisation to occur and, by all means, let things go in the direction they want to go.

After everyone feels satisfied that they've fully enacted the dream, discuss sensations, revelations, ideas, or anything else that was stimulated by the experience. When that discussion is finished, sit again in a circle and again the facilitator will ask if anyone has a dream.

After several dreams have been enacted, it's sometimes fun to combine dreams to make a small play. Decide upon the flow of the action, the roles to be played, the use of space, and the transition devices. Then launch a final rehearsal followed by a performance. It's not uncommon that everyone in the group is participating and there are little to no spectators.

THE OBJECT EXERCISE

A week prior to this class, the participants are asked to bring in two objects that have some meaning for them. The objects may not be extremely fragile, large, or valuable.

Participants are to take one of their objects and to simply warm up with it in their hands. Afterwards, the leader should instruct them to engage in an abstract sound and movement journey with the object. A sound and movement journey could start anywhere and go in any direction. It might start, for example, with an attempt to be the object or to be a dancer inspired by the object or by making the sounds of the emotions associated with the object and letting that lead to movements. There really are no rules except that the object must be incorporated and related to in some manner.

Let this exercise continue past the first layer of frustration. If participants feel they've exhausted their ideas regarding the object, the leader should remind them they're only now on the threshold of creativity and must keep working. They have only now come to the end of their personal cliches and might be ready to discover some-thing quite remarkable about their object and their process.

In nearly all cases, this renewed effort to engage in an organic dialogue with the object results in some very creative and non-cliche action. Let this effort continue for five minutes or so and then bring the exercise to a close.

Allow a few moments for the group to write in their journals if they feel so inclined and then repeat the exercise with the next object. The second object exercise should proceed as it did with the first object, except this time, they're to search for a "sound and move-ment metaphor."

The process of finding a metaphor is identical to the original exploration at first: A sound and movement exploration with the object ensues, going from one idea or experience to the other in an associative flow. The difference is that, at some point, the person must halt the associative exploration and settle upon one repeatable sequence of sound and movement. This sequence is then fully invested with feeling and commitment.

As the person repeats and refines the sequence, they must endow it with greater and greater commitment until, regardless of the external abstraction, the internal emotional content is focused and unambiguous.

To give you an example, I had a student once who brought to class a small plastic shovel. The exploration he worked on was dynamic and full and yet too vague to be effective as a metaphor. With a little prodding on my part, I got him to connect to the dig-ging movements he was doing around the chest as if digging, really digging into his heart; matching gesture with concrete personalized imagery. Immediately I saw a vast improvement and I watched, spellbound, as he transformed his piece from something banal into a thrilling and gut wrenching work of art. His digging motions took on mythological proportions as he found deeply personal connec-tions to this simple action. With each scoop he seemed to be dump-ing out more shame, more hurt, more self-disgust, until finally after an amazing and intense journey, he stood, unmoving, shovel in hand, radiant, and astonishingly whole.

The class need only witness one of these metaphors and then the whole level of work lifts considerably. After ample exploration time, each participant should demonstrate their object metaphor. Constructive feedback from the group is encouraged if it's aimed at helping the person reconcile their inner sensations with what's being communicated externally.

At the end, the leader should explain that the day's work was exploratory and a means to teach the process. They must now use what they know to create and present a finished solo theatrical object metaphor. They can use one of the objects they brought to class or find a new one. I allow them to use music if it does not overwhelm the action of the piece. The due date is up to the leader, but it should be within two weeks of this exercise to be effective.

BREATH — THE UNIVERSAL LINK

ZEN TARGET BREATH

Although inspired by the Oriental meditation practices of Zen Buddhism, there's nothing particularly exotic about this exercise. In fact, it's been used by acting and singing teachers in various forms unrelated to Zen for ages. The technique then is obviously universal. Personally, I like to connect it to Zen, because it raises questions about Buddhism that I find useful in terms of my goal of expanding cultural awareness. It also reminds everyone that breath is a universal link, a fundamental human action that is appreciated, studied, and even utilized spiritually all over the world.

The beauty and consequent difficulty of this exercise is its utter simplicity. People, especially talented people, often have a predisposition toward complexity. If an exercise does not feel difficult or complex, the value quickly drops and the attention given the work quickly wanes. It's important to challenge the participants to master simplicity. I often ask them to ask themselves if they can't do justice to a simple exercise, how can they expect to master more complex ones.

The assignment is to write or find a poem or piece of writing that moves you in some way. It should be no longer than a single page, double spaced. Once a selection has been prepared, sit in a chair with the spine long and balanced. Let the stomach relax totally. This isn't as easy as it sounds, particularly for women who've been conditioned to hold their stomachs in at all cost. Rubbing the tummy sometimes helps to relax it. Next, they're to breathe in a gentle relaxed way, focusing their attention on their breath and sensing when the impulse to breathe begins and ends.

After a few minutes of this (it's best to avoid staying at this stage for very long as it can quickly lead to a meditation session) have everyone read their selection out loud. Invariably, there'll be one extreme where people force the words in an attempt to sound dramatic or the other where people drone the words in order to match their notion of simplicity, and everything in between.

Let this first rendition play out. Afterwards, ask that the group look at their text and select the operative words from each sentence or phrase. Operative in this case means the word that best reflects the meaning of the sentence. Then invite them to read this sentence several times, putting emphasis on the operative word as they do so.

After several trials, remind them that emphasis can be made with melody, texture, and the attack on the word. Ask that they look again at their word and limit their emphasis to a logical syllable of that word, so they don't feel the need to emphasize the entire word each time. Inform them that they may change to a new word if their first choice did not effectively express the true intent of the phrase. After these latest adjustments, ask that they try the phrases again.

This time there's usually more authentic readings of the material. Ask that they don't bury their faces in the text, but rather look out at an imaginary horizon line. After a few more readings, ask everyone to take a few minutes and go through their selections and underline the accent syllables of each target word they choose.

When they're finished or near enough to finishing, repeat the directions and invite everyone to practice their readings. Stop the practice after a few minutes and explain that now, they're to concentrate on only one simple thing, they must sit aligned and simply breathe in a deeply relaxed manner and read their text aloud.

No gesture, no dramatics or comic turns are allowed. By the same token, no droning zombies are allowed either. Instead, everyone is asked to find that meeting ground where the breath is relaxed and supportive and the words are alive with expression without a lot of unnecessary interference.

Relish the inhale, exhale and speak, paying attention to subtle emphasis given to the target syllables and simply observing any nuances occurring as the entire selection is read aloud. After several repetitions of this, have everyone read their selections out loud for the whole group.

One at a time, let everyone simply sit and read their work. Make any corrections necessary and insist that participants keep their renditions simple, but alive.

Once the pressure of being watched enters the equation, there

PHOTOS RIGHT AND BELOW: MARK OLSEN

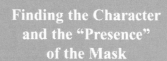

**Finding the Character
and the "Presence"
of the Mask**

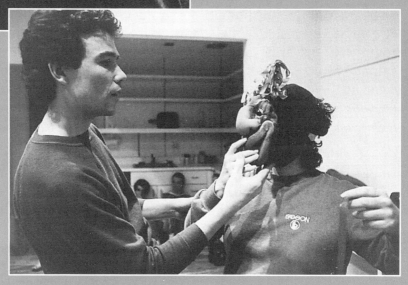

PHOTO: CAROL LEWINSTON

are distinct problems that arise.   First of all, people might feel shy and frightened by the attention they get.   Secondly, some people might feel distorted by the attention and overproduce out of excitement.   Thirdly, some of them might fidget and openly display expressions of irritation, which is a sign that the stored anger is being released by the deep relaxed breathing.

Regardless of the manifestations, let the text selections speak for themselves.   Imagine the belly as a target with the bull's-eye being the navel and another target being the syllables of emphasis.   Then, while keeping one part of consciousness monitoring the breath, let the other simply speak the text.

As simple as it may seem in this description, the actual exercise is far from lifeless. The various texts flow beautifully from these vulnerable open bellies, untainted by unconscious gestures or cliche attempts to express anything other than the values inherent in the words themselves.

CHARACTER MASKS

Having had some experience with life masks as a foundation, the group is ready to experience the poignancy and hilarity of character masks.   Greek and Roman theatre made frequent use of character masks in both their legitimate and fringe theatre endeavors.   The theatre most associated with character masks, however, is the Italian commedia dell'arte.   Many stock characters such as Arlecchino, Pantaloon, or Pulcinella were recognized by the distinct shape and color of their masks.   Unlike the large and somewhat cumbersome masks of previous epochs, Commedia character masks were leather half-masks that allowed the actor to speak and improvise freely.

I enjoy the Commedia masks very much and I have often employed them in my performing and teaching. Currently, however, due to availability of new materials and the latest advances in the world of movement theatre, I hold a much broader definition of a character mask. I now define a character mask as anything that can be attached or worn by the body that evokes the presence of a character.

It could be an odd-shaped bucket, a torn shoe, a construction of papier-mache, or plastic cups, virtually anything. The charm in freeing the materials from the tradition of wood and leather is that we're reminded of the fundamental aliveness of all things, even everyday objects. And when given a little shape or just a bit of highlighting, the greater, more mysterious character presence of these objects is drawn out.

This "presence" is a critical feature in character mask. Therefore, I usually start this unit of work with a discussion on the difference between decorative masks and character masks: Many masks are produced as purely decorative objects, meant to be hung on walls or displayed for aesthetic purposes. Unfortunately, some people, usually foreigners ignorant of native customs, mistake character masks for decorative masks. They end up hanging wonderfully expressive character masks on their walls as decoration, never allowing them to come to life. This is a tragedy to me. I am always saddened to see strong character masks sit lifelessly on a wall.

I am equally upset, however, when I witness performers who wear decorative masks as if they were character masks. Dancers are particularly guilty of donning masks and then dancing as if the mask were an extension of their costume, which unfortunately in many cases it is.

A character mask should invoke the presence of another being, another rhythm and mood sensibility that must be reckoned with in some way. It's not meant to draw attention to itself as an art object. Instead, it's a kind of lens, helping to focus a specific group of characteristics.

Decorative masks are meant to enhance the aesthetics of a room, to give an exotic or mysterious flair to the atmosphere of a particular space, and perhaps in some cases to honor the culture or country where the mask is made. They're usually highly stylized, beautifully painted or carved, and somewhat two-dimensional. A beautifully painted mask may be nice to look at, but it may also be void of character spirit.

A good character mask is somewhat of a mystery. There's no formula that can insure that a mask creation will transcend decoration and become a lens. Nevertheless, it's possible to say in general terms that a good character mask is one in which the design elements don't dominate or extinguish the expression. We the viewer should not be so taken with the design of the mask that we lose sight of the total presence of a character. Therefore, my only dictum regarding the construction of masks is: Don't sacrifice expression for design.

Native cultures the world over have long used masks for religious and ceremonial purposes. Some of them are decorative and used to evoke a sense of celebration and "other worldliness." Some masks, on the other hand, are considered sacred because they're thought to have the power to invoke deities. These masks are usually more aligned with what I consider theatrical character masks. In cultures where theatre and the dominant religion are still closely linked, the sacred masks are particularly vibrant. I'm thinking primarily of the remarkable Balinese masks, and the masks of the traditional Noh drama in Japan.

While most masks, ceremonial and theatrical, are carved from wood or made from leather, modern theatrical maskwork has lately departed from those traditional materials. I had the good fortune at one point in my life to perform as a member of the Swiss Mime/Mask troupe, Mummenschanz. They made masks out of writing pads, toilet paper, Jerry cans, pastry dough, balloons, and much much more. I've constructed a number of masks myself out of a wide variety of materials: paper, buckram, plastic, wire, latex, gauze, glue, leather, nylon, rubber, aluminum . . . you name it and I probably made a mask out of it.

I tend to like foam rubber, because it's lightweight, takes punishment, and breathes fairly easily. My experience has proved to me, however, that it's not the material that's of primary consequence. Instead, it is the creation of something that looks and acts like a living creature and can be relied upon for repeated showings.

MASK DEMONSTRATION

I bring in about ten masks and allow a few students to hold them and to see their construction. After answering any questions about the masks I prepare for a brief demonstration. I tend not to demonstrate the masks myself for fear that what I do will too strongly influence the student. Occasionally, and very rarely, I will don a mask and demonstrate a few fine points. My experience is that a teacher's style of mask playing can sometimes limit the student's own creative impulses.

What I prefer to do is to take two volunteers and put the masks on them as I talk them through a few paces. The first mask I have anyone wear in the demonstration is a simple paper plate mask. This is a paper plate with an expression drawn on it and string attached to hold it to the face. Very simple. There aren't even any eyeholes.

The purpose of these paper plate masks is to demonstrate to the class that even something as limiting and mundane as a paper plate can come alive in surprising and usually hilarious ways. This also helps to ease the anxieties in some students who may have a fear of any assignment that threatens to become an "art project."

THE PAPER PLATE MASK

Take two plain white paper plates and draw on each very simple expressions with a bold black marker. By simple, I mean draw only the eyes, eyebrows, nose, and mouth. Make the expressions contrasting. I often rely on two plate masks where one expression has an anxious worried look and the other has a smirking smile with both eyes cocked upwards and to the side a bit, expressing an ambiguous mix of insecurity and lasciviousness.

Get two chairs and two volunteers. Sit the volunteers down and tie the plate masks onto their heads. *Do not let the volunteers see the expressions on the mask!* The leader should then stand back and ask one of them to move while the other stays fixed, then reverse that after a moment or two. After they both have had a moment to try out some movement behind the masks, ask that they keep the masks flat and fully exposed to the spectators while they try to determine the relationship between them.

In all cases it takes very little time for the mask players to discern from the reactions of the spectators what indeed the relationship should or at least could be. Gradually, as the confidence improves, a good mask player will begin to refer to a vocabulary of postures that seem to support the relationship supposition. When it's obvious the players have a sense of their character, the leader should stop the exercise and invite them to remove the mask and look at the expression.

It's either a complete surprise, which indicates that the player was playing the contra-mask (all masks have several contrasting expressions within them) or it happily verifies the player's suspicions.

AVAILABLE CHARACTER

This exercise is useful only if there's a quantity of available masks to use. First lay the masks out on a table or on the floor in order to display their expressions. Ask the class to browse through looking at the masks and then to select one they think they want to try out.

If two people want to use the same mask, assure them they'll have another chance at it but that one should find another mask. When everyone has selected a mask, they should sit down and create for themselves a private circle of concentration where they can commune with the mask.

Some masks have peculiar limitations. I often construct a mask where the vision is obscured or the player is looking out of the mask's mouth. Sometimes a mask will cover most of the body and demand unusual physical contortions or breathing will be restricted. Make sure that the participants are fully aware of the challenges in their mask and that when they compensate for the limitations, they do so safely and effectively.

After five minutes of contemplation, the leader should ask that they all turn away from the center of the room and put on the mask. Ask that everyone make sure the mask will fit well enough to keep it from falling off or from breaking. When everyone has secured their mask and there is silence and stillness, ask that they stand and then turn toward the group.

Mirrors are helpful at this stage in order to guide the players into an understanding of how their body works to enhance or detract from the expression. However, I usually limit the mirror work to ten or fifteen minutes. Too much mirror awareness becomes addictive and reduces the chances for contact with other masks.

I then ask them just to play, to encounter each other and communicate in silence; or, if they have a half-mask, in limited sound. It's best at this stage for the leader to withdraw, leaving the group to work their way into the characters and out of any residue of self-consciousness.

Let the work unfold free-form, taking breaks from the mask from time to time to watch the others and then re-entering when it seems appropriate.

When the improvisations start to lose momentum or when the group begins to waver in attention, ask that they turn away from the center of the room, remove the masks, and return them to their original spot. Once everyone has had a small break, they can select another one and repeat the exercise.

NEWLY CREATED MASKS

After some exposure to a few available masks, the class should be given a week to come up with some of their own mask creations. On the assigned mask day, the leader should organize a brief showing of each mask so that everyone gets a chance to see them all. Then, just as with the available masks, they're to put on their masks and move about the space relating to one another and letting situations unfold. (Be especially careful if wearing masks with little or no vision or those that restrict breathing)

At the end of the session, discuss the various scenarios that emerged through the masks. Then, set them all on the table and let the class discuss them one at a time. The discussion should be limited to the subject of expression and its relationship to the design elements in the mask.

Discuss any problems with the masks themselves. Very often the elastic is not sufficient, or the eye holes have been poorly placed, or the mask is simply not practical and cannot be worn without falling apart.

The leader should encourage experimentation and by all means invite them to make as many masks as they like. For those who have a penchant for overdesigning their masks, insist that they start with a paper plate or with a rumpled up bag with eye holes torn out and features held together with tape. When they begin to see the value

PHOTOS: MARK OLSEN

Newly Created Masks with objects

of simplicity and soulful handling of the materials, their masks will improve immensely.

Next, let smaller groups of four or five put on their masks and improvise while being observed by the class. The leader should remind the players to keep the masks available to the spectators and to keep their interplay slow, clear, and simple.

These observed improvisations are always somewhat awkward. But they're also very charming and allow the masks to respond to the performance situation. After each improv allow the class to react to what they saw. In each improvisation will be a seed for an etude or study. It's up to the observers to inform the parformers where the seed was revealed.

It might occur, for example, that at one point the masks were vaguely milling around as if confused or frightened and someone watching the improvisation realizes it would be effective to use the behavior in another setting like a police station.

The point is, that the participants may be so concerned with playing their character and responding to the others around them, that they'll have missed the chance to focus the improvisation. Feedback and suggestions engages the observers so they don't just sit back as an audience, but help the mask players begin to recognize the potential of their individual masks and their group dynamic.

As each improvisation occurs and is discussed, it should become obvious that character masks need direction and feedback. Scenarios need definition. Instant improvisation, although challenging and useful in producing the seeds of an idea, is definitely limited.

The next step therefore is for the groups to take a seed idea and develop it into an etude that has a beginning, middle, and an end. The leader should decide upon the time frame for this. Some situations may call for half an hour preparation before performing it, others may allow two or three days, or a week.

One assumes that the longer the allowed preparation time the better the results, but that's not always the case. Very often the immediate pressure of a short time span produces remarkable work. I suggest experimenting with several lengths of preparation time and see which unit of time best suits the chemistry of the class.

Have a presentation of the scenes and allow the leader as well as the observers to give feedback to each performance group, giving as much detailed and positive feedback as possible. After the exercise is complete, the class can choose to work on another version of their presentation, create a new piece, or go on to the next exercise.

The final application of work for the character masks is to team up in groups of two or three and present a highly exact and well-constructed performance. The teams are to spend ample time in preparation so that the scenarios they perform have a finished quality to them.

The performance is wide open as long as all of the following restrictions are met: Each of them must have a clear beginning, middle, and end. Music is allowed *if* it doesn't dominate the scene. The scenes can be narrative or abstract and should be around five to eight minutes long. The themes and locations of the presentations must be chosen from the following list. This insures a focused approach to the work. It also keeps the emphasis on the performing of the characters rather than on the cleverness of the plot.

Players can mix and match between these two lists, selecting no more than three selections from each list:

THEMES	LOCATIONS
Transformation	Bedroom
Saying Goodbye	Elevator
Overcoming FearIce	Cream Store
Nightmare	The Theatre
Revenge	Holy Shrine
Blind Love	At the Races
Saving a Life	Library
Love Conquers All	Hospital
Going Home	Restaurant
Crime Does Not Pay	On a Bus
Pleasing the King	Art Museum
Exposing Cruelty	Court of Law

PHOTO LEFT : MORRIS LAMONT

PHOTOS: MARK OLSEN

The Smallest Mask

THE SMALLEST MASK

Jacques Lecoq, the renowned French movement teacher, refers to the clown nose as the mask. I tend to agree with this perspective, because once it's applied to the face, it acts like a mask by affecting the internal rhythms of whoever is wearing it. With a clown nose on, a person cannot help but become a character. The nose cannot be ignored.

The added beauty of the clown nose mask is that it transcends status expressions. It allows the wearer to adopt virtually any kind of behavior, including deeply sincere behavior, without any regard to social status. It's a simple and powerful statement of anarchy, foolishness, wisdom, and idiocy all rolled into one tiny mask.

The following are descriptions of class exercises I like to use in teaching clown. Clown character work is highly personal and extremely revealing, that is why it is important to create an atmosphere where students can feel free to take risks and to allow the secret, vulnerable part of themselves to emerge. The search for the inner clown is a serious one and needs a combination of strict demanding leadership from the teacher and an atmosphere of loose derisive freedom, simultaneously.

These clowns are not clowns who perform acrobatics or make silly faces and parade their traits. They are not festival clowns. They are fully developed characters with exaggerated and absurd points of view. Their body rhythms and shapes and manner of speaking and relating is sheer, joyous, lunacy. It is divine lunacy, however, rooted in exquisite timing and the struggle to overcome the obstacles of the "normal" world.

The lunacy of this clown world's collision with our world is impossible to describe. Suffice to say that the freedom and relief from needing to do it right and the joy of finding and living true to the world of the clown is the most liberating and most poignant of all character work. I have seen painfully shy folks jump into these exercises, open some new door within themselves, and emerge bolder, more confident, and beaming with joy.

WAITING FOR INSPIRATION.

In this exercise, the person puts on the red nose, stands in front of the class and lets anything happen. I encourage each character to strip away unessential qualities and to be increasingly vulnerable and simple.

This exercise immediately separates those who are liberated by the lack of structure from those who desperately need structure. All of them, however, will begin to display flickerings of their essential clown nature. This information is good for the participant and for the leader, both of whom must work hard to focus and then set free the inner clown.

The participant's only rule, and this goes for each and every exercise, is not to hurt themselves, the props, or any of their fellow participants. Otherwise, the field is wide open and they are invited to literally follow any and all impulses.

TRYING TO BE FUNNY

In this one I ask that each character, one at a time, stand in front of the class and try to be funny. This is the hardest thing in the world to endure for both performer and spectator. The lesson, however, is indelible and well worth the pain. This exercise demonstrates how pathetic it is when someone tries to be funny. The effort of trying robs the clown of its necessary buoyancy and vitality. The effort to be funny will crush the fragile comic timing and flatten any chance of genuine laughter to emerge in the spectators.

GETTING SERIOUS AND SINCERE

This exercise is designed to prove to the student that clown characterization comes from a deeper place than one might assume. True comedy comes from the sincere struggle of the clown who just happens to live by his own rules. The clown is fearless even in his fear and is the most positive creature even in despair. In this exercise, I have the students, again one at a time, sing a serious ballad, or do a serious monologue, or recount a serious childhood event, or express their anger at whatever notion seems to be current. When the nose is allowed to do its work, the juxtaposition of serious intent and the absurdity of this big round red nose creates the foundation of a comic character.

When the foundation of the clown is recognized, it's sometimes useful to give the character a name or an occupation or both. With these titles the clown can begin to develop a mental attitude, a vocabulary, and a physical characterization. The character can be drawn to certain props and costume pieces and very soon will develop a "look" that is unique and appropriate to the character.

Regardless of how the clown is shaping up in terms of character, all clowns at this stage I call "can–do clowns." That is to say, they're completely convinced they can do anything to which they set their minds. They're fully and completely in charge of the situation. The only hitch is that they haven't the slightest idea how to go about doing anything. They invent complex ways of accomplishing the simplest tasks and delight in their accomplishments no matter how idiotic.

The leader need only set up a few improvisation situations and the clown characters will take it from there. They will go in whatever direction they want and create total hilarity in their attempts to do whatever is asked of them.

CLOWNS FROM HELL

In this exercise, I set the clown characters to a task like cleaning up the workspace, or finding a lost quarter, whatever.

They understand that they're not to follow any logic and to only do the task according to the absurd rules of their bizarre character. They also know that at some point I'll call out the words, "Go Odd!" At this command, they kick their activity over into hyperdrive, they go completely wacko and let chaos reign complete. They've been warned beforehand that although they're going out on the edge, they must still be aware of not hurting themselves or anyone else in the space.

After a minute of this high–pitched frenetic energy, I call out, "Come back!" several times until the level returns to its original pitch. They're to continue from where they are with their task until I next choose to call out, "Go Odd!" I usually do four or five shifts to give them a chance to fully explore the two states of their character.

THE ENSEMBLE MASK

This is a concept that grew out of some experiments I've done with a large piece of fabric. I use a rectangle of Qiana, the dimensions of which are approximately 20 X 25 feet. I like Qiana because it flows like silk but is much cheaper, doesn't wrinkle, and stands up to the handling of a group of people. Other fabrics could be used, I suppose, like parachute silk or cotton. I just have a preference for Qiana.

I refer to this huge swatch of fabric as an ensemble mask because, like any mask, it transforms the inner rhythms of everyone who comes in contact with it while serving as a conduit for expression. It has a character of its own can stimulate remarkable creativity and cooperation among the group.

Before doing anything, the group should remove all jewelry and their shoes. This will keep the Qiana clean and prevent snags in the material. Next, I have the group carefully unfold the fabric, lay it on the floor face up and then "breathe" it awhile. Breathing is simply getting everyone around it or on opposite sides of it and lifting it into the air and then allowing it to billow naturally as it falls slowly back to the floor.

It helps if the leader has had some previous experience with the fabric, but it is by no means a prerequisite. Because of my experience, I'll direct some of the early experiences in order to demonstrate the capabilities of the fabric and to clarify points of care and safety. Afterwards, I withdraw and let the group explore for a while on their own.

When the group has gathered a modicum of confidence in handling the fabric, the leader should announce that for the next hour or so, everyone must remain silent, communicating through the fabric and with each other without the use of words.

The limitation of silence is frustrating at first, but it soon becomes liberating as the group establishes their signals and learns to listen to the ensemble mind over individual desires. This exploratory stage is wonderful and can go on for many hours.

Next, I introduce music into the atmosphere and let the group work with the fabric as they respond to the music. I prefer instru-

The Ensemble Mask

PHOTOS: MARK OLSEN

Making Something From Nothing, — atmosphere is important.

The Ensemble Mask in Performance

(*PERICLES*, HOUSTON SHAKESPEARE FESTIVAL.
DIRECTED BY CAROLYN BOONE.)

PHOTOS THIS PAGE: JIM CALDWELL

mental music so that the words of a song don't interfere with the imagery being created with the fabric. I make sure that there are contrasting music choices to stretch the imagination and to keep the creativity fresh.

After ample exploration time (a subjective measure that must be decided by the leader), it should be explained that the leader will leave the room for half an hour and when he or she returns, the group must have created a short performance piece with the ensemble mask. They're to remember all they know from traditional maskwork, whatever discoveries were made in the exploration, and any ideas that may surface while working, and apply it to this assignment.

It's very satisfying, for everyone, to create a piece that has a beginning, middle, and end with a huge ensemble mask. The material becomes the star of the show and the players facilitate the flow of imagery as dictated by the demands of the fabric and their imagination. This egoless performance experience can be extremely satisfying and a valuable education in ensemble theatre.

MAKING SOMETHING FROM NOTHING

We are beings that like to create. We also do our share of destroying, to be sure. But most of man's noblest intentions are linked with the urge to create something of value, something that will improve life, that will inspire or educate, that will stand the test of time and contribute to humanity.

At long last, after physical, vocal, mental and emotional preparations, after countless exercises, the group must now face the ultimate creative challenge. The assignment is simple: Create a fifty minute ritual theatre event using the tools you've learned and incorporating your individual and collective creativity.

The great thing about this assignment is that a total win/win situation. Regardless of the outcome, working together on a project of this magnitude can teach a group more than any collection of exercises could ever hope to teach. This is the final test. Can the group really function as an ensemble? Can they go beyond discrete classroom studies and create something that they all feel is worthy of their understanding?

What follows is a guide to assist in the creation of this ritual. Although each group will inevitably invent their own process, the guide can help to structure the work and thereby help the group to avoid some of the more common pitfalls.

FINDING AN AIM

The first step in creating a ritual is to clarify the intention behind the creation. The question to ask is, "What's the aim of this ritual?"

A music ensemble often finds an aim by gathering together under the umbrella of their common tastes in music, or their common training, or their common reaction for or against the current fads in music. And so it must be with any group that wishes to function as an ensemble. There must be a unifying aim in order to sustain the focus.

A true aim for a group is a rare and precious thing. Usually, a group will form under the aegis of producing a service. The service itself then may have a variety of aims related to profits, safety, information sharing, and so on. Often a group is formed with the lure of mutual reciprocal benefits including, but not limited to, making money. There is nothing intrinsically wrong with making money, but that is only a half-baked aim. Most people have difficulty getting to the next step, the step that focusses in on the ultimate uses of the money.

Any group, particularly a group endeavoring to produce ensemble theatre of any kind, must find an aim meaningful enough and powerful enough to sustain them. This isn't an easy task. Very often the leader must help the group sort through a sea of personal problems and unresolved issues before the first glimmers of a true aim begin to emerge.

Some of the time-tested aims formulated by ritual groups in the recent and ancient past are related to one or more of the following:

HEALING

RITES OF PASSAGE

HONORING THE DEAD

HONORING THE NEWBORN

EXPOSING HYPOCRISY

CELEBRATING LIFE

Each one of these aims could also be focused even more clear-ly. Healing, for example, could be focused with the following questions: What kind of healing? Why? For whose benefit?

Is it healing or more specifically purging? Or perhaps, confessing? Or is the aim to motivate toward healing?

Questions are used to help redefine the common denominator from a general interest in rituals and theatre, to a common denominator so precise it can cut away all obstacles that stand in the way of the creative process.

As the questions get refined during the process of creating a piece of ritual theatre, the work will become increasingly more unique and specific. If everyone remains committed to the stated aims, the ensemble will soon find itself powered by enormous resources unleashed by the increasing clarity of their goal.

Once everyone has landed on a clear mission for the ritual, they stand at the threshold of unbridled creative inspiration. Then, upon enactment of a successful piece of ritual theatre, the ensemble may enjoy the unparalleled sensation of having accomplished something truly meaningful.

FRAMING

While the aim is the process of becoming more securely formulated, the group should create some "frames" for the piece as mentioned in the Joseph Campbell exercises. Frames are devices that can help to separate the project into manageable units. There are countless ways to frame something and at the outset they can be purely arbitrary. I've witnessed one ritual that was framed into four distinct kinds of dreams; another was constructed into three units of Yin, Yang, and the two combined; another was constructed according to childhood, maturity, old-age, death, and after-death; another was constructed according to movement from the intellect, movement from the heart, movement from the primal center, and movement from the funny bone. The choices are endless.

The first decision, therefore, should be to choose the structure of the piece in terms of definite framing devices. Once this decision has been made, the process becomes immediately easier.

DEADLINES

The next step is to set deadlines for when certain phases of the project are to be completed. Start at the opening and work backwards as you consider the necessary rehearsal time, when masks or special props need to be introduced, when music needs to be selected, when publicity of any kind needs to be arranged, and so forth. Pay special attention to the time and place of the opening.

Openings are important because they pull the work through death valley. All projects, regardless of scale, seem to have a burst of energy in the beginning that carries the work forward. After a time, when the build up of demands are all in the foreground the initial energy has been spent and the work will bog down into a version of Death Valley; things look grim if not utterly hopeless. That's when an opening and a series of deadlines help artificially to boost the energy output. The energy shifts from inspiration to fear of humiliation and finally, if things go well, back to inspiration again.

If there is no deadline for a performance, the creative process won't have the necessary pressure it needs to sharpen the research and rehearsal and to focus the resources of everyone. Therefore, if a performance hasn't been scheduled, create an arbitrary date and stick to it.

RESOURCES

Take an inventory of available resources and from that deduce how realistic the initial goals seem to be. If the planning stages called for a huge ladder, seven video monitors, two cats, three Max Ernst prints, and a tub of tapioca, now is a good time to assess from where these items will come. If a flyer is going to be made to announce the ritual event, find out who has graphic skills or access to printing materials. Cover as many bases as possible. Are costumes needed, masks, recorded music? Try to think of everything that will be needed.

After all the available resources have been listed, look at what remains and discern how much more can be done to secure any other resources, without sacrificing valuable rehearsal time. Delegate and share the work load and try to give jobs to those people who have an aptitude for a particular task.

THE ARC OF THE EVENING

Even with a good framing device, it's necessary to consider how the evening's ritual is going to unfold in terms of energy and mood. Is the work going to progress along the very effective and time-honored Aristotelian lines where the ritual must open with something captivating, then introduce characters and expository elements, build gradually to a climax, fall to a resolution?

Perhaps the shape of your ritual will want to be more circular, where the opening turns out to be the ending. Perhaps the shape will be a constant barrage, or a long contemplative journey, or a series of climaxes with no resolution. The choices are endless.

It may seem premature to select a shape before the work has even begun, but my experience has proven that having a shape that later gets reshaped, for whatever reason, is far better than roughing it through without any notion of the arc of the evening. It is difficult to prioritize moments if they're not assigned weight according to the desired shape of energy.

OBJECTIVE

An objective is a unit of action unto itself, although it's related to the overall aim or what could be called the super objective of the ritual. The objective is, in fact, a smaller more manageable aim that is entirely rooted in the moment to moment reality of the ritual. For example, if the stated aim of the ritual is to Honor the Dead, the participant can't spend every moment trying to do something in the abstract like honoring. Instead, it must be clear to the player what the immediate action is, perhaps, drawing a perfect circle in the sand. Drawing a circle may in fact contribute to the aim of the ritual, but the objective for the player is to draw a perfect circle.

A series of objectives will flow one into the next and allow the player to be fully engaged in the action of the ritual, without the burden of trying to carry the weight of philosophic overtones. Each participant must trust that their focused contribution in the form of specific objectives adds up with all the others to create a fusion that indeed serves the aim of the entire ritual.

Many a worthy ritual has been doused by the vague and weighty actions of participants who are mesmerized by their own intent to fulfill a noble aim. The results are deadly, not unlike some musicians who destroys Beethoven with their reverence. It's as if they are playing music with one part of their attention and then shouting "I am playing Beethoven!" with the other. The combination kills any chance of allowing the music to enter into the hearts of the listener on its own merit.

An audience isn't stupid. They sense when a performance is on the sell and they instinctively withdraw. "After all," they say to themselves, "if the performance was any good why must they try and sell it?" Therefore avoid being pretentious or sanctimonious. It's a strong temptation in ritual work, particularity if the aim of the ritual is deeply important to the players. A noble aim is very necessary, but it happens to be an aim and not a given. So play the singular objectives and let the superobjective, like the symphony, enter into the hearts of the listener.

This is not to imply, however, that rituals cannot be direct or even confrontational. Quite the opposite. Subliminal messages and symbols drenched in beauty are great, but so are stark, roaring, raw, and shocking elements of the street. Play only what can be accomplished, the objective, and let the aim emerge as the resonance.

PREPARATION

Many different kinds of preparations are necessary to insure the success of a ritual. The individual players need to prepare themselves internally in order to align with the aims and objectives of the piece.

This is particularly important if the player is still wrestling with issues or sees the ritual differently. Once the train starts moving, you're either on it or not. It's best to prepare the internal states to commit fully to the work at hand. Half–hearted commitments will sabotage the whole effort and ultimately be self defeating.

It's also necessary to prepare the rehearsal and performance space. Both must be cleaned, decorated or arranged in order to evoke the correct mood, and checked for security and safety of both players and public.

Preparation of the ritual itself means plenty of rehearsal. In the early stages it's best to work on one frame at a time. Building the objectives, moments, and images that fill one frame and lead to the next one. Transitions of any kind, including getting furniture or props or even costumes on and off should be rehearsed. And, of course, the ritual should be rehearsed in its entirety numerous times to establish the overall tempo and to allow the players to sense the arc of the evening.

FILLING THE MOMENTS

Even in rehearsal, the players should practice filling the moments. To fill a moment means to commit fully to every second of action as well as every moment of inaction. It means finding ways to link up internally with every external event while at the same time remaining extremely alert and responsive to the flow of energy between players.

A moment un–filled falls flat. It's as if the player is skipping over moments in order to get to the ones that feel good or that are fully understood. Each moment must be given full presence. That's not to imply every second of the ritual is equally important or needs to be saturated with the weight of pith.

Filling a moment is related to the quality of attention. One can behave with ease and even toss off a throw–away line with quality attention.

It comes down, as do most things, to love. If there is love for each and every moment of the ritual, the moments will be filled and the energy will flow and expand to encompass everyone.

PRESHOW RITUAL

It has long been a tradition in the theatre to create a pre-show ritual. Not all theatres do this and not all plays would necessarily benefit from it. Nevertheless, those plays that create and nurture an effective pre-show ritual stand a better than average chance of achieving ensemble coherency once the play (or ritual) has begun.

The ritual before the performance of an ensemble work should provide the players with a means to settle nerves, to share feelings, and to reaffirm the commitment to the ensemble and the overall aim of the work. It shouldn't be elaborate, but should be deep and sincere enough to do the job.

Although I have participated in and have helped create numerous pre-show rituals in my time, I wouldn't presume to instruct anyone on how to create one.

It should be the special invention of the people involved and grow organically out of the impulses and imaginations of the members of the ensemble.

I would only add that once a ritual has been established, keep it in place and only change or improve upon it if there's a long run and the original ritual shows signs of losing potency.

THE GUESTS ARRIVE

How the audience enters the space, where they sit, what they sit on, what the atmosphere is of the space, and everything connected to the arrival of the audience is part of the whole event and should be considered.

Some ensembles have walked the audience through a labyrinth of images before arriving at their seat. Some ensembles greet each and every member of the audience and personally usher them to their pillows on the floor. Some invite the audience to sit anywhere they like, even on the stage if they desire. One ritual event gathered the audience in the center of the performing space, circled them while dancing and playing music and then rushed them to their seats. The possibilities are endless.

It is important to remember that the point is not to be clever, but to take responsibility for the sequence of impressions that eventually lead up to the actual start of the ritual. Treat the audience as honored guests, for it is their presence that completes the circle of energy necessary for a successful ritual.

CLOSURE

End the ritual with closure for both the audience and the players. A gesture, sound, curtain call, tableau, anything can serve as the closure device. The performers need this in order to step out of their circle of concentration and to return to ordinary reality.

Audiences need it too. Not supplying this can erode the trust established between the performance and the performers. The audience has been served a feast of impressions, they have in effect gone through a hypnotic induction and a soulful sojourn and they will need for the magicians to say, "The magic is over. When you hear the snap you will awaken and remember everything."

Find the appropriate closure that will free everyone from the spell, but not the resonance of the spell. You want them to digest and to radiate the fullness of their experience. Close the curtain in actual or metaphorical manner to leave them in their stirrings. The journey is over and the vehicle should land clearly and securely. This stirring in their soul is important and can do much to awaken the lift the spirit.

FINAL WORDS

I feel a strong desire to say a few final words to you, the unique individual who has, for whatever reasons, made it to this point; the end of the text. Endings, even for an acting text are a bit like saying goodbye. Therefore, forgive my words if they seem sentimental or rhapsodic. (Why do I suddenly feel like Polonius?)

This book is a guide, a reference, a menu, and even a bit of a map. Common sense, safety, and a dose of humor are essential to all facets of the work herein contained. It is my heartfelt wish that you and others like you who have a nagging desire to devote yourself to a worthy endeavor, manage to create, if even for a short time, moments of true ensemble flow.

This can be accomplished within the limitations of almost any situation, including film. The challenges are different, but the principles are the same. If you have absorbed the values and the training elements suggested by this text, you will be respected and perhaps even admired by audiences and fellow actors. Hopefully, you will have gained courage and the kind of insight that will mature and season your work.

If you are lucky and manage to be a member of a company dedicated to ensemble work, it is my hope that you stay together long enough to mature as a group. When a group matures, when it assumes a character, an identity, a way of working, a style, and the beginnings of a body of work, it has evolved beyond just a group that enjoys moments of ensemble flow. It becomes a true ensemble, a beacon of artistry and hope. Each actor in this instance becomes the actor with a thousand faces.

When that level is attained, neophytes and young artists will come to the performances or even to the studio looking for inspiration. Audience members will become loyal fans, discussing nuances and avidly, passionately, soaking up all that you present. With perseverance and luck, the work may nurture an audience that will allow the ensemble to develop and take risks.

When and if this happens, new challenges will emerge. The expectations will continue to mount. The struggle to exceed or at least match each new success will enter the equation; as will the struggle to sustain the creative fire. And do not be deceived, it is a struggle, it is a sacrifice, it is hard, yet thrilling work.

And as in all things in life, the only constant is change. The complexion of the group will change, the focus of the work will change, audiences will change, times will change, technology will change, approaches will change, and through it all, the group must remain fluid to survive and grow with that change.

What sustains the ensemble through all the struggle and flux is the same thing that sustains the audience and motivates them to leave their computers and televisions, to buy a ticket, get a sitter, or make whatever effort needed to make their pilgrimage to the theatre. What sustains it all, is the presence of that invisible, ineffable, something; that unique and sublime artistic liftoff. It's the launch of the players and the audience into the unknown that we crave. It is also the rare, but inspirational electric flash of a life–changing insight in the dark, a shuddering "aha" moment. The epiphany.

And, at the very least, it is the subliminal message sent by all groups who dare to surrender to the power of working smoothly, openly, ecstatically, triumphantly, together. The message, simple but powerful, can be described in three words. Three words that can calm the fear, still the chattering mind, encourage the desperate, and activate the complacent. These three words are simple and unas-suming, and carry enormous power.

The words are: *This is possible.*

SUGGESTED WARM–UP SEQUENCES

The following are suggested sequences for applying some of the exer-cises described in part I. These are useful as warm–ups and have lim-ited value in terms of expression. All of them, however, can be aug-mented with other elements such as music or dance to provide more creative applications. Work on these warm–ups sensibly and with regard to ability and readiness to do the more demanding ones. Feel free to adjust the order or overall number of exercises as the need arises.

I

Circular Warm–through

Sparkling Hands

Tossing the Dice

The Dragon

Painting the World

Bear Crawl

Rockefeller Center

Tortoise on its Back

Squat

II

The Slap Out

The Shake Out

Squat

Circle Warm–Through

Circle Run

Home Base

III

Yogic Full Breath

Clearing the Six Dimensions

Moving Walls

Circular Warm–Through

Breath Machine

IV

The Slap Out

Circular Warm–Through

Solo Arm Wrestle

Squat

Squat Hops

Singing Push–Ups

The Bridge

The Back Arch

Frog Jumps

ACKNOWLEDGMENTS

To begin, I'd like to acknowledge three individuals whose interest and support for this book motivated them to allocate grant funds necessary to complete the photographs: Mr. Robert Edwards who serves at the director of the Penn State University Institute for the Arts and Humanistic Studies, Ed Williams, Associate Dean of Graduate Research at Penn State University College of Arts and Architecture, and Dan Carter, Chair of the Penn State University School of Theatre.

I'd like to thank photographer and director Tom Polumbo, for his photographs and the walking tour of The Actor's Studio. Eric Picard, graduate and Penn State University photography major deserves thanks for helping out during the on-site photo shoot.

Special thanks to Sidney Berger and the University of Houston School of Theatre for allowing me to continue my research and experiments in this unusual and non-traditional direction.

My most humble and enthusiastic thanks to the true heros of this book, the many students who have studied with me and opened their hearts to this work through the years at the following schools and institutes:

The Open Center, New York City

The Omega Institute, Rhinebeck, N.Y.

Ryerson Theatre School, Toronto

Carnegie Mellon University Department of Drama, Pittsburgh, PA.

Wright State University Department of Theatre Arts, Dayton, OH

Antioch College Theatre Program, Yellow Strings, OH

University of Houston School of Theatre, Houston, TX

Webster Movement Institute, St. Louis, MO

Penn State University School of Theatre, State College, PA

I'd like to acknowledge the many teachers who've directly and indirectly contributed to the content of this book: Samuel Avital, Richard Armstrong, Paul Baker, Robert and Anne Britton, E.J. Gold, Jonathan Hart, Ann Mathews, Stephan Niedzialkowski, Moni and Mina Yakim, and many others.

Particular thanks to Glenn Young and the staff at Applause Books who've shepherded this work through the years and guided it to this completed edition.

MONOLOGUE WORKSHOP
From Search to Discovery
in Audition and Performance
by Jack Poggi

To those for whom the monologue has always been synonymous with terror, *The Monologue Workshop* will prove an indispensable ally. Jack Poggi's new book answers the long-felt need among actors for top-notch guidance in finding, rehearsing, and performing monologues. For those who find themselves groping for a speech just hours before their "big break," this book is their guide to salvation.

The Monologue Workshop supplies the tools to discover new pieces before they become over-familiar, excavate older material that has been neglected, and adapt material from non-dramatic sources (novels, short stories, letters, diaries, autobiographies, even newspaper columns). There are also chapters on writing original monologues and creating solo performances in the style of Lily Tomlin and Eric Bogosian.

Besides the wealth of practical advice he offers, Poggi transforms the monologue experience from a terrifying ordeal into an exhilarating opportunity. Jack Poggi, as many working actors will attest, is the actor's partner in a process they had always thought was without one.

paper • ISBN: 1-55783-031-2

DUO!

The Best Scenes for the 90's

Edited by John Horvath & Lavonne Mueller

DUO! delivers a collection of scenes for two so hot they sizzle. Each scene has been selected as a freestanding dramatic unit offering two actors a wide range of theatrical challenge and opportunity.

Every scene is set up with a synopsis of the play, character descriptions, and notes. DUO! offers a full spectrum of age range, region, genre, character, level of difficulty, and non-traditional casting potential. Among the selections:

**EMERALD CITY · BURN THIS · BROADWAY BOUND
EASTERN STANDARD · THE HEIDI CHRONICLES
JOE TURNER'S COME AND GONE
RECKLESS · PSYCHO BEACH PARTY
FRANKIE & JOHNNY IN THE CLAIR DE LUNE
COASTAL DISTURBANCES · THE SPEED OF DARKNESS
LES LIAISONS DANGEREUSES · LETTICE AND LOVAGE
THE COCKTAIL HOUR · BEIRUT
M. BUTTERFLY · DRIVING MISS DAISY · MRS KLEIN
A GIRL'S GUIDE TO CHAOS · A WALK IN THE WOODS
THE ROAD TO MECCA · BOY'S LIFE · SAFE SEX
LEND ME A TENOR · A SHAYNA MAIDEL · ICE CREAM
SPEED-THE-PLOW · OTHER PEOPLE'S MONEY
CUBA AND HIS TEDDY BEAR**

paper · ISBN: 1-55783-030-4